Contemporary Issues in Human Resource Management

We live in a time of chaos, marked by
breathtaking technological advances,
tectonic cultural and political shifts, and
vigorous international competition.
Our workforce grows more diverse every
day, while our attitudes about work are
constantly changing. At the same time
customers are demanding intensive
service and near-perfect quality.
Everything has to be better, cheaper,
faster.

Robert H. Rosen with Paul B. Brown, 1996.
Leading people: transforming business from the inside out.
New York, Viking Penguin, p. 10.

Contemporary Issues in Human Resource Management

Gaining a Competitive Advantage

Chris Brewster
Peter Dowling
Pieter Grobler
Peter Holland
Surette Wärnich

OXFORD
UNIVERSITY PRESS

OXFORD
UNIVERSITY PRESS

Great Clarendon Street, Oxford OX2 6DP

Oxford University Press is a department of the University of Oxford.
It furthers the University's objective of excellence in research, scholarship,
and education by publishing worldwide in

Oxford New York

Athens Auckland Bangkok Bogatá Buenos Aires Calcutta
Cape Town Chennai Dar es Salaam Delhi Florence Hong Kong Istanbul
Karachi Kuala Lumpur Madrid Melbourne Mexico City Mumbai
Nairobi Paris São Paulo Shanghai Singapore Taipei Tokyo Toronto Warsaw

with associated companies in Berlin Ibadan

Oxford is a registered trade mark of Oxford University Press
in the UK and certain other countries

Published in South Africa
by Oxford University Press Southern Africa, Cape Town

Contemporary Issues in Human Resource Management:
Gaining a Competitive Advantage

ISBN 0 19 571850 X

The moral rights of the author have been asserted
Database right Oxford University Press (maker)
First published 2000
Reprinted 2000

Designer: Mark Standley
Indexer: Jeanne Cope

Published by Oxford University Press Southern Africa
PO Box 12119, N1 City, 7463, Cape Town, South Africa

Set in 10pt on 12pt Plantin by Compleat Typesetters
Reproduction by Compleat Typesetters
Cover reproduction by The Image Bureau
Printed and bound by Clyson Printers, Maitland, Cape Town

Abridged table of contents

Contents

6   Integrating total quality management and human resource management   107

7   Management of intellectual capital within organisations – the HR challenge   134

8   International human resource management   158

9   Labour relations in multinational firms   183

Acknowledgements

Many people deserve thanks for the successful completion of this project, and we would particularly like to thank acquisitions editor Eloise Wessels (originally from International Thomson Publishing, and now with Oxford University Press), who accepted our project, for her warm guidance and friendship; Professor P.D. Gerber, who initiated the project; Cecilia du Plessis, who performed important library and background research; and Babs Marais, who assisted with the typing. We would also like to thank South Western Publishers from Cincinnati, Ohio, USA, for their permission to use Chapter 8 (Labour Relations) from the text *International Human Resource Management: Managing people in a multinational context* (3rd edition, 1999) by P.J. Dowling, D.E. Welch and R. Schuler. It is much appreciated!

The authors

Introduction

This book is intended to give line managers and human resource management (HRM) practitioners insight into the changing role of the HRM function and to indicate how it can contribute towards enhancing the competitiveness of a company. Although there are numerous titles giving a solid account of the various functional areas in which HRM operates – such as recruiting, placement, human relations, performance appraisal, compensation and training – it is essential for the HR manager to find the optimum framework in which each of these functional areas can contribute towards the competitiveness of the organisation. For example, to be truly effective requires a strategic approach which links the HR strategies with the total organisation strategy.

In this text, due cognisance will be taken of discussions included in books such as *Human resource champions, Tomorrow's HR management, The human equation, Global impact, The ultimate advantage, Leading people, Competitive advantage through people* and *Intelligent enterprise.*[1-8] Concepts such as the competitive advantage, total quality, flexibility, the strategic role of HR, intellectual capital, leadership, and international HR and labour relations management will be integral to the search for guidelines to optimise the impact of HR.

The resource-based theory[9] suggests that companies have resources or capabilities that constitute their strategic assets. By utilising these assets in an effective way, they can contribute towards gaining a competitive advantage. Three types of resources can be distinguished within companies:

- physical (plant, technology, location);
- organisational (organisation structure, systems of planning and control, social relations within the organisation); and
- human (employees' competencies, experience and knowledge).[10]

The focus in this text will be on the human assets. The function of HR is increasingly being viewed not simply as a set of practices and policies that should fit into the overall corporate or business strategy, but as a crucial component in the total organisation strategy.[11] The function of managing human assets has also become the focus of attention for senior managers.

In a Towers Perrin survey,[12] executives were asked to rank the importance of both people-related issues and business priorities. Almost 98 per cent of the respondents agreed that improved employee performance was a key to improved business results; 73 per cent also noted that their company's most important investment was in people. To state it plainly, achieving organisational excellence must be the work of HR.

The changing role of HR has led to a shift in activities and objectives, which has been the result of a number of new challenges:

- globalisation – the restructuring of world markets;
- technology and structure – work roles and skill requirements, work teams, the role of managers, company structures, information.
- social – the changing composition of the labour market, employee values, legislation, skill deficits; and
- quality – meeting customers' needs, service needs and product needs.

These are crucial influences on the world of business and the world of HR, and they will be addressed in the chapters that follow.

References

1   Ulrich, D. 1997. *Human resource champions: The next agenda for adding value and delivering results*. Boston, Mass., Harvard Business School Press.

2   Ulrich, D., Losey, M.R. & Lake G. (eds.) 1997. *Tomorrow's HR management*. New York, John Wiley & Sons.

3   Pfeffer, J. 1998. *The human equation: Building profits by putting people first*. Boston, Mass., Harvard Business School Press.

4   Odenwald, S.B. & Matheny, W.G. 1996. *Global impact: Award winning performance programs from around the world*. Chicago, Irwin Professional Publishing.

5   Lawler, E.E. III 1992. *The ultimate advantage: Creating the high-involvement organisation*. San Francisco, Jossey-Bass Publishers.

6   Rosen, R.H. & Brown, P.B. 1996. *Leading people: Transforming business from the inside out*. New York, Viking, Penguin Group.

7   Pfeffer, J. 1994. *Competitive advantage through people: Unleashing the power of the work force*. Boston, Mass., Harvard Business School Press.

8   Quinn, J.B. 1992. *Intelligent enterprise*. New York, The Free Press, A Division of Macmillan.

9   Barney, J. 1991. Firm resources and sustained competitive advantage. *Journal of Management*, vol. 17, pp. 99–120.

10   Jackson, S. & Schuler, R. 1995. Understanding human resource management in the context of organisations and their environment. *Applied Review of Psychology*, vol. 46, pp. 237–264.

11   Schuler, R.S. & Rogovsky, N. 1998. Understanding compensation practice variations across firms: the impact of national culture. *Journal of International Business Studies*, vol. 29, no. 1 (First Quarter).

12   Towers Perrin. 1992. *Priorities for competitive advantage. Statistical supplement*. London, Towers Perrin.

1

Human resource management's role in the evolving paradigm

1.1 Introduction

The role played by human resource management (HRM) within organisations has changed dramatically. Having been excluded from participating actively in business decisions for most of its existence, HR is now required by organisations to play an active role in the fight to be successful and remain competitive.[1-2] The HR function is being asked to respond by cutting costs and finding creative ways to add value to the business. Doing so, however, appears to require a repositioning of the HR department which will involve not only new roles but also new competencies, new relationships and new ways of operating[3] (see Chapters 2–9). To understand the role of HRM, one must first understand its historical evolution and, second, the challenges facing HR today. In this chapter the following issues will be addressed:

- The origins of HRM.
- The present role of HRM.
- The new employee/employer relationship.
- Innovative approaches to HRM.

1.2 The origins of HRM

Although some HR activities had been taking place in the early 1800s in areas such as agriculture and small family businesses, more formal HR practices evolved only at the beginning of the Industrial Revolution, when factories required large numbers of employees with specific skills to operate their machines.[4] To recruit and train these workers, companies started employing persons who would be responsible for these activities. Since then, rapid changes within organisations have taken place which have had a profound impact on the role played by the HRM professional.[5-6]

A researcher, Kathryn D. McKee,[7] has successfully described these paradigm shifts in business life and has also identified the evolving role of the HRM function during these periods. Before we take a closer look at McKee's work, it may be appropriate to briefly define what is meant by "a paradigm". According to the futurist Joel Barker (1989), as quoted by James Belohlav,[8] the term "paradigm" can be described as a set of rules and regulations that define boundaries and tell us what to do to be successful within those boundaries. Thus, the term "paradigm" refers to a particular way of thinking about, seeing and doing things within one's environment.

The categories of change within businesses which McKee has identified can be grouped into four distinct periods, namely (1) mechanistic, (2) legalistic, (3) organistic and (4) strategic. We will take a brief look at these periods and their impact on the role of the HRM professional.

- **Mechanistic period.** This period can be associated with the 1940s and 1950s, when manufacturing was the driving force in industry. During this period, we saw the birth of the personnel/industrial relations profession. The main focus of the HR function was of an administrative nature, for example interpreting union contracts, keeping manual records and hiring and paying people. This period also saw the emergence of benefit programmes as an area of interest.[9]

- **Legalistic period.** The 1960s and 1970s saw an unprecedented amount of legislation in the social and employment area, which had a major impact on the workplace and the roles and responsibilities assumed by the personnel officer. This legislation began a trend towards the regulation of the workforce beyond that of the union contract and company rules. Training and development began to emerge as a separate and specialised area of HR, and to this day it plays an important and vital role. Also in the early 1970s, the first HR information systems application (the computerisation of the salary database) was started.[10]

- **Organistic period.** Tremendous organisational change started to take place in the 1980s. Here we think of globalisation, mergers, acquisitions, re-engineering and downsizing. These activities brought about radical changes in the workplace and created an environment in which the HRM function faced numerous challenges (e.g. an increasingly diverse workforce, and an increase of awareness of work and family issues). During this period the movement towards cost and profit centres became an important issue for HRM, as did the implementation of more command and control policies and procedures to save the organisation from failing to deal with the turbulent environment. This period can also be seen as the height of HRM specialisation.[11]

- **Strategic period.** The period of the 1990s has become known as the strategic period. During this time strategic thinking and planning emerged as the most prominent activity to deal with the continual change faced by the corporate organisation. We find in this period that organisations are in flux, with structures ranging from webs to networks and matrices. Due to fierce competition, organisations turned to the HRM function to assist them in their struggle to remain successful and competitive. HRM now becomes a true strategic partner, reporting to the CEO and interacting with the Board of Directors. The HR professional also plays an active role in determining the future direction of the organisation.[12]

For the future – that is, beyond 2000 – McKee projects the present trends described above and calls this period the catalytic period. In this period, she argues, the following issues will play a major role:[13]
- an increase in cross-border employment;
- a workforce that will be comfortable in, and with, other cultures;
- fewer organisations as a result of continued mergers and acquisitions;
- the use of just-in-time professional workers;
- an increase in outsourcing of administrative functions;
- more innovative compensation practices;
- a more selective approach by employees regarding their careers;
- telecommuting and other forms of flexible work being widely introduced; and
- teams playing a major role.

Thus, to summarise, the good old days of HRM are over, and in the future human resource management will emerge as an even more critical factor in developing and maintaining a company's competitive edge. However, to play this significant part successfully, it is important to take a look at the function's present role and how it is adapting to meet the needs of the future.

1.3   The present role of HRM

As indicated in the previous section, rapid changes have taken place within the organisation as well as in the role to be played by HR professionals. Thus, few successful businesses can continue to rely on past policies and practices, while their HR professionals can ill afford to continue to be functional experts.[14-16] Management and HR professionals must become partners in decision making and share accountability for organising the work to be performed – including where it is to be performed. To be successful, the HR professional will have to:[17]

- become involved with line managers in strategy formulation and implementation, resulting in the design of HR strategies that will support the overall company strategy;
- become an expert in the way work is organised and executed;
- become involved in reducing costs through administrative efficiency, while at the same time maintaining high quality. This can be achieved by delivering state-of-the-art, innovative HR practices;
- become a reliable representative for employees when putting their concerns to management;
- become involved in efforts to increase the employees' contribution to the organisation; and
- become an agent for continuous transformation, shaping processes and culture to help organisations improve their capacity for change.

If all these issues are done well, the HR professional will receive the recognition he or she deserves within the organisation.

The strategic alliance between management and HR has received substantial attention in both popular and academic literature. However, a study of these articles reveals a focus on the strategic partnership role (e.g. getting to know the needs of the business and where it is going), while no mention is made of HR's past operational role.

In his popular book *Human Resource Champions*, Dave Ulrich[18-19] warns about this one-sided view and proposes a multiple role model for HRM which addresses these as well as other issues. Ulrich is of the opinion that for HR to be successful, it will have to play at least four different roles, namely strategic partner, administrative expert, employee champion and change agent.[20] He also proposes that HR professionals should first focus on what they can deliver, before they look at the activities or work of HR. As his model has been successfully implemented by major corporations around the world (e.g. Hewlett-Packard, General Electric and Sears) it would be wise to take a closer look at the model.

The axes of Ulrich's model (see Figure 1.1) represent two aspects, namely focus (i.e. short and long term) and activities (managing processes – HR tools and systems – and managing people). The HR roles mentioned earlier are depicted in the four quadrants of the model. To clarify these roles, each quadrant also contains the outcome of each role as well as the activities to be performed by the HR professional. A closer look at each of the roles follows:

- **Top left quadrant (Cell 1).** In this cell (management of strategic human resources) the HR manager works to be a strategic partner by focusing on the alignment of HR strategies and practices with the overall business

Figure 1.1 HR roles in building a competitive organisation

Future/strategic focus (short–long term)

Cell 1 Management of strategic human resources	**Cell 3** Management of transformation and change
Deliverable/outcome Executing strategy	**Deliverable/outcome** Creating a renewed organisation
Activity Aligning HR and business strategy: "organisational diagnoses"	**Activity** Managing transformation and change: "ensuring capacity for change"
Role Strategic partner	**Role** Change agent
Cell 2 Management of firm infrastructure	**Cell 4** Management of employee contribution
Deliverable/outcome Building an efficient infrastructure	**Deliverable/outcome** Increasing employee commitment and capability
Activity Re-engineering organisation processes: "shared services"	**Activity** Listening and responding to employees: "providing resources to employees"
Role Administrative expert	**Role** Employee champion

(left axis: **Processes**; right axis: **People**)

Day-to-day/operational focus

SOURCE: Adapted and reprinted by permission of Harvard Business School Press. From *Human resource champions: the next agenda for adding value and delivering results*, by Ulrich, D. Boston, MA. 1997. This figure is a combination of Figure 2.1 on page 24 and Table 2-1 on page 25 of the text. Copyright © 1999 by the President and Fellows of Harvard College, all rights reserved.

strategy (see Chapter 3 for more detail). By fulfilling this role, HR professionals increase the capacity of the business to execute its strategies.[21]
- **Bottom left quadrant (Cell 2).** This role (management of firm infrastructure) requires HR professionals to design and deliver efficient HR processes, e.g. staffing, training, appraising, rewarding and promoting. HR professionals must ensure that these organisational processes

are designed and delivered efficiently. This process is of an ongoing nature.[22]

- **Top right quadrant (Cell 3).** The third key role to be played by the HR professional is management of transformation and change. This entails making fundamental cultural changes within the organisation.[23]
- **Top right quadrant (Cell 4).** The employee contribution role of HR professionals encompasses their involvement in the day-to-day problems, concerns and needs of employees. Where, for example, intellectual capital becomes a critical source of a company's value, HR professionals should be active and aggressive in developing this capital (see Chapter 7).[24]

Thus, by turning the four HR roles into specific behaviours and actions, a world-class HR organisation can be created, as seen in companies such as Hewlett-Packard and some of the others already mentioned. According to Ulrich, the business partner concept has changed to become a more dynamic, all-encompassing equation, thus replacing the simple concept of business partner (that is, working only with general managers to implement strategy) with:

Business partner = strategic partner + administrative expert + employee champion + change agent.[25]

In conclusion, being an effective HR professional does not mean simply moving from operational to strategic work as the new challenges demand; it means learning to master both operational and strategic processes and people. For today's HR professionals to deliver value to a company, they must fulfil multiple – not only single – roles.

1.4   The new employee/employer relationship

From the discussion thus far, it has become clear that organisations that want to be successful and competitive will be those that are able to turn their strategies into action quickly, manage their processes efficiently and maximise their employees' contributions and commitment. For this to be possible, the old way of doing things must be abolished and new practices implemented. This can take place through re-engineering, restructuring, downsizing and other activities.

These changes will inevitably result in employees being dismissed – not only those working in factories, but also those who traditionally were offered a long-term career within the organisation. Thus the psychological contract –

what employees and employers want and expect from each other[26-27] – will change dramatically in the new work environment. The question now is: what will this new contract look like?

We see that the psychological contract that is dynamic, voluntary, subjective and informal accomplishes two tasks: first it defines the employment relationship; second, it manages the mutual expectations.[28-29]

Perhaps the most significant change in the new work environment is the lack of job security offered to employees. In the old paradigm, an employee's current and future position was very clear and predictable, which resulted in employee loyalty being fostered. For this loyalty, employers would provide good pay, regular promotion and benefits, and would also invest in the training and development of their staff. The relationship between the employer and the employee was a good one. However, this happy marriage has become strained in the new work environment, in which cutting costs and improving productivity are management goals. The flexible, de-layered, slimmer organisation is constantly changing to suit volatile and shifting markets, and can logically no longer sustain secure career progression.[30]

What is interesting is that, while these changes are occurring from the employer's side, new values, trends and workplace demographics have resulted in revised expectations from the employees themselves. For example, there seems to be a significant shift in employees' attitudes and values as regards career management, leadership style, motivation and working conditions. This highly educated new generation of workers want more opportunities for development, autonomy, flexibility and meaningful experiences. They also value independence, imagination, tolerance and responsibility.[31]

Thus, with changes taking place on the employer as well as employee side, a new type of psychological contract is emerging – one that is more situational and short term, and assumes that each party is much less dependent on the other for survival and growth.

According to Jean-Marie Hiltrop, this new contract can be defined as follows:[32-33]

> There is no job security, the employee will be employed as long as he/she adds value to the organisation, and is personally responsible for finding new ways to add value. In return the employee has the right to demand interesting and important work, has the freedom and resources to perform it well, receives pay that reflects his or her contribution and gets the experience and training needed to be employable here or elsewhere.

As the old employment contract, which is based on security and predictability, is withdrawn, it will be replaced with one of faint promises. Thus employees will give their time but not much more.

1.5   Innovative approaches to HRM

There is no doubt that each of the factors mentioned in this chapter thus far is creating a number of new challenges for HR management. Jean-Marie Hiltrop summarises these challenges skilfully when he asks:[34]

- How can we attract and retain people who can live with and often thrive upon uncertainty?
- How can we get and maintain the loyalty and commitment of our employees when job security, promotion opportunities and career entitlements are declining?
- How can we meet career expectations of employees who expect rapid promotions in an organisation that is becoming flatter and leaner and is not expanding enough?
- How can we encourage (older) employees to take more responsibility for their own personal and professional development?
- How can we develop procedures and processes that help a group of managers and specialists understand and commit themselves to working together?
- How can we build an organisation culture and structure in which employees feel satisfied, challenged and empowered?

To manage this complex and challenging environment, HR professionals have not only adopted new roles within the workplace, as mentioned earlier, but have also designed, in conjunction with line managers, some innovative HR approaches. In this section a closer look will be taken at some of the more important ones: self-managed work teams, alternative workplaces and virtual HRM.

1.5.1 Self-managed work teams (SMWT)

Although not totally new, self-managed work teams (SMWT) have again recently come to the fore as a method to improve employee commitment and thus the general well-being of the organisation.[35] In Europe, these teams are used by companies such as Volvo, SAAB, and (in Spain) the Mondragon co-operative movement, resulting in significantly larger profits and productivity gains than the average operator. These teams are also used in other parts of the world.[36]

As the term "self-managed" implies, these teams within the work environment are responsible for determining what they want to do, how they want to do it, and also when they want to do it. The teams are thus empowered to use their initiative in solving problems and managing themselves. The advantage of these teams is that they can respond quickly to the needs of a particular situation, which is of great importance for companies finding themselves in a turbulent environment.

Team members participate in decisions such as who to hire for their teams, what equipment to purchase, and also what training is necessary to operate the equipment.

The most profound implication for establishing these teams appears to be in the overall role of HRM.[37] Moving from a centralised functional staff position, as indicated earlier in the chapter, the HR professional now becomes a coach/counsellor/advisor to the team. For example, when hiring/selecting people for the company, the team members will play an important role in deciding whether the applicants will be good team members or not. Also, in the job analysis process the team will play an important role.[38] Not only are certain behaviours necessary to perform a specific job, but the team members will also have to learn new sets of behaviours to be able to work together successfully. These behaviours will have to be identified during the job analysis stage. In training, the self-managed work teams will assess their own training needs and, with the input and advice from the HR professional, participate in the design, delivery and evaluation of the training programmes. Besides their own job training requirements, the team will also need training in communication, listening and supervisory skills, conflict resolution, decision making, running meetings and time management. For overall business responsibility they will need to learn customer relations, and how to deal with suppliers as well as unions.[39]

Due to the teams' unique situation, changes will also have to be made to the compensation system within the company. In the past, individuals were paid according to the job category in which they were classified. Now, however, with teams, the most prevalent pay system used is pay for knowledge. Thus, team members are paid according to how many team tasks they can perform. Other compensation system innovations for teams include gain-sharing or suggestion system payments in order to encourage team initiative.[40]

New procedures to determine the critical factors of performance for teams must also be implemented. Team members must become involved in both the design and the appraisal itself. The team will also be responsible for its own work schedule and vacation policy.

It is clear that the development of team-based work systems has the potential to create a more productive, creative and individual-fulfilling working environment and thus plays a critical role in the new challenges facing HRM.

With the greater availability of technology within companies, the self-managed work teams have now also evolved into virtual teams.[41] According to Townsend *et al.*, these teams can be defined as follows:[42]

> Virtual teams are groups of geographically and/or organisationally dispersed co-workers that are assembled using a combination of telecommunications and information technologies to accomplish an organisational task. They rarely meet face to face, they may be set up as temporary structures existing only to accomplish a specific task or may be more permanent structures to address ongoing issues.

These types of teams have become important for a number of reasons, including the following:[43]

- the change in organisation structures to flat or horizontal formats;
- the emergence of environments that require inter-organisational co-operation as well as competition;
- changes in workers' expectations regarding their involvement in organisations; and
- the globalisation of trade and organisation activity.

We also see that the virtual team formation can expand the telecommuting potential (to be discussed shortly) by allowing employees involved in highly collaborative teamwork to participate from remote locations. However, these teams will be successful only if all the members became proficient with a wide variety of computer-based technologies and learn new ways to express themselves and understand others in an environment with a diminished sense of presence. Also, in many organisations, virtual-team membership will cross national boundaries, involving a variety of cultural backgrounds which will require additional team development in areas such as cultural diversity.[44]

1.5.2 Alternative workplace (AW)

Besides the self-managed work teams and virtual teams, other approaches have been developed to increase employee commitment and productivity. The alternative workplace is such an effort by HR management to transform the workplace by moving the work to the worker instead of the worker to the work.[45] The alternative workplace approach is a combination of nontraditional work practices, settings and locations that is beginning to supplement traditional offices. It can also give companies an edge in vying for talent as well as keeping it. Today, AT&T in the US is just one among many organisations pioneering the alternative workplace. Although different companies use different variations on the alternative workplace theme to tailor work arrangements to their own needs, Mahlon Apgar IV has identified a number of options available, namely:[46]

- **placing workers on different shifts or travel schedules,** thus enabling them to share the same desk and office space;
- **replacing traditional offices with open-plan space**;
- **implementing the concept of "hotelling".** As in other shared office options, "hotel" work spaces are furnished, equipped and supported with typical office services. These spaces can then be reserved by the hour, day or week instead of being permanently assigned. In addition, a concierge may be appointed to provide employees with travel and logistical support;
- **creating satellite offices**. Such offices are the result of breaking up large, centralised facilities into a network of smaller workplaces that can be located close to the customer or employees' homes;
- **introducing telecommuting.** This is one of the most commonly recognised forms of alternative workplace and has been used for some time. Telecommuting – that is, performing work electronically wherever the worker chooses – generally supplements the traditional workplace rather than replacing it.

Although these different forms of alternative workplace have been identified separately, they are sometimes also found in combination within organisations (e.g. shared offices and telecommuting). It is also interesting to note that a dynamic, non-hierarchical, technologically advanced organisation is more likely to use these practices than a highly structured, command-driven company.

One of the most critical HR issues in setting up these alternative workplace practices is that of measuring the employees' performance. It is very clear that the traditional approaches will not work and new methods will have to be devised. This also applies to the manner in which employees are rewarded. As a result of the different locations at which the employees will be working, a culture change within the company will be necessary as employees learn new ways of connecting with one another.[47]

The decision to implement alternative workplace practices is normally based on a number of assumptions, for example that certain jobs either do not depend on specific locations and types of facilities or depend only partly on them. For the successful implementation of the different workplace practices, Mahlon Apgar IV suggests asking the following questions:[48]

- What function does the job serve?
- Is the work performed over the phone?
- How much time does the employee have to spend in direct contact with other employees/customers and business contacts?
- Is the location of the office critical to performance?
- Is it important for others to be able to reach the employee immediately?

Having answered the above questions satisfactorily, the company will also have to look at a number of other issues before proceeding with the implementation of alternative workplace programmes. One such aspect that needs attention is the attitude of middle management. These employees normally see their roles being diminished with their subordinates working at home. Informing them of the positive contribution these programmes can make to the company – as well as their crucial role therein – will be vital. Programmes that are undertaken with only partial support from the staff will only result in confusion and frustration for the employees at home, with a consequent drop in productivity.[49]

The company will also have to look at the cost aspects of implementing the programmes. These programmes need hardware, software and other support which can involve large sums of money. Ongoing costs such as allowances, phone charges and technical support must also be budgeted for, as well as the time necessary to reorientate and train the employees involved.[50]

Besides these problems, certain external barriers may exist. For example, in Japan people's homes are so small that they cannot contain a home office. Also, in many other countries around the world, the homes of some citizens either do not have electricity or are structures that are not conducive to housing highly sophisticated technical equipment. Thus, when an employee at home cannot communicate with other employees or clients, gain access to the right information or easily reach a help desk to solve a technology problem, the initiative is destined to fail.[51]

Thus, to improve the chances of an alternative workplace programme, those involved must be armed with a full set of tools, relevant training and appropriate flexible administrative support.

If all the above problems/issues have been solved satisfactorily, the company is then in a position to implement such a programme. It is advisable to start with simple activities before moving to more complex ones, for example functions such as telemarketing and personal sales. It is also important to inform the employees involved of how their performance will be monitored. Setting clear goals from the outset and agreeing on what will be monitored is critical. The success of a programme will also depend on how successfully the individuals can differentiate between their work and family at home.[52]

A major US company, Merrill Lynch, has reduced its people risk by setting up telecommuting laboratories at a number of its offices. After extensive pre-screening, employees spend about two weeks at work in a simulated home office. Here, the prospective telecommuters communicate with their managers, customers and colleagues by phone, e-mail or fax. If they do not like this way of working, they can drop out. This approach has proved very valuable to Merrill Lynch in minimising the risk of placing people in jobs they do not like. Interestingly, approximately 17 per cent of IBM's total worldwide workforce is sufficiently equipped and trained to work in alternative workplace programmes.[53]

1.5.3 Virtual HRM

One of the more innovative methods of managing employees efficiently is that of using the World Wide Web for HR applications. Although it is still limited in its application, HR departments worldwide are showing a keen interest in this development. Virtual HR management includes a wide range of functions ranging from something as simple as making a company's HR policies and procedures available through its intranet to managing the development and deployment of the company's most strategic skills.

In this section we will focus on the work of James F. Letart, an employee at the TALX Corporation. This company is responsible for the design and implementation of interactive Web and IVR solutions for HR. It is based in St Louis, USA.[54]

According to Letart, five stages of Web deployment can be found within organisations. Using these stages, companies can determine where they stand at present. A brief look at the different stages follows.

- **Stage I – information publishing.** Many companies find themselves at this stage of development. Here the HR policies and procedures of the company are published for general scrutiny. Other information also available includes the company history, a directory of services and information on the management team. This is a very cost-effective way of making up-to-date company information available to employees.[55]
- **Stage II – database inquiry.** Like the previous level, this level also provides one-way communication to employees. However, increased security requirements now exist, as the user is given the opportunity to gain some personal information from the system. Examples include current benefit coverage, personal demographic data and work schedules. The advantage of this stage of development is that it reduces phone calls and e-mails to the HR department, which ultimately can have a major impact on staffing needs. This level begins to change the way business is conducted.[56]

- **Stage III – simple HR transactions.** At this stage, paperwork is replaced with transactions using electronic input. Here the employee updates personal information such as bank particulars for salary deposits on the HR database available in the company. This is the first step in HR transaction processing and represents a much bigger change in the way HR departments work.[57]
- **Stage IV – complex HR transactions.** Stage IV applications differ from those of the previous stage in the complexity of the interaction between the user and the HR transactions being processed. In addition to updates, calculations or other internal processing of data takes place – for example, an employee may access the employee benefits database and make a selection of items which will be calculated by the system, approved within the budget limits allowed and confirmed by e-mail to the employee.[58]
- **Stage V – HR workflow over the Web.** This is the ultimate stage of development. Here HR executives give employees and managers a way to administer their own HR data and processes without paperwork or administrative support. The users are walked through all the steps necessary to complete whole processes rather than just discrete transactions. For example, an employee who gets divorced may need to change his or her address, contacts, income tax particulars, benefits profile and pension contributions.[59]

It is clear that the Web application for HR departments is enormous. Not only can it lead to improved services, better communication and cost reduction, but also to the ultimate goal of making the organisation more successful and more competitive, especially when deployed globally, where it will increase the capability to manage a global workforce.

1.6   Summary

In this chapter we have seen an evolution within both the management of organisations and the role played by the HR professional. The old way of doing business has gone forever, and a new flexible, fluid and ever-changing environment is a reality. Changes are taking place not only within the organisation but also in the people working in them. Gone are the days of job security and numerous fringe benefits. Companies are only prepared to employ individuals who can add value, and individuals are only interested in selling their labour to the highest bidder. Thus, the challenges facing HR are multiple. The HR professional has responded with innovative ideas to address challenges, such as self-managed work teams, creating virtual teams with available technology, and implementing alternative workplace programmes, all of which offer profound opportunities to benefit both the individual and the company. HR has also moved into the area of the World Wide Web to deliver its own services.

References

1   Ulrich, D., Brockbank, W., Yeung, A.K. & Lake, D.G. 1995. Human resource competencies: An empirical assessment. *Human Resource Management* (Winter), vol. 34, no. 4, pp. 473–495.

2   Pfeffer, J. 1995. Producing sustainable competitive advantage through the effective management of people. *Academy of Management Executive*, vol. 9, no. 1, pp. 55–68.

3   Schuler, R.S. 1990. Repositioning the human resource function: transformation or demise? *Academy of Management Executive*, vol. 4, no. 3, pp. 49–59.

4   Sims, R.R. & Sims, S.J. 1994. *Changes and challenges for the human resource profession*. Westport, Connecticut: Quorum Books, p. 2.

5   Ulrich, D. 1998. A new mandate for human resources. *Harvard Business Review*, (January/February), pp. 124–134.

6   Capelli, P., Bassi, L., Katz, H. Knoke, D., Osterman, P. & Useem, M. 1997. *Change at work*. New York: Oxford University Press.

7   McKee, K.D. 1997. The human resource profession: Insurrection or resurrection? In Ulrich, D., Losey, M.R. & Lake, G., *Tomorrow's HR Management* (Chapter 18). New York, John Wiley & Sons, pp. 182–189.

8   Belohlav, J.A. 1996. The evolving competitive paradigm. *Business Horizons* (March/April), vol. 39, no. 2, pp. 11–19.

9   McKee, K.D. 1997, p. 185.

10   *Ibid.*, pp. 185–186.

11   *Ibid.*, p. 186.

12   *Ibid.*, pp. 187–188.

13   *Ibid.*, pp. 188–189.

14   Morton, M.S. 1995. Emerging organisational forms: work and organisation in the 21st century. *European Management Journal* (December), vol. 13, no. 4, pp. 339–345.

15   Laabs, J.J. 1996. Eyeing future HR concerns. *Personnel Journal* (January), vol. 75, no. 1, pp. 28–37.

16   Jackson, S.E. & Schuler, R.S. 1995. Understanding human resource management in the context of organisations and their environments. *Annual Review of Psychology*, pp. 237–264.

17   Ulrich, D. 1998. A new mandate for human resources. *Harvard Business Review* (January/February), pp. 124–134.

18   Ulrich, D. 1997. *Human Resource Champions: The next agenda for adding value and delivering results*. Boston, Massachusetts, Harvard Business School Press.

19   Dawson, P. 1995. Redefining human resource management. *International Journal of Manpower*, vol. 16, no. 5/6, pp. 47–55.

20   Ulrich, D. 1997, pp. 24–25.

21   *Ibid.*, pp. 25–27.

22   *Ibid.*, pp. 27–28.

23   *Ibid.*, pp. 30–31.

24   *Ibid.*, pp. 29–30.

25   *Ibid.*, p. 37.

26   Hiltrop, J-M. 1995. The changing psychological contract: The human resource challenge of the 1990s. *European Management Journal* (September), vol. 13, no. 3, pp. 286–294.

27   Hiltrop, J-M. 1996. The impact of human resource management on organisational performance: Theory and research. *European Management Journal* (December), vol. 14, no. 6, pp. 628–637.

28 Hiltrop, J-M. 1995, p. 287.
29 Overman, S. 1994. Reengineering HR. *HR Magazine* (June), pp. 50–53.
30 Hiltrop, J-M. 1995, p. 287.
31 *Ibid.*
32 *Ibid.*, p. 289.
33 Cappelli, P., Bassi, L., Katz, H., Knoke, D., Osterman, P. & Useem, M. 1997. *Change at Work*. New York, Oxford University Press, pp. 203–204.
34 Hiltrop, J-M. 1995, p. 288.
35 Banner, D.K., Kulisch, W.A. & Peery, N.S. 1992. Self-managing work teams (SMWT) and the human resource function. *Management Decision*, vol. 30, no. 3, pp. 40–45.
36 *Ibid.*, p. 40.
37 *Ibid.*, p. 41.
38 *Ibid.*, p. 41–44.
39 *Ibid.*
40 *Ibid.*
41 Townsend, A.M., De Marie, S.M. & Hendrickson, A.R. 1998. Virtual teams: Technology and the workplace of the future. *Academy of Management Executive*, vol. 12, no. 3, pp. 17–29.
42 *Ibid.*, p. 18.
43 *Ibid.*
44 *Ibid.*, pp. 19–29.
45 Apgar IV, M. 1998. The alternative workplace: Changing where and how people work. *Harvard Business Review* (May–June), pp. 121–136.
46 *Ibid.*, pp. 122–124.
47 *Ibid.*, p. 125.
48 *Ibid.*
49 *Ibid.*, pp. 126.
50 *Ibid.*, pp. 127–130.
51 *Ibid.*, pp. 126–127.
52 *Ibid.*, pp. 134.
53 *Ibid.*, pp. 135–136.
54 Le Tart, J.F. 1998. A look at virtual HR: How far behind am I? *HR Magazine* (June), pp. 33–42.
55 *Ibid.*, p. 36.
56 *Ibid.*
57 *Ibid.*, pp. 36–37.
58 *Ibid.*, p. 38.
59 *Ibid.*, pp. 36–39.

2

Human resources and the competitive advantage

2.1 Introduction

It is an accepted fact that governments do not make profits, but only create the environment in which organisations and employees can interact to the advantage and benefit of all concerned. Thus, the well-being of the citizens of any country is inextricably linked to the effectiveness of their organisations. However, for organisations to achieve their goals, they must constantly look for better ways to organise and manage their work.[1] Although this is not an easy task, a substantial body of evidence exists indicating that many organisations can obtain a competitive advantage by adopting a management style that involves employees in the business of their organisation.[2] Employee involvement and most of the management practices that are part of it have been shown to have significant positive effects on organisational effectiveness.[3] There is thus a growing recognition that a primary source of competitive advantage derives from a company's human resources; also that this source of advantage may be more inimitable and enduring than a particular product.

As indicated in Chapter 1, this has not always been the case, as human resources – both as labour and as a business function – have traditionally been seen as a cost to be minimised. However, the new interest in HR as a strategic lever that can have economically significant effects on a company's bottom line appears to be shifting the focus more towards value creation.

In this chapter, the following issues will be addressed:

- What is a competitive advantage?
- Sources of competitive advantage.
- HR's role in gaining a competitive advantage.

Before we look at the role of HR in gaining a competitive advantage, it is important to understand what is meant by the phrase "competitive advantage".

2.2   What is a "competitive advantage"?

As observed in the literature, understanding the phrase "competitive advantage" is an ongoing challenge for many decision makers.[4] Historically, competitive advantage was thought of as a matter of position, where companies occupied a competitive space and built and defended their market share.[5] With this strategy, the competitive advantage depended on the area in which the business was located and where it chose to provide its goods and services. This was known as the strategic model.

This strategy seemed to work well in a stable environment, especially for large and dominant organisations.[6] However, with rapid competition appearing, it outlived its popularity and a new meaning of the phrase "competitive advantage" started to appear.

One of the earlier researchers in this area was Jay Barney, who, besides defining the concept, also provided some interesting insight into the total area of competitive advantage.[7-8] Barney defined the term as follows:[9]

> A firm is said to have a competitive advantage when it is implementing a value creating strategy not simultaneously being implemented by any current or potential competitors. A firm is said to have a sustained competitive advantage when it is implementing a value creating strategy not simultaneously being implemented by any current or potential competitors and when these other firms are unable to duplicate the benefits of this strategy.

From the above description, it appears that company resources have a major role to play in obtaining the competitive advantage. Companies cannot create strategies if they do not utilise their resources in the process. This approach is known in the literature as the resource-based view (RBV), and is based on two assumptions:[10] first, that companies within an industry or group may be heterogeneous with respect to the strategic resources they control; and, second, that these resources may not be perfectly mobile across the industry or group. If this is not the case, companies will be able to retain a competitive advantage only for a very short period; they will also have to be the first to utilise their resources in the marketplace to make this possible.

2.3   Sources of competitive advantage

As indicated in the previous section, the resource-based view (RBV) plays a key role in achieving a competitive advantage. This view describes a company as a bundle of resources (see Figure 2.1) that enables it to conceive and implement strategies that will lead to above-average industry returns.[11-12]

Figure 2.1 An example of a strategic specialised bundle*

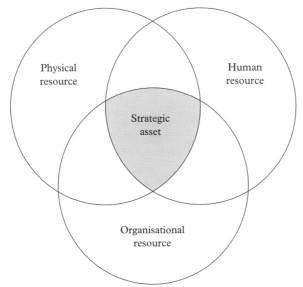

*Please note that numerous similar bundles can be found at any one time in the organisation.

SOURCE: Winfrey, F.L., Michalisin, M.D. & Acar, W. 1996. The paradox of competitive advantage. *Strategic Change*, vol. 5, p. 206. Copyright John Wiley & Sons Ltd. Reproduced with permission.

Thus the differences in company resources across an industry will be reflected in the variability in profits generated by them. No two companies are alike, because no two companies have had the same set of experiences, acquired the same assets and skills or built the same organisation culture. Each company, therefore, is truly unique.[13]

It is also important to note that the resource-based view of competitive advantage differs from the traditional strategy paradigm mentioned earlier, in that the resource-based view is company-focused, whereas the traditional strategic analysis has an industry environment focus.[14] The traditional strategy model also sees company resources as homogeneous and mobile across companies in an industry – that is, companies can purchase or create resources held by a competing company – which is not the case with the resource-based view.[15]

Barney indicates that a company's resources can be classified into four groups, namely:[16]

- **financial capital resources** – including debt, equity-retained earnings.
- **physical capital resources** – including physical technology, machines, manufacturing facilities and buildings.
- **human capital resources** – including knowledge, experience, insight and wisdom of individual managers and workers associated with a company.
- **organisational capital resources** – the history, relationships, trust and organisational culture that are attributes of groups of individuals associated with the company. A company's formal reporting structure, explicit management control systems and compensation policies.

However, not all these resources can be classified as strategic resources (assets). For example, some might even prevent the company from implementing valuable strategies. To determine a resource's value, managers must address four questions[17] concerning value, rarity, imitability and organisation. These questions will be briefly discussed.[18]

- **The question of value.** The first question that must be asked is: do a company's resources add value by enabling it to exploit the opportunities and/or neutralise the threats in the company's environment? By answering this question, managers link the analysis of internal resources with the analysis of environmental opportunities and threats. This is important as the resources of a company cannot be valuable in a vacuum; the company must be able to exploit opportunities and/or neutralise threats.[19]
- **The question of rarity.** The second question that needs to be answered is: how many other companies already possess the valuable resources? The valuable resources must be rare among the competing companies in order to be a source of competitive advantage. However, this does not mean that a common but valuable resource is not important; it might be essential for a company's survival.[20]
- **The question of imitability.** The third question that can be asked is: do companies without a resource face a prohibitive cost disadvantage in obtaining the resources other companies already possess? Having a valuable and rare resource can at least provide a company with a temporary competitive advantage. However, if a competing company does not find it too expensive to imitate this resource, the competitive edge will soon disappear. If imitation is too expensive, the first company will retain its competitive advantage. According to Barney, imitation can occur in at least two ways: by duplication or by substitution. Duplication occurs when an imitating company builds the same kind of resources it has established the competitor possesses; while, in the case of substitution, a similar

resource may be found that provides the same result. It is important to note that some competing companies might find the imitation of a company's resources difficult as a result of historical reasons. For example, many resources are built up over years through trial and error within companies, making them unique reflections of personalities, experiences and relationships that can exist only in one company. Another obstacle might be the social integration of resources through trust, friendship, teamwork and culture, which will make them virtually impossible to imitate.[21]

- **The question of organisation.** The fourth question that can be asked is: is a company organised to exploit the full competitive potential of its resources? As indicated thus far in this chapter, a company's competitive advantage potential depends on the value, rarity and imitability of its resources. However, to fully realise what it has, a company needs a proper organisation structure. Issues that are important in this regard are a formal reporting structure, explicit management control systems, and compensation policies. These components are referred to in the literature as complementary resources, as they have – in isolation – only a limited ability to generate a competitive advantage. In combination with other resources, however, they are capable of releasing a company's full competitive advantage.[22]

In Figure 2.2, Barney provides a model that indicates the relationship between resource heterogeneity and immobility, value, rarity, imitability and substitutability. The model can be applied in analysing the potential of a broad range of company resources to be sources of sustained competitive advantage. It not only specifies the theoretical conditions under which sustained competitive advantage may exist, but also suggests questions that must be addressed before the relationship between a particular company resource and sustained competitive advantage can be understood.[23]

Before we conclude this section of the chapter, it is important to look at the aspect of flexibility, which has not been mentioned. By aligning a company strategy and its resources with the environment, a company can achieve superior performance. In the literature this alignment is termed strategic fit.[24-28] However, with the rapid external and internal changes taking place, this strategic fit becomes more challenging (see Chapter 4). The ability of a company to adjust to these changes is referred to as strategic flexibility.[29-35]

Winfrey, Michalisin & Acar[36] make a number of suggestions that will help a company sustain strategic fit while simultaneously enjoying flexibility in a hypercompetitive environment. One of their proposals is to give a system flexibility within the company, which will allow it to create batches of unique products quickly, at a relatively low cost, as and when required. Galbraith,[37]

Figure 2.2 The relationship between resource heterogeneity and immobility, value, rarity, imperfect imitability, substitutability and sustained competitive advantage

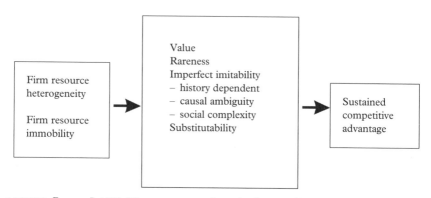

SOURCE: Barney, J. 1991. Firm resources and sustained competitive advantage. *Journal of Management*, vol. 17, no. 1, p. 112. Used with permission.

as quoted by Winfrey *et al.*, notes that its transferability makes the flexible system a valuable resource. To enhance this system, companies must also strive to acquire flexible (knowledge) workers and organic structures which in a hypercompetitive environment will play a crucial role. The basis for this flexibility can be made possible by installing a company culture based on creativity and quick response.

2.4   HR's role in gaining a competitive advantage

The role that HR can play in gaining a competitive advantage for the organisation is empirically well documented.[38-46] A number of paradigms in the literature describe the contribution of HR to company performance. The first assigns value to a company's stock of human intellectual capital as a way of measuring the contribution of HR to the company's performance (see Chapter 7).[47] The human intellectual capital researchers attempt to formalise, capture and leverage this asset (intellectual capital) to produce higher-value products. This approach can be captured in the resource-based view. The second paradigm attempts to identify HR's best practices. Researchers in this movement specify and measure the bundles of typologies of HR practices associated with the high performance of labour.[48-49] The third and last paradigm is a new perspective, designed by

Raphael Amit and Monica Belcourt,[50] which is anchored in both the resource-based view and the best practices theory, and is known as the "process" approach. This perspective integrates economic considerations with social legitimacy aspects.

Before we look at these different perspectives on the role of HR in a competitive advantage paradigm, it might be useful to evaluate the HR component against the measures of sources of competitive advantage. For this discussion we will look at the important work done by Wright & McMahan and published in their article "Theoretical perspectives for strategic human resource management".[51]

- **The value of HR.** For human resources to exist as a sustained competitive advantage they must provide value to the company. It is thus assumed that there is a heterogeneous demand for labour (i.e. companies have jobs that require different types of skills) and a heterogeneous supply of labour (i.e. individuals differ in their skills and level of skills). Under these circumstances, human resources can add value to the company.[52]

- **The rarity of HR.** If it is to be a sustained competitive advantage, a resource must be rare. Wright & McMahan note that, due to the normal distribution of ability, human resources with high ability levels are by definition rare. For example, the basic premise of a selection process is to select only the individuals who possess the highest ability.[53]

- **The inimitability of HR.** Human resources must be inimitable to be considered a sustained competitive advantage. Wright & McMahan use the concepts mentioned earlier in the chapter – namely unique historical conditions, causal ambiguity and social complexity – to demonstrate the inimitability of human resources. Unique historical conditions are the historical events that shape the development of a company's practices, policies and culture. Causal ambiguity describes a situation where the causal source of the competitive advantage is not easily identified, and social complexity recognises that in many situations (e.g. team projects) competitive advantage has its origins in unique social relationships that cannot be duplicated. Thus, Wright & McMahan argue that, due to the fact that many competitive advantages that might be based on a company's human resources are characterised by unique historical conditions, causal ambiguity and social complexity, it is highly unlikely that well-developed human resources could easily be imitated.[54]

- **The substitutability of HR.** For a resource to be considered a sustained competitive advantage it must not have substitutes. For example, if a company has the highest-ability individuals, who constitute a competitive advantage, and a competitor develops new technology that provides vast productivity increases – greater than the productivity differences in the company's ability – it will be only a matter of time before the company obtains the same technology, and then its human resources will again exist as a competitive advantage.[55]

From the foregoing discussion it is clear that human resources can serve as a competitive advantage for the company. As mentioned earlier in this section, a number of paradigms exist in the literature regarding the contribution of HR to company performance. A brief discussion of each of these paradigms will follow.

2.4.1 The resource-based paradigm

This approach suggests that HR systems can contribute to a sustained competitive advantage by facilitating the development of competencies that are company-specific.[56] However, one of the biggest problems facing the resource-based approach, especially regarding human resources, is the possibility of employee turnover.[57-59] Building competencies that do not stay long can have a negative effect on the competitive advantage enjoyed by the company. To limit the damage that can occur as a result of losses, companies can design and implement turnover management strategies. Other approaches that can be implemented include the allocation of a bigger portion of the profits to employees by means of gain-sharing or share-options. To further enhance this process, a culture of belonging can also be created within the company.[60]

2.4.2 The best practices paradigm

This approach implies that there is a direct relationship between particular HR approaches and company performance.[61] In the literature a fair amount of evidence is found that certain HR practices can be related to company performance – such as compensation, selection and training activities.[62] More recently, however, researchers have found that bundles or systems of HR practices have more influence on company performance than individual practices working in isolation.[63] Although support for a best practices approach to HR exists, there are notable differences across studies as to what constitutes a best practice. It is found that most studies focus on enhancing the skill base of employees through HR activities – selective staffing, comprehensive training and broad developmental efforts like job rotation and cross-utilisation.[64] Other issues also found include the promotion of empowerment, participative problem solving and teamwork. An aspect closely linked to the use of best practices is that of creating role behaviours. Company strategies dictate certain unique attitude and role behaviours from employees, and HR practices are the primary means to make this happen. However, because role behaviours of employees are observable and also transferable from one organisational setting to another, they may be easily duplicated and may not be an enduring competitive advantage.[65]

2.4.3 The process paradigm

This approach, as mentioned earlier, is anchored in both the resource-based view and the best practices theory.[66] The creators of this approach, Raphael Amit and Monica Belcourt, refer to HR processes as the deeply embedded company-specific dynamic routines by which a company attracts, socialises, trains and motivates, evaluates and compensates its HR.[67] Company-specific HR processes are established by developing and exchanging information throughout the entire organisation. This process, sometimes called organisation learning, creates transfers and institutionalises knowledge throughout the organisation, which increases its adaptability.[68] From the foregoing it can be deduced that HR processes within a company are evolutionary – in other words, they are continuously evolving and adapting by drawing on past experiences to refine the effectiveness of processes and to meet the changing needs of the organisation. Indeed, the HR processes can become one of the company's strategic assets if they are able to help it realise superior profitability.[69]

Thus, to summarise, it is clear that the HR process is the engine of renewal that can be used to continually adjust the way in which a company selects, trains, socialises and evaluates its human capital, and that enables a company to execute its strategy effectively. The universal adoption of best practices leads to company homogeneity, as people come and go, but processes remain and improve the company. Thus HR processes are about how things are done, not what is produced.

2.5 Summary

In this chapter, attention has been given to the growing importance of human resources as a source of competitive advantage. The phrase "competitive advantage" was defined and sources of competitive advantage were identified. Measures to identify sources of competitive advantage were also discussed. The different paradigms that exist in the literature regarding the contribution of HR to company performance, i.e. the resource-based view, the best practices approach and the process approach, were also considered.

References

1   Lawler, E.E. III 1992. *The ultimate advantage: creating the high involvement organisation.* San Francisco, Jossey-Bass Publishers, p. xi.
2   *Ibid.*
3   *Ibid.*
4   Duncan, W.J., Ginter, P.M. & Swayne, L.E. 1998. Competitive advantage and internal organisational assessment. *Academy of Management Executive*, vol. 12, no. 3, p. 7.
5   *Ibid.*
6   *Ibid.*
7   Barney, J. 1991. Firm resources and sustained competitive advantage. *Journal of Management*, vol. 17, no. 1, pp. 99–120.
8   Barney, J. 1995. Looking inside for competitive advantage. *Academy of Management Executive*, vol. 9, no. 4, pp. 49–61.
9   Barney, J. 1991, p. 101.
10   *Ibid,* p. 100.
11   Collis, D.J. & Montgomery, C.A. 1995. Competing on resource strategy in the 1990s. *Harvard Business Review* (July/ August), pp. 118–128.
12   Coff, R.W. 1997. Human assets and management dilemmas: coping with hazards on the road to resource-based theory. *Academy of Management Review*, vol. 22, no. 2, pp. 374–402.
13   Collis *et al.* 1995, p. 119.
14   Wright, P.M. & McMahan, G.C. 1992. Theoretical perspectives for strategic human resource management. *Journal of Management*, vol. 18, no. 2, pp. 295–320.
15   *Ibid.,* p. 301.
16   Barney, J. 1991, p. 101.
17   *Ibid.,* pp. 105–106.
18   Barney, J. 1995, pp. 50–61.
19   *Ibid.,* pp. 50–51.
20   *Ibid.,* p. 52.
21   *Ibid.,* pp. 53–55.
22   *Ibid.,* pp. 56–57.

23   Barney, J. 1991, pp. 112–114.
24   Venkatraman, N. & Camillus, J.C. 1984. Exploring the concept of "fit" in strategic management. *Academy of Management Review*, vol. 9, no. 3, pp. 513–525.
25   Drazin, R. & Van de Ven, A.H. 1985. Alternative forms of fit in contingency theory. *Administrative Science Quarterly*, vol. 30, pp. 514–539.
26   Venkatraman, N. 1990. Environment-strategy coalignment: an empirical test of its performance implications. *Strategic Management Journal*, vol. 11, pp. 1–23.
27   Chorn, N.H. 1991. The "alignment" theory: creating strategic fit. *Management Decision*, vol. 29, no. 1, pp. 20–24.
28   Nath, D. & Suharshan, D. 1994. Measuring strategy coherence through patterns of strategic choices. *Strategic Management Journal*, vol. 15, pp. 43–61.
29   Harrigan, K.R. 1985. *Strategic flexibility: A management guide for changing times.* Lexington Books, Lexington.
30   Noori, H. 1990. Economies of integration: a new manufacturing focus. *International Journal of Technology Management*, vol. 5, no. 5, pp. 577–587.
31   Harrigan, K.R. & Dalmia, G. 1991. Knowledge workers: The last bastion of competitive advantage. *Planning Review* (November/December), pp. 4–9, 48.
32   Goldhar, J.D. Jelinek, M. & Schie, T.W. 1990. Flexibility and competitive advantage – manufacturing becomes a service industry. *International Journal of Technology Management, Special Issue on Manufacturing Strategy*, vol. 6, no. 3/4, pp. 243–259.
33   Sarge, A. 1991. Strategic fit and societal effect: interpreting cross-national comparisons of technology organisation and human resources. *Organization Studies*, vol. 12, no. 2, pp. 161–190.

34 Parthasarthy, R. & Sethi, S.P. 1992. The impact of flexible automation on business strategy and organization structure. *Academy of Management Review*, vol. 17, no. 1, pp. 86–111.

35 D'Aveni, R.A. 1994. *Hypercompetition: Managing the dynamics of strategic maneuvering.* The Free Press, New York.

36 Winfrey, F.L., Michalisin, M.D. & Acar, W. 1996. The paradox of competitive advantage. *Strategic Change*, vol. 5, p. 206.

37 Galbraith, C.S. 1990. Transferring core manufacturing technologies in high-technology firms. *California Management Review* (Summer), pp. 56–70.

38 Becker, B. & Gerhart, B. 1996. The impact of human resource management on organisational performance: progress and prospects. *Academy of Management Journal*, vol. 39, no. 4, pp. 779–801.

39 Delery, J.E. & Doty, D.H. 1996. Modes of theorizing in strategic human resource management: Tests of universalistic contingency and configurational performance predictions. *Academy of Management Journal*, vol. 39, no. 4, pp. 802–835.

40 Youndt, M.A., Snell, S.A. Dean, J.W. & Lepak, D.P. 1996. Human resource management, manufacturing strategy and firm performance. *Academy of Management Journal*, vol. 39, no. 4, pp. 836–866.

41 Arthur, J.B. 1994. Effects of human resource systems on manufacturing performance and turnover. *Academy of Management Journal*, vol. 37, pp. 670–687.

42 Cutcher-Gershenfeld, J.C. 1991. The impact on economic performance of a transformation in workplace relations. *Industrial and Labour Relations Review*, vol. 44, pp. 241–260.

43 Huselid, M.A. 1995. The impact of human resource management practices on turnover, productivity and corporate financial performance. *Academy of Management Journal*, vol. 38, pp. 635–672.

44 Gerhart, B. & Milkovich, G.T. 1990. Organizational differences in managerial compensation and firm performance.

Academy of Management Journal, vol. 33, pp. 663–691.

45 MacDuffie, J.P. 1995. Human resource bundles and manufacturing performance: Organizational logic and flexible production systems in the world auto industry. *Industrial and Labor Relations Review*, vol. 48, pp. 197–221.

46 Amit, R. & Shoemaker, J.H. 1993. Strategic assets and organisational rents. *Strategic Management Journal*, vol. 14, pp. 33–46.

47 Stewart, T.A. 1997. *Intellectual capital.* New York, Doubleday/Currency.

48 Becker, B. & Gerhart, B. 1996. The impact of human resources management on organizational performance: Progress and prospects. *Academy of Management Journal*, vol. 39, pp. 779–801.

49 Koch, R. & Gunter-McGrath, R. 1996. Improving labour productivity: HR policies do matter. *Strategic Management Journal*, vol. 17, pp. 335–354.

50 Amit, R. & Belcourt, M. 1999. Human resources management processes: A value-creating source of competitive advantage. *European Management Journal*, vol. 17, no. 2, pp. 174–181.

51 Wright, P.M. & Mc Mahan, G.C. 1992. Theoretical perspectives for strategic human resource management. *Journal of Management*, vol. 18, no. 2, pp. 295–320.

52 *Ibid.*, p. 301.

53 *Ibid.*, p. 302.

54 *Ibid.*

55 *Ibid.*, p. 303.

56 Lado A.A. & Wilson, M.C. 1994. Human resource systems and sustained competitive advantage: a competency-based perspective. *Academy of Management Review*, vol. 19, no. 4, p. 700.

57 Casio, W.F. 1991. *Costing human resources: The financial impact of behaviour in organisations.* Boston, PWS Kent.

58 Chiang, S.H. & Chiang, S.C. 1990. General human capital as a shared investment under asymmetric information. *Canadian Journal of Economics*, vol. 23, pp. 175–188.

59 Steffy, B.D. & Maurer, S.D. 1988.
    Conceptualizing the economic effective-
    ness of human resource activities.
    Academy of Management Review, vol. 13,
    pp. 271–286.
60 Coff, 1997, pp. 380–382.
61 Becker *et al.* 1996, pp. 779–780.
62 Youndt *et al.* 1996, pp. 837–838.
63 *Ibid.*
64 *Ibid.*, p. 839.
65 Lado *et al.* 1994, p. 701.
66 Amit *et al.* 1999, p. 174.
67 *Ibid.*, p. 175.
68 *Ibid.*, p. 176.
69 *Ibid.*, pp. 177–179.

3

Human resources and leadership

3.1 Introduction

Up to now, this book has examined the new role that HR has to play to enable the company to gain and sustain its competitive advantage. Being a good manager in today's flexible, innovative and dynamic environment is not enough; all managers (HR included) also need to play a leadership role as part of the top management team.[1] In this chapter, the following important issues pertaining to this vital component will be discussed:

- What is leadership?
- Why is leadership important?
- Individual models of leadership.
- Group models of leadership.
- Leadership training techniques.
- The leadership role of HR.

Before we address the leadership role of HR, it is important to take an overall look at what the literature in general has to say about the concept of leadership.

3.2 What is leadership?

A large number of definitions of leadership can be found in the literature.[2] Nevertheless, they all say essentially the same thing – namely that leadership is:

- the activity of influencing people to strive willingly for group objectives;[3]
- the process of influencing the activities of an individual or a group in efforts towards goal achievement in a given situation;[4]
- a process of giving purpose (meaningful direction) to collective effort, and causing willing effort to be expended to achieve such a purpose;[5]
- getting people to move in directions, make decisions and support paths they would typically not have selected;[6]

- the process of making sense of what people are doing together, so that they will understand and be committed;[7] and
- the process of articulating visions, embodying values and creating the environment within which things can be accomplished.[8]

These definitions highlight a number of important issues. Firstly, it is clear that leadership is a process and not a position; secondly, it involves a relationship between a leader and followers in a given situation.[9] Thus, leadership can be seen as a complex phenomenon involving the leader, the followers and the situation.

The question that can be asked when studying these definitions is: what is the difference between leadership and management? According to Hinterhuber & Krauthammer,[10] the sources of leadership are alertness to opportunity and the imagination and vision to exploit or capitalise on it, thereby creating value for all the stakeholders – people, society, customers and shareholders. On the other hand, they see management as creative problem solving that works within the system and that is easier to learn than leadership. They are also of the opinion that, in a time of uncertainty, leadership is more important than management. In Figure 3.1 their views on the complementarity of leadership and management are illustrated.

Similar views are also echoed by Hughes, Ginnett & Curphy, who indicate that the term *management* suggests words like procedures, control and regulations, while the term *leadership* is more associated with words like risk taking, creativity, change and vision.[11] They come to the conclusion that leadership and management are closely related but distinguishable activities and do not view leaders and managers as different types of people. Thus, the same individual can fulfil both roles.[12]

Warren Bennis,[13] an authority on leadership, also draws a distinction between the two concepts by saying that "managers administer and leaders innovate, managers control and leaders inspire, and managers accept the status quo, while leaders change it".

Gary Howard, as quoted by Bill Leonard,[14] expands on the concept of leadership when he remarks:

- leaders do not just develop visions of what an organisation is, they develop visions of what an organisation can be;
- leaders do not just inform people about new visions, they energise people to accept and work towards making those visions come true;
- leaders do not just formulate new programmes and policies, they initiate improvements that last by changing organisational culture; and
- leaders do not just manage organisations, they seek ways to transform them.

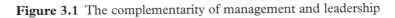

Figure 3.1 The complementarity of management and leadership

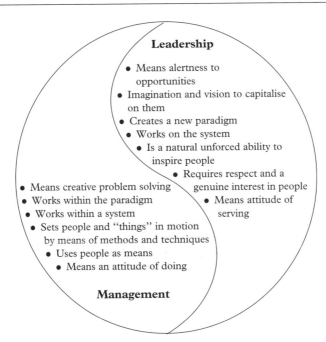

SOURCE: Hinterhuber, H.H. & Krauthammer, E. 1998. The leadership wheel: The tasks entrepreneurs and senior executives cannot delegate. *Strategic Change*, vol. 7, no. 7 (May), p. 150. Copyright John Wiley & Sons Ltd. Reproduced with permission.

It is thus clear from the discussion that leadership and management complement each other and that both are vital to organisational success.

However, to be an effective leader, some critical competencies are required. Today there is a growing agreement on some of these competencies, which, according to Ketterer & Chayes,[15] include vision, managing complexity, industry and business insight, a general management perspective, a drive for success, personal integrity, flexibility, self-awareness, active learning, influencing without authority, developing talent and teamwork. Expanding on this list, two of the leading experts in leadership, James Kouzes and Barry Posner,[16] indicate five practices and 10 commitments needed for exemplary leadership (see Table 3.1). The table indicates how leaders are able to achieve extraordinary things within the organisation. From the content of this table it is obvious that, to be successful, the leader must win the hearts and minds of the followers and also needs a guiding vision and clear idea of what he or she wants to accomplish.

Table 3.1 The five practices and ten commitments of leadership

Practices		Commitments
Challenging the process	1	*Search out* challenging opportunities to change, grow, innovate and improve.
	2	*Experiment,* take risks, and learn from the accompanying mistakes.
Inspiring a shared vision	3	*Envision* an uplifting and ennobling future.
	4	*Enlist* others in a common vision by appealing to their values, interests, hopes and dreams.
Enabling others to act	5	*Foster* collaboration by promoting co-operative goals and building trust.
	6	*Strengthen* people by giving power away, providing choice, developing competence, assigning critical tasks, and offering visible support.
Modelling the way	7	*Set* the example by behaving in ways that are consistent with shared values.
	8	*Achieve* small wins that promote consistent progress and build commitment.
Encouraging the heart	9	*Recognise* individual contributions to the success of every project.
	10	*Celebrate* team accomplishments regularly.

SOURCE: Kouzes, J.M. & Posner, B.Z. 1995. *Leadership challenge: How to keep getting extraordinary things done in organisations.* San Francisco, Jossey Bass Publishers, p. 18. Used with permission.

Besides the competencies, practices and commitment, a further ingredient is necessary to successful leadership – namely effective communication.[17] Knowing what to do, but not being able to communicate this to others, can be a major drawback for effective leadership. According to Martina Platts & Anne-Marie Southall,[18] organisations need complete, coherent and efficient communication systems in which essential information is channelled upwards, downwards and laterally between employees. William Sonnenschein[19] defines communication as "understanding each other as individuals and as members of larger groups".

It is important to note that a number of barriers to good communication must be taken care of. These include poor communication skills, distortion or omission of information flowing through the various levels within the organisation, people hearing only what they expect to hear, and lack of trust between the sender and the recipient.[20] On the other hand, the literature has identified a number of common characteristics in organisations that do communicate well. The following keywords describe these characteristics:[21]

- top management commitment
- open and honest
- planned and deliberate
- interesting, significant content
- systematic
- two-way
- relevant
- sufficient time and money
- reliable
- regular and well timed
- upwards, downwards, sideways
- supported by training
- agreed objectives
- right amount
- support in preparation
- flexible
- think message then medium
- supportive attitudes
- within recipients' horizon
- constantly reinforced.

3.3   Why is leadership important?[22]

A number of studies have indicated that effective leadership can make a difference to organisational performance.[23-42] But the determinants of leadership success are not as clear-cut. For example, which is more significant: leadership traits or leadership as a group activity? What is clear is that successful organisational leadership relies on a combination of traits, skills, attitudes and environmental and intra-organisational conditions (see sections 3.4 and 3.5 in this regard). When one or more of these combinations is missing, leadership goes awry.[43]

Despite these observations, we agree with Sarros & Woodman that certain leadership attributes do exist and that these are related to organisational performance. This view is shared by numerous other authors as well.[44-47] Which leadership attributes account for which organisational outcomes, however, is still difficult to determine. In Figure 3.2, Sarros & Woodman have tried to answer this question by indicating the relationship of a number of leadership attributes to organisational outcomes. Their findings, which have limitations, are based on a study involving 282 executives undertaken in Australia over a nine-month period.

Figure 3.2 Relationships among leadership attributes and organisational outcomes

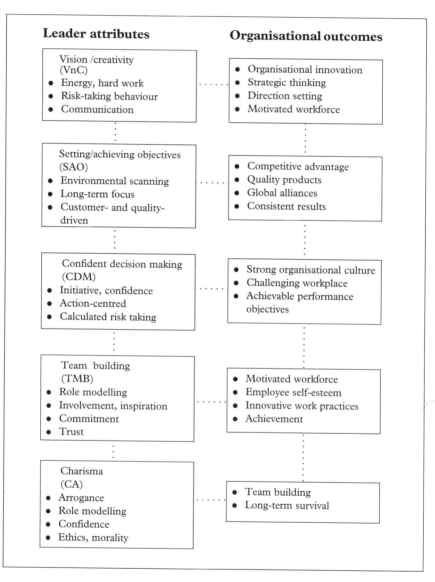

SOURCE: Sarros, J.C. & Woodman, D.S. 1993. Leadership in Australia and its organisational outcomes. *The Leadership & Organisational Development Journal*, vol. 14, no. 4, p. 5. Reproduced with permission.

3.4   Individual models of leadership

It is quite amazing to think that during the 20th century (1900–2000) more than 8 000 studies on leadership have emerged.[48-50] However, when one takes a closer look at all the published work, two main streams of research emerge, one looking at individual models of leadership, and the other at group models of leadership. In this section we will briefly discuss a number of the individual models, and in section 3.5 a number of models found in the "group" category will be considered.

3.4.1 Traits-based approach

The early studies on leadership looked at the various issues concerning the individual leader in the workplace.[51] They began with a focus on traits or characteristics (physical or mental), followed by a focus on skills (ability to carry out tasks), and moved on to behaviours (performing in specific ways).[52] A very extensive literature on leadership traits (so-called traits-based leadership) exists.[53] Figure 3.3 summarises the traits into four categories, namely physical, social, personality and intellectual. However, the trait theory was not very successful, as it was found that no particular set of personality characteristics had recurred in leaders. As Hunt correctly states, "the reverse is more likely to be true – leaders are noted for being different from each other in personality traits".[54]

3.4.2 Situational-based approach

The second approach to be developed expanded on the trait theory to include tasks to be completed, the factors affecting the situation both leader and followers are in, and the personality traits of the followers.[55] This theory became known as the situational theory. Although it had some shortcomings, the situational theory was a useful way to get leaders to think about how leadership effectiveness may depend somewhat on being flexible with different subordinates – that is, not acting the same way towards them all.[56] This approach was developed by Paul Hersey and Kenneth Blanchard.

3.4.3 Behavioural-based approach

The third major development was the behavioural approach. Here researchers tried to discover leadership styles that would be effective across all situations.[57] Most of the studies undertaken in this area used question-

---

Figure 3.3 Leadership traits

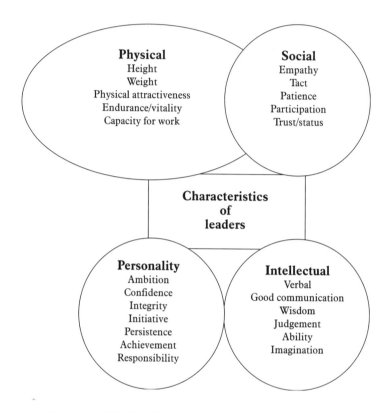

Physical
Height
Weight
Physical attractiveness
Endurance/vitality
Capacity for work

Social
Empathy
Tact
Patience
Participation
Trust/status

**Characteristics
of
leaders**

Personality
Ambition
Confidence
Integrity
Initiative
Persistence
Achievement
Responsibility

Intellectual
Verbal
Good communication
Wisdom
Judgement
Ability
Imagination

SOURCE: Swierczek, F.W. 1991. Leadership and culture: Comparing Asian managers. *Leadership & Organization Development Journal*, vol. 12, no. 7, p. 7. Reproduced with permission.

naires measuring task-orientated and relations-orientated behaviour. These studies were conducted to see how these behaviours correlated with criteria of leadership effectiveness such as subordinate satisfaction and performance. Unfortunately the results from the massive research efforts have been mostly contradictory and inconclusive.[58]

As a result of the various problems experienced with the traits-based, situational and behavioural approaches, newer individual models started to appear. Some of the most popular were models of transactional, transformational and charismatic leadership.[59]

3.4.4 Transactional-based approach

In the transactional leadership approach, leaders are characterised by contingent-reward and management-by-exception styles of leadership.[60] Exchanges or agreements with followers are developed which point out what the followers will receive if they do something right as well as wrong. The transactional leadership approach thus lasts only as long as the needs of both leader and follower are satisfied by the continuing exchange process. It is consequently not a relationship that binds the leader and follower together in a mutual and continuing pursuit of higher purpose. Thus, in a sense one can say that a purely transactional style of leadership may be counter-productive.[61]

3.4.5 Transformational-based approach

In direct contrast to the transactional approach, in which the status quo within the organisation is maintained, the transformational-based approach raises both leaders and followers to higher levels of motivation and morality with a view to changing the present situation by focusing primarily on the external environment. According to Bass, as quoted by Steers *et al.*,[63] transformational leadership consists of four behavioural components – namely (1) charisma, (2) inspiration, (3) intellectual stimulation and (4) individual consideration. Charisma is viewed as the process through which leaders arouse strong emotions in followers, while inspiration refers to leader behaviours such as articulating an appealing vision. Intellectual stimulation, on the other hand, encourages followers to be creative in solving problems, while individual consideration includes leader behaviours that provide special support to followers, such as expressing appreciation for a job well done.

3.4.6 Charismatic-based approach

Where transformational leadership seeks to empower and elevate followers, charismatic leadership seeks to keep followers weak and dependent and to instil personal loyalty rather than commitment to ideals. The existence of charismatic leadership within an organisation is normally rare, as it will occur only when there is a collapse of formal authority to deal with a severe crisis.[64]

3.4.7 Managerial-based approach

A new leadership model – a combination of both transactional and transformational leadership – which appeared in the literature recently also deserves some attention. This model is known as managerial leadership.[65] Flanagan & Thompson, who designed this model, found in their extensive research that the pendulum was clearly swinging back from the emphasis on transformational leadership.[66] According to them, this swing could be the result of the exclusive emphasis on the creative component in the transformational leadership approach. It would appear that a combination of both these leadership styles (i.e. transactional and transformational) might be the answer. Empirical research has indicated that the same leader can display both the transactional and transformational leadership behaviours in varying degrees and intensities, and also in a complementary way.[67-72] Besides encompassing transactional and transformational leadership components, the proposed model also includes a third major component, situational sensitivity. The managerial leadership model enables management to diagnose the organisational situation and deploy the appropriate leadership response – that is, the right combination of transformational and transactional leadership. It is important to note that the precise mix will vary from one organisation to the next and also from one time to another. Working from the basic factors of transformation, transaction and the situation, Flanagan & Thompson found it possible to derive a range of components from these factors – for example:[73]

- **Transformational leadership skills**
  - create a vision
  - communicate meaning
  - inspire
  - empower
  - take risks
  - stir
- **Transactional management skills**
  - agree on objectives
  - communicate information
  - motivate
  - bargain
  - promote security
  - stabilise
- **Situational sensitivity**
  - scans organisation
  - reads jobs
  - understands self.

To be successful, managers will need to have those three macro components, by acquiring their underlying capabilities. Once managers have these skills, they must exercise them holistically; and if their actions and behaviour are in harmony with the demands and expectations of the situation, they will be successful.[74]

It is important to note that each of the components in the model builds progressively on the others. For example, once a vision has been created, it is important to agree on specific objectives that will build that vision. A further critical aspect is that, after this process has been completed, the vision and objectives must also be communicated to the employees. This will give meaning to their work.[75] However, hard facts and information will also be required to set further individual objectives against which to measure performance. We also see that if employees see meaning in what they do, this can inspire them to greater efforts. This process should be accompanied by the empowerment of employees. Devolution of authority will enable employees to stir things up and be innovative, thereby resulting in employees taking risks in exploring new ways of managing new situations that will provide opportunities to adapt to change. If the activities mentioned are not in tune or harmony with the company's environment, they will not be successful.[76]

3.4.8 Strategic-based approach

To conclude our discussion on individual models of leadership, we will look at another new approach that recently appeared in the literature – namely that of strategic leadership. According to Ireland & Hitt,[77] strategic leadership can be defined as "a person's ability to anticipate, envision, maintain flexibility, think strategically, and work with others to initiate changes that will create a viable future for the organisation". From this definition it is clear that this approach will enable an organisation to achieve superior performance when competing in turbulent and unpredictable environments. CEOs who apply practices associated with 21st-century strategic leadership can create sources of competitive advantage for their organisations (see Table 3.2).[78] However, they (the CEOs) will have to cease viewing their leadership position as one with rank and title, but rather as a position of significant responsibility to a range of stakeholders.[79]

In this process, the CEOs will also have to satisfy the requirements associated with six key effective leadership practices, namely:
1   determining the company's purpose or vision;
2   exploiting and maintaining core competencies;
3   developing human intellectual capital;
4   sustaining an effective organisational culture;
5   emphasising ethical practices; and
6   establishing balanced organisational controls.[80]

Table 3.2 Strategic leadership practices for the 21st century

20th-century practices (past)	21st-century practices (future)
Outcomes focused	Outcome and process focused
Stoic and confident	Confident, but without hubris
Sought to acquire knowledge	Seeks to acquire and leverage knowledge
Guided people's creativity	Seeks to release and nurture people's creativity
Work flows determined by hierarchy	Work flows influenced by relationships
Articulated the importance of integrity	Demonstrates the importance of integrity by actions
Demanded respect	Willing to earn respect
Tolerated diversity	Seeks diversity
Reacted to environmental change	Acts to anticipate environmental change
Served as the great leader	Serves as the leader and as a great group member
Views employees as a resource	Views organisational citizens as a critical resource
Operated primarily through a domestic mindset	Operates primarily through a global mindset
Invested in employees' development	Invests significantly in citizens' continuous development

SOURCE: Republished with permission of Academy of Management Executive, from Ireland, R.D. & Hitt, M.A. 1999. Achieving and maintaining strategic competitiveness in the 21st century: The role of strategic leadership. *Academy of Management Executive*, vol. 13, no. 1, p. 54. Permission conveyed through Copyright Clearance Center, Inc.

3.5   Group models of leadership

The leadership models discussed thus far in this chapter worked reasonably well within a fairly stable internal environment. However, as indicated in Chapters 1 and 2, this environment has undergone radical changes during the last number of years. Issues that have had a major impact on the company's internal environment include downsizing, rightsizing, restructuring (implementing matrix structures and flatter organisations), the introduction of teams and the empowerment of employees. The acceptance of the resource-based approach as a method to improve the organisation's competitive advantage has also refocused the leadership researchers to look at new approaches in the field.[81]

An important movement in this regard has been the implementation of group leadership approaches and the movement away from the old power control paradigm (using coercive, expert, referent, legitimate power) to the empowering of others.[82] This new leadership style will require the transformation of the role of managers at all levels within the company, with more time being spent on initiating problem solving among team members and absorbing internal and external information to ensure the best possible decision making.[83]

Thus the formal authority, as the cornerstone of leadership, is nearly obsolete. Leadership should no longer be restricted to one individual who happens to be entrenched in a formal hierarchical position, but must be dispersed across a wide range of diverse individuals, some of whom will not even be within the organisation. This view is shared by Mitch McCrimmon in his thought-provoking article entitled "Bottom-up leadership".[84] According to McCrimmon, such dispersed leadership should not only be spread across more individuals, but should also be broken down into components which will allow everyone to show some aspect of leadership, however small.[85] He thus suggests that an end should be made to characterising leadership solely in terms of personality or behavioural attributes and a start made with thinking about leadership acts. McCrimmon defines such an act as "any initiative which influences how an organisation does business".[86] Thus, an individual may not be classified as a leader according to the old leadership paradigm, but his or her initiatives which lead to an improvement in the functioning of the organisation are definitely leadership acts. McCrimmon remarks as follows in this regard: "In any given team, each member might exhibit technical leadership acts on different projects. If each team member has reasonably effective interpersonal skills he or she may also display people leadership acts from time to time".[87]

Besides considering the leadership acts to be performed by numerous individuals, McCrimmon is of the opinion that it will also be useful to think of leadership functions. Most leadership acts will fall into one or more leadership categories, such as developing new products, enhancing quality and convincing people to contribute to a new plan. According to McCrimmon, some of these categories should be formalised as leadership functions which would be seen as essential for competitive success. These functions can be fulfilled by a variety of senior executives who can exhibit leadership by ensuring that all critical leadership functions are fulfilled by as many people as possible.[88]

With the foregoing discussion as background, we can now look at approaches involving group leadership. Three models of group leadership will be discussed: the cross-functional team leadership model, the self-managed team leadership model, and the executive team leadership model.

As indicated in Chapter 1, a growing trend in organisations today is to give more responsibility to teams rather than individuals.[89] These teams have considerable discretion as to how to execute their duties and have a common purpose, interdependent roles and complementary skills. Although various types of teams can be found, we will concentrate on only three of the more popular types – namely cross-functional teams, self-managed teams and executive teams.

3.5.1 Cross-functional teams

Organisations are increasingly using cross-functional teams with a view to improving co-ordination of the independent activities among specialised sub-units.[90] This type of team usually includes employees from each of the functional sub-units. These teams allow flexible, efficient deployment of personnel and resources to solve problems as they occur. As a result of the different backgrounds of the team members, they are normally creative in generating different ideas and also in providing interesting solutions to various problems.[91] Although cross-functional teams are beneficial to organisations, they do have a number of negative aspects. For example, it is not always possible to get the members to participate sufficiently, and time-consuming meetings may result. A further problem is the possibility of role conflicts as a result of the competing demands of team members.[92]

According to Barry,[93] as quoted by Gary Yukl,[94] four leadership functions can be identified that appear to be essential for cross-functional teams that solve problems, manage projects or develop policy. These are:

- **envisioning** – articulating strategic objectives or a vision and encouraging the team to consider innovative performance strategies;
- **organising** – planning and scheduling team activities;
- **social integration** – encouraging mutual trust and open communication;
- **external spanning** – monitoring the external environment to identify client needs and emerging problems, and promoting a favourable image of the team to outsiders.

3.5.2 Self-managed teams

As indicated in Chapter 1, much of the responsibility and authority for making important management decisions is turned over to self-managed teams.[95] These teams are normally responsible for producing a distinct product or service. While the parent organisation usually determines the mission, scope of operations and budget, self-managed teams are responsible for setting their own performance goals and quality standards.[96] The internal leadership role of these teams involves management responsibilities assigned to the team and shared by the group members. It is typical for self-managed teams to have an internal team leader who is responsible for co-ordinating the team activities. However, it is not unknown for self-managed teams to rotate this position among several team members.[97] According to Yukl, shared leadership in self-managed teams can take many different forms besides the rotation of the team leader position. For example, group decisions about important issues can be made at any time, and members may also assume responsibility for providing co-ordination and direction for specific team activities. Some supervisory functions may also be performed collectively by members and some administrative responsibilities distributed to individual members.[98]

3.5.3 Executive teams

The third group model to be discussed is that of executive team leadership. Much of the earlier leadership literature was mainly concerned with supervisors and middle managers in organisations. However, with the rapid changes taking place within organisations, and the intensifying of competition between companies, the attention has shifted towards the CEO and the top management executive team.[99]

Although the traditional top management structure is still popular, a new approach has developed in which the CEO shares power with the top management team. The advantage of this approach is that team members can compensate for weaknesses in the skills of the CEO.[100] Thus, leadership is becoming a team sport. A set of executives now takes on the responsibility for providing leadership to the whole organisation.[101]

The development of the executive leadership teams has a number of advantages which, according to Nadler & Spencer, include the generation of more ideas, increased ownership of products, increased commitment and motivation, a wide range of views and perspectives, sharing of risks, transfer of expertise and social support.[102]

The quality of team performance at the executive level is critical, not just because of the obvious impact of the team's decisions on organisational performance, but also because of the team's leadership role as a model of appropriate behaviour.[103]

A model designed by Carlos Rivero containing elements of executive team effectiveness appears in Table 3.3.

Table 3.3 Elements of executive team effectiveness

Element	Description
Team design	
Composition	Mix of skills and experiences, values, perspectives, and other characteristics
Structure	Includes the size of the team, the boundaries (who's in and out, the specific formal roles, the nature of team and individual roles)
Succession	Team members' perceptions and expectations of how their performance and behaviour affect their succession prospects
Core processes	
Work management	How the team organises and manages itself to perform work
Relationship management	How the team manages the nature and quality of relationships among its members
External boundary management	How the team deals with elements outside the team and beyond the organisation
Team performance	
Production of results	The team's ability to consistently meet the performance demands on it
Maintenance of effectiveness	The team's ability to meet members' needs and for members to work together over time

SOURCE: Rivero, J.C. 1998. The role of feedback in executive team effectiveness (Chapter 10). In Nadler, D.A. & Spencer, J. L. (eds.), *Executive teams*. San Francisco, Jossey Bass, p. 182. Used with permission.

This model can be used to diagnose threats to the team's effectiveness, and also indicates the team's opportunities. It is important to note that the different elements of the model are linked with one another. For example, the skills and experience of the team have a great impact on core processes such as how information is shared and how decisions are made.[104] Another link is that between core processes and performance. The team's performance is, for example, directly influenced by the quality, effectiveness and appropriate management of the team's work, relationship and external boundaries.[105]

For the executive team to lead the organisation successfully, it must, according to Nadler & Spencer, perform at least four leadership activities successfully. These activities include the following:[106]

- **Governance.** This involves a number of activities such as (1) determining and monitoring the company identity and mission, (2) developing internal policies, processes and rules, (3) managing external and internal relationships, and (4) ensuring future executive capability.
- **Developing strategy.** Developing strategies and choosing the best one is vital for the retention of the company's sustained competitive advantage.
- **Leading strategic change teams (SCTs).** These teams, which are appointed by the executive team, are responsible for driving critical business priorities and initiatives by means of generating innovative solutions for tough issues that strongly affect the organisation's future capabilities, performance and competitive position in the marketplace. Designing effective strategic change teams involves four important steps, namely:
  — establishing the team charter;
  — selecting team members;
  — agreeing on key work processes;
  — embedding a quality assurance process into the work of the team.
  Figure 3.4 gives more detail regarding the above issues, which will not be further discussed.
- **Creating a high-performance operating environment.** To be successful, the executive team must also create a new operating environment that will support the successful implementation of the business strategy. Thus, just as operating plans are needed to implement strategies, appropriate operating environments to execute these plans are also required. According to Thies & Wagner,[107] this process will involve changing how decisions are made, how people deal with each other, patterns of leadership behaviour, how people operate individually and collectively, how people think about customers, competitors and employees, and how the organisation is perceived by the external environment.

Figure 3.4 Strategic change teams building framework

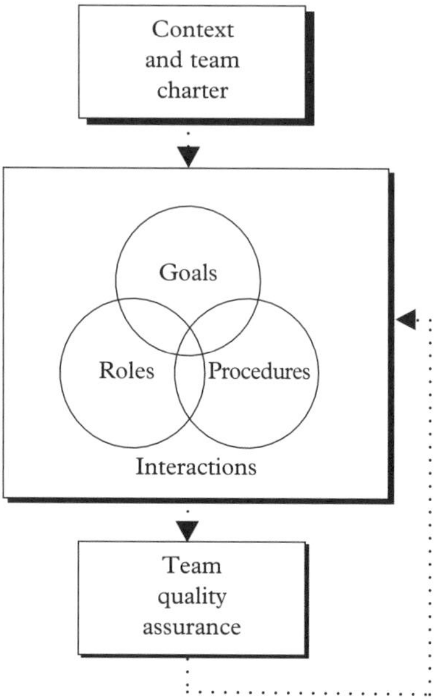

1   **Context and team charter**
   - What is the role of this team in the larger system?
   - What are the team's performance requirements?
   - What are key relationships with other teams?
   - What are the team's rewards and consequences?

2   **Goals**
   - What is the value-added work of the team?
   - What is the core content of the team's agenda?
   - What are the measures of team success?

3   **Roles**
   - What is expected or required of team members?
   - What are the special roles (for example, leadership)?
   - What do subgroups require of each other?

4   **Procedures**
   - How are meetings structured?
   - How is the team's agenda created and managed?
   - How are decisions made?
   - How is team output managed?

5   **Interactions**
   - What behaviour is expected or required of members?
   - Which operating principles will govern behaviour?

6   **Team quality assurance**
   - How will the team be initiated or launched?
   - How are work sessions started?
   - How are work session process reviews conducted?
   - How are periodic process reviews conducted?

SOURCE: Delta Consulting Group, 1991, as it appeared in Ketterer, R.F. & Spencer, J.L. 1998. Leading strategic change teams. In Nadler, D.A. & Spencer, J.L. (eds.), *Executive teams* (Chapter 13). San Francisco, Jossey Bass, p. 254. Used with permission.

3.5.4 New developments

From the discussions in sections 3.4 and 3.5 thus far, it is clear that the subject of leadership has received much attention over the years. However, the type of leadership applied during periods of change has only recently attracted serious attention. What has emerged is the application of a special kind of leadership that appears to be critical during periods of discontinuous organisational change. As a result of this new development, the authors find it appropriate to discuss this issue briefly. The focus for this discussion will be on the interesting work done by David A. Nadler *et al.* and published in the book *Discontinuous change: Leading organizational transformation.*[108]

Nadler *et al.* identify four different types of change that can occur within the organisation. These are:[109]

- **Tuning.** Here organisations initiate incremental change in anticipation of environmental events. There is thus no immediate need for change. According to Nadler *et al.*, this type of change maintains or enhances the fit between strategy and organisation.
- **Adaptation.** While tuning is initiated internally and is proactive in nature, adaptation takes place as a result of external conditions and is reactive in nature.
- **Reorientation.** Here the company initiates change as a result of an emerging environmental shift that is perceived. This will involve redefining the company's identity, vision and mission.
- **Recreation.** As companies do not always have visionary leaders, they are sometimes caught unaware regarding certain changes that are taking place. In this situation they must move quickly and change all the basic elements of the organisational system if they want to survive.

Focusing on the reorientation type of organisation change, Nadler *et al.* suggest that, for success under these circumstances, two types of leadership are required, one "heroic" and the other "instrumental".[110] The heroic leader will excite the employees, shape their aspirations and direct their energy, while the instrumental leader will make sure that the individuals throughout the organisation do indeed behave in ways needed for the change to occur.[111] It thus appears that effective organisational change (reorientation change) will require both heroic and instrumental leadership.

Although individuals may exist who can fulfil both roles, it may be wise also to involve other employees in the leadership roles. According to Nadler *et al.*,[112] the best option is to extend the leadership role beyond the individual leader and create institutionalised leadership. They consequently suggest extending the leadership to at least three groups – namely the senior team, the broader senior management group and, lastly, throughout the entire organisation.[113] (See Figure 3.5.) This makes the challenge of leadership in the organisation even more exciting!

Figure 3.5 Institutionalised leadership

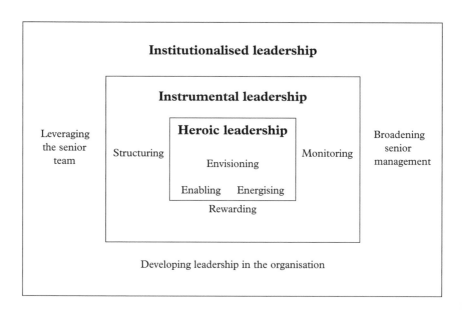

SOURCE: Nadler, D.A., Shaw, R.B. & Walton, A.S. 1995. *Discontinuous change: leading organizational transformation.* San Francisco, Jossey Bass, p. 225. Used with permission.

3.6 Leadership training techniques

Creating an effective selection process is a prerequisite to developing enduring leadership capability within the organisation. However, it is not enough that the managers with requisite skills are identified, they must also be given a chance to broaden and develop their skills through systematic job-related training and developmental experiences.[114]

A large variety of methods have been successfully used for leadership training, including lectures, demonstrations, procedural manuals, videotapes and equipment simulations.[115-118] Interactive computer tutorials are used to learn technical skills, while cases, exercises, business games, simulations and videotapes are used to learn conceptual and administrative skills. Lectures, case discussions, role playing and group exercises are normally used to learn interpersonal skills.

Techniques for leadership development have also been identified in the literature. They include special assignments, job rotation, action learning, mentoring, multi-source feedback workshops, developmental assessment centres, outdoor challenges and personal growth programmes.[119]

Further interesting information pertaining to the development of leaders appears in a summary of the results of a survey of Fortune 1000 companies by the Saratoga Institute in Santa Clara, California (see special report on p. 50).

3.7   The leadership role of HR

Being a business partner, the HR professional plays a crucial role in unlocking the organisation's people potential to help it achieve world-class status.[120] However, this will not be possible if it does not shed its control and bureaucratic role and act like a true leader. Thus, instead of orientating employees to their current roles, HR leaders must disorientate them so that they can take on new roles, new relationships, new values, new behaviours and new approaches to work.[121] To be successful in this regard, activities such as creating an HR vision, developing an overall corporate HR strategy and instilling new values in employees are essential.[122]

Within the work context, developing and maintaining the technology infrastructure to support the organisation's HR programmes and establishing and managing proper communications to and from managers and employees, to name but a few activities, are essential. These activities can all be seen as leadership activities when evaluating the content of this chapter. Thus, according to Kenneth Alvares,[123] HR officers who play a leadership role are held accountable for the bottom line and are less control-orientated.

Using the model designed by Rosen & Brown[124] (see Figure 3.6), we suggest that HR leaders should start their own leadership orientation with some basic assumptions about human nature and organisational life. These assumptions will then influence their values and beliefs about people and organisations. They must then continue to develop an operating style and build relationships with others that reflect these basic beliefs. From there, HR leaders should create a work environment of strategies, systems and practices that grow naturally out of these philosophies. When this is done, all the stakeholders – whether employees, customers, shareholders or society – will benefit.[125]

SPECIAL REPORT

DEVELOPING LEADERS FOR THE 21st CENTURY

Providing or creating a vision is the key difference between managing and leading. Managers administer policies, set practices, maintain systems and direct activities. Leaders inspire and acquire followers with a vision.

This type of behavior or leadership style has not always been the norm. For many leaders in profit-oriented organizations, the modus operandi was simply to increase revenue, decrease expenses and raise the profit margin. Redirecting the organization and its operating philosophy to a more balanced, humanistic and financial vision and style is a recent occurrence.

Saratoga Institute surveyed Fortune 1000 companies to obtain a view of the changes both in style and development of today's leaders. Following is a sampling of those findings, and what high-performing companies are doing to enable their leaders to develop the requisite skills necessary for the 21st century.

1 CHANGING THE ROLE OF THE LEADER.
Outside forces are now major drivers for the new leadership. Eighty-eight percent of the participants indicated that both the nature of leadership and the method for developing leaders had changed. Successful leaders are embracing a "people first – activities second" style. They are putting trust in the human asset to develop and achieve, as opposed to controlling the workforce.

2 CEO & CORPORATE CULTURE.
Over half of all participating companies feel that the CEO is the driving force for determining or changing the culture of the organization. The CEO's behavior is emulated by the rest of the organization's leaders – the more visible the CEO, the greater the impact.

3 PERFORMANCE FACTORS.
Those who lead successful companies take a cohesive, holistic approach to organizational management. The three most important words used to describe leadership were "values, inspiration and beliefs." More organizations are focusing on communicating and teaching company core values and beliefs, and value systems are being reestablished.

4 A GUIDE FOR EFFECTIVE LEADERS.
Participating organizations chose six leadership skills or traits that identify a great leader. They are: vision; values and beliefs; teamwork and collaboration; business and technical knowledge; communication; and personal attributes.

5 FOCUSING ON THE NEXT GENERATION.
Identifying the next generation of leaders requires foresight. Potential leaders exist throughout the organization, yet the process of identification and development is often inadequate. Considering technology, customers, competition and employees is a prime asset. Beyond that, flexibility, openness and communication skills are important.

6 APPROACHES TO LEADERSHIP DEVELOPMENT.
Leadership training is now a corporate priority. Over 70 percent of participants indicate that their organization has a formal leadership development program. New approaches and topics are indicated by many participating organizations, and case studies outline how several organizations are using these new training approaches.

7 EVALUATING LEADERSHIP EFFECTIVENESS.
How will you know that your company's leadership style is effective? Data provides a picture of how organizations can and will measure leaders. The five highest-ranked factors were: profitability; customer satisfaction; employee attitudes/satisfaction; sales revenue increases; and company reputation.

8 THE FUTURE DIRECTION OF LEADERS.
What will the 21st century bring in leadership development training? It requires the complete development of a broad array of leadership abilities. Sixty-two percent of companies report future changes to the leadership development process, and indicate how in the report.

....

This article is based on Saratoga Institute's special report, "Leadership Development," published by AMACOM. Saratoga Institute, Santa Clara, Calif., is known for its pioneering research and reports on performance measurement and improvement. ©Saratoga Institute 1997. To order the full report, call 800-262-9699 or e-mail your order to cust_serv@amanet.org. ARTICLE #8951

Figure 3.6 Reorientating HR for its leadership role

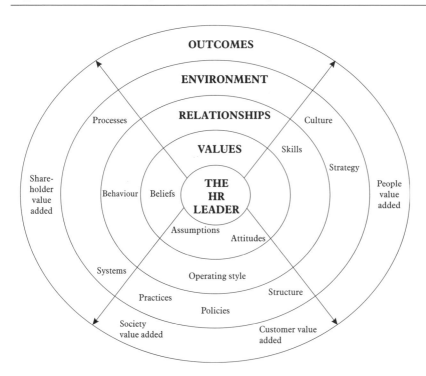

SOURCE: From *Leading People* by Robert Rosen. Copyright © 1999 by Robert H. Rosen. Used by permission of Viking Penguin, a division of Penguin Putnam Inc.

3.8   Summary

In this chapter it has become clear that business as usual will not generate a competitive edge, but that something significantly different – namely effective leadership – is needed. Leaders inspire the creation of a shared and compelling vision, and once this is established, they articulate it, keep it current and enrol others in its vigorous support. Various leadership approaches to achieve this goal are available. In this chapter we have looked at individual models of leadership as well as group models, and their contribution to company performance as well as training and development methods to enhance an organisation's leadership capability. The leadership role of HR and how to improve it was also addressed.

References

1 Nathanson, C. 1993. Three ways to prove HR's value. *Personnel Journal*, vol.. 72, no. 1 (January), p. 19.

2 Schriesheim, C.A. & Neider, L.L. 1989. Leadership theory and development: the coming "New Phase". *Leadership & Organisation Development Journal*, vol. 10, no. 6, pp. 17–26.

3 Ulrich, D. & Lake, D. 1990. Organizational capability: Competing from the inside out. New York, John Wiley & Sons, p. 259.

4 *Ibid.*, p. 259.

5 Jacobs, T.O. & Jaques, E. 1990. Military executive leadership. In Clark, K.E. & Clark, M.B. (eds), *Measures of leadership*. West Orange, NJ, Leadership Library of America, p. 281.

6 Lippitt, M. 1999. How to influence leaders. *Training and Development*, vol. 53, no. 3, p. 18.

7 Drath, W.H. & Paulus, C.J. 1994. *Making common sense – leadership as meaning-making in a community of practice*. Greensboro, NC, Center for Creative Leadership.

8 Richards, D. & Engle, S. 1986. After the vision: suggestions to corporate visionaries and vision champions. In Adams, J.D. (ed), *Transforming leadership*. Alexandria, VA, Miles River Press, p. 206.

9 Hughes, R.L., Ginnett, R.C. & Curphy, G.J. 1999. *Leadership: enhancing the lessons of experience* (third edition). Singapore, Irwin McGraw-Hill, p. 1.

10 Hinterhuber, H.H. & Krauthammer, E. 1998. The leadership wheel: the tasks entrepreneurs and senior executives cannot delegate. *Strategic change*, vol. 7, p. 149.

11 Hughes *et al.* 1999, p. 11.

12 *Ibid.*

13 Bennis, W.G. 1989. *On becoming a leader*. Reading, M.A., Addison-Wesley, p. 18.

14 Leonard, B. 1999. From management to leadership. *HR Magazine*, vol. 44, no. 1, p. 34.

15 Ketterer, R. & Chayes, M. 1995. Executive development: Finding and growing

champions of change. In Nadler, D. Shaw, R. Walton, A.E. & Associates (eds), *Discontinuous change*. San Francisco, Josey Bass, pp. 190–216.

16 Kouzes, J.M. & Posner, B.Z. 1995. *The leadership challenge: How to keep getting extraordinary things done in organisations*. San Francisco, Jossey Bass Publishers, pp. 17–18.

17 Yukl, G. 1998. *Leadership in organizations* (fourth edition). New Jersey, Upper Saddle River, Prentice Hall, p. 19.

18 Platts, M. & Southall, A-M. 1994. Employee communications and effective involvement. In Michael Armstrong (ed), *Strategies for human resource management*. London, Kogan Page, pp. 150–164.

19 Sonnenschein, W. 1997. *Workforce diversity*. Lincolnwood, Illinois, NTC Business Books.

20 Platts *et al.* 1994, p. 153.

21 *Ibid.*, p. 154.

22 This section is based on the work done by one of the authors (Prof. P.A. Grobler) and published in the book Carrell, M.R., Elbert, N.F., Hatfield, R.D., Grobler, P.A., Marx, M. & Van der Schyf, S. 1997. *Human resource management in South Africa*. Cape Town, Prentice Hall, p. 608.

23 Meindl, J.R., Ehrlich, S.B. & Duckerich, J.M. 1985. The romance of leadership. *Administrative Science Quarterly*, vol. 30, pp. 78–102.

24 Miller, D. & Toulouse, J.M. 1986. Chief executive personality and corporate strategy and structure in small firms. *Management Science*, vol. 32, no. 11, pp. 1389–1409.

25 Thomas, A.B. 1988. Does leadership make a difference to organisational performance? *Administrative Science Quarterly*, vol. 33, pp. 388–400.

26 Seltzer, J. & Bass, B.M. 1990. Transformational leadership; beyond initiation and consideration. *Journal of Management*, vol. 16, no. 4, pp. 693–703.

27 Niehoff, B.P., Enz, C.A. & Grover, R.A. 1990. The impact of top-management

actions on employee attitudes and perceptions. *Group and Organisational Studies*, vol. 15, no. 3, pp. 337–352.

28 Kotter, J.P. 1990. *A force for change: How leadership differs from management.* New York, The Free Press.

29 Kirkpatrick, S.A. & Locke, E.A. 1991. Leadership: do traits matter? *Academy of Management Executive*, vol. 5, no. 2, pp. 48–60.

30 Sarros, J.C. & Woodman, D.S. 1993. Leadership in Australia and its organisational outcomes. *The Leadership and Organisational Development Journal*, vol. 12, no. 4, pp. 3–9.

31 Ulrich, D. & Lake, D. 1990. *Organizational capability: Competing from the inside out.* New York: John Wiley & Sons, pp. 259–293.

32 Carnall, C.A. 1995. *Managing change in organizations* (second edition). London, Prentice Hall International, pp. 184–196.

33 Beer, M., Eisenstat, R.A. & Spector, B. 1990. *The critical path to corporate renewal.* Boston, Harvard Business School Press, pp. 179–208.

34 Nadler, D.A., Shaw, R.B. & Walton, A.E. 1995. *Discontinuous change: Leading organisational transformation.* San Francisco, Jossey Bass Publishers, pp. 190–276.

35 Kanter, R.M. 1997. *Frontiers of management.* Boston, Harvard Business Review, pp. 5–26.

36 Rosen, R.H. & Brown, P.B. 1996. *Leading people: Transforming business from the inside out.* New York, Penguin Books, pp. 1–353.

37 Nadler, D.A. & Spencer, J.L. 1998. *Executive teams.* San Francisco, Jossey Bass Publishers, pp. 257–287.

38 Farkas, C.M. & De Backer, P. 1996. *Maximum leadership.* New York, Henry Holt and Company, pp. 17–26.

39 Murphy, E.C. 1996. *Leadership IQ?* New York, John Wiley & Sons.

40 Katzenbach, J.R. & the RCL Team. 1995. *Real change leaders: How you can create growth and high performance at your company.* New York, Random House (Times Business).

41 Hesselbein, F., Goldsmith, M. & Beckhard, R. 1996. *The leader of the future: New visions, strategies and practices for the next era.* San Francisco, Jossey Bass Publishers.

42 Simons, G.F., Vazquez, C. & Harris, P.R. 1993. *Transcultural leadership.* Houston, Gulf Publishing Company.

43 Sarros & Woodman 1993, p. 4.

44 Kenny, D.A. & Zaccaro, S.J. 1983. An estimate of variance due to traits in leadership. *Journal of Applied Psychology*, vol. 68, no. 4, pp. 678–685.

45 Ehrlich, S.B., Meindl, J.R. & Viellieu, B. 1990. The charismatic appeal of a transformational leader – an empirical case study of a small high-technology contractor. *Leadership Quarterly*, vol. 1, no. 4, pp. 229–248.

46 Conger, J.A., 1991. Inspiring others: The language of leadership. *Academy of Management Executive*, vol. 5, no. 1, pp. 31–45.

47 Howell, J.M. & Avolio, B.J. 1992. The ethics of charismatic leadership: Submission or liberation. *Academy of Management Executive*, vol. 6, no. 2, pp. 43–54.

48 Steers, R.M., Porter, L.W. & Bigley, G.A. 1996. *Motivation and leadership at work* (sixth edition). New York, McGraw-Hill.

49 Hughes *et al.* 1999, p. 236.

50 Yukl, G. 1998, p. 82.

51 Steers *et al.* 1996, p. 167.

52 Hunt, J.W. 1992. *Managing people at work* (third edition). Berkshire, McGraw-Hill, pp. 241–242.

53 Steers *et al.* 1996, p. 167.

54 Hunt, J.W. 1992, p. 241.

55 *Ibid.*

56 Hughes *et al.* 1999, p. 62.

57 Steers *et al.* 1996, p. 167.

58 Yukl, G. 1998, p. 64.

59 Steers *et al.* 1996, p. 181.

60 Bass, B.M. & Avolio, B.J. 1994. Transformational leadership and organisational culture. *International Journal of Public Administration*, vol. 17, no. 3 & 4, pp. 541–554.

61 Carrell *et al.* 1997, p. 612.

62 Hunt, J.W. 1992, p. 255.

63 Steers *et al.* 1996, p. 181.

64 Yukl, G. 1998, pp. 326–327.

65 This section of the chapter is based on the work done by one of the authors (Prof. P.A. Grobler) and published in Carrell *et al.*, pp. 612–615.

66 Flanagan, H.D. & Thompson, D.J.C. 1993. Leadership: the swing of the pendulum. *The Leadership & Organizational Development Journal*, vol. 14, no. 1, pp. 9–15.

67 Bass, B.M. 1985. *Leadership and performance beyond expectation*. New York, Free Press.

68 Avolio, B.J. & Bass, B.M. 1988. Charisma and beyond. In Hunt, J.G., Baliga, B.R., Dachler, H.P. & Schriesheim, C.A. (eds), *Emerging leadership vistas*. Lexington, M.A. Heath.

69 Bass, B.M. & Avolio, B.J. 1990. *Manual for the multifactor leadership questionnaire*. Palo Alto, CA, Consulting Psychologists Press.

70 Bass, B.M. & Avolio, B.J. 1994. Transformational leadership and organisational culture. *International Journal of Public Administration*, vol. 17, no. 3 & 4, pp. 541–554.

71 Koh, W.L., Terborg, J.R. & Steers, R.M. 1991. *The impact of transformational leadership on organizational commitment, organizational citizenship behaviour, teacher satisfaction and student performance in Singapore*. Paper presented at the Annual Academy of Management Meeting, Miami, Florida.

72 Howell, J.M. & Avolio, B.J. 1993. Transformational leadership, transactional leadership, locus of control and support for innovation: key predictors of consolidated business unit performance. *Journal of Applied Psychology*, vol. 78, no. 6, pp. 891–902.

73 Flanagan & Thompson, 1993, p. 10.

74 *Ibid.*, pp. 10–11.

75 *Ibid.*, pp. 12–13.

76 *Ibid.*, pp. 14–15.

77 Ireland, R.D. & Hitt, M.A. 1999. Achieving and maintaining strategic competitiveness in the 21st century: The role of strategic leadership. *Academy of Management Executive*, vol. 3, no. 1, p. 43.

78 *Ibid.*, p. 54.

79 *Ibid.*, p. 47.

80 *Ibid.*, p. 49–52.

81 *Ibid.*, p. 47.

82 Ulrich *et al.* 1990, p. 260.

83 *Ibid.*

84 McCrimmon, M. 1995. Bottom-up leadership. *Executive Development*, vol. 8, no. 5, pp. 6–12.

85 *Ibid.*, p. 10.

86 *Ibid.*

87 *Ibid.*, p. 11.

88 *Ibid.*

89 Yukl, G. 1998, p. 351.

90 *Ibid.*, p. 356.

91 *Ibid.*, pp. 356–357.

92 *Ibid.*, p. 357.

93 Barry, D. 1991. Managing the bossless team: Lessons in distributed leadership. *Organisational Dynamics* (Summer), pp. 31–47.

94 Yukl, G. 1998, p. 358.

95 *Ibid.*, p. 359.

96 *Ibid.*

97 *Ibid.*, p. 360.

98 *Ibid.*

99 Nadler & Spencer, 1998, p. 3.

100 Yukl, G. 1998, p. 409.

101 Nadler & Spencer, 1998, p. 1.

102 *Ibid.*, p. 5.

103 Rivero, J.C. 1998. The role of feedback in executive team effectiveness (Chapter 10). In Nadler, D.A. & Spencer, J.L. (eds), *Executive teams*. San Francisco, Jossey Bass, p. 181.

104 *Ibid.*

105 *Ibid.*

106 Nadler & Spencer, 1998, pp. 193–284.

107 Thies, P.K. & Wagner, D.B. 1998. In Nadler, D.A & Spencer, J.L. (eds), *Executive Teams* (Chapter 14). San Francisco, Jossey Bass, p. 258.

108 Nadler, D.A., Shaw, R.B. & Walton, A.S. 1995. *Discontinuous change: Leading organizational transformation*. San Francisco, Jossey Bass, pp. 217–231.

109 *Ibid.*, pp. 25–29.

110 *Ibid.*, pp. 218–224.

111 *Ibid.*, p. 222.

112 *Ibid.*, p. 224.

113 *Ibid.*, p. 225.

114 *Ibid.*, p. 206.

115 Bass, B.M. 1990. *Handbook of leadership: A survey of theory and research.* New York, Free Press.

116 Burke, M.J. & Day, R.R., 1986. A cumulative study of the effectiveness of managerial training. *Journal of Applied Psychology*, vol. 71, pp. 232–246.

117 Latham, G.P. 1988. Human resource training and development. *Annual Review of Psychology*, vol. 39, pp. 545–582.

118 Tetrault, L.A., Schriesheim, C.A. & Neider, L.L. 1988. Leadership training interventions: A review. *Organizational Development Journal*, vol. 6, no. 3, pp. 77–83.

119 Yukl, G. 1998, p. 477.

120 Markowich, M.M., 1995. HR's leadership role in the third wave era. *HR Magazine* (September), p. 93.

121 Yeung, A.K. & Ready, D.A. 1995. Developing leadership capabilities of global corporations: A comparative study of eight nations. *Human Resource Management*, vol. 34, no. 4 (Winter), pp. 529–547.

122 Heifetz, R.A. & Laurie, D.L. 1997. The work of leadership. In Kerr, S. *Ultimate rewards: What really motivates people to achieve* (Chapter 4). Boston, A Harvard Business Review Book, pp. 113–132.

123 Alvares, K.M. 1997. The business of human resources. *Human Resource Management*, vol. 36, no. 1 (Spring), pp. 9–15.

124 Rosen, R.H. & Brown, P.B. 1996. *Leading people: Transforming business from the inside out.* New York, Penguin Books, pp. 365–376.

125 *Ibid.*, p. 367.

4

The strategic role of human resource management

4.1   Introduction

There is no doubt that dramatic changes in both internal and external environments of companies during the past few decades have presented HR professionals with new and important challenges.[1] To address these challenges, the HR function has evolved from playing a limited administrative role to entering into a business partnership with line managers.

As indicated in Chapter 1, HR professionals – in their capacity as business partners – must play a number of new roles to be successful, one of them being the strategic partner role, which involves linking the human resource management practices, systems and policies with the strategic initiatives of the company.[2] In the literature, this process is known as strategic human resource management (SHRM).[3-4]

A number of benefits can be derived from this process, including:[5-6]

- contributing to the goal accomplishment and survival of the company;
- supporting and successfully implementing given corporate and business strategies of the company;
- creating and maintaining a competitive advantage for the company;
- improving the responsiveness and innovation potential of the company;
- increasing the number of feasible strategic options available to the company;
- participating in strategic planning and influencing the strategic direction of the company as an equally entitled member of top management, and
- improving co-operation between the HRM department and line managers.

However, despite these benefits, the strategic use of human resources within companies frequently remains an afterthought.[7]

This chapter will discuss a number of issues relating to how the HRM function can be linked to the company strategy to gain the desired competitive advantage. The following issues will be addressed:

- The basic principles of SHRM.
- The relationship between strategic management and SHRM.
- The development of an HRM strategy.
- The various models of SHRM.

4.2   The basic principles of SHRM

Before we look at some of the basic principles of SHRM, it is necessary to provide a few brief definitions of the concept. One of the early definitions to be found in the literature is that of Tsui, who describes the concept as follows:[8-9]

> The concept of strategic human resource management tends to focus on organization wide human resource concerns and addresses issues that are related to the firm's business, both short-term and long-term. It is particularly useful for designing specific human resource programs, policies, systems or management practices at the organisational or business level. It also suggests that the line executive is the most important constituent for the human resource function.

What is interesting about this definition is that it supports the "proactive" approach to be found within the literature. With this approach HR professionals participate in the strategic planning process and can, as a result of limitations in the company's HR situation, potentially influence the formulation of the company strategy.

In another definition, Dyer & Holder provide more substance to the concept when they remark:[10]

> Strategic human resource management consists of three major tasks. The first task, which arises during the formulation of business strategies, is to assure that the HR issues and implications of various alternatives or proposals are fully considered (their desirability and feasibility). The next task involves establishing HR goals and action plans – that is HR strategies (at all levels) – to support the business strategies. And the final task requires working with line managers as principal clients to ensure that established action plans are indeed implemented.

From the above definitions it is clear that two major issues or aspects need to be in place within the organisation before the SHRM process can function successfully. The first of these is the presence of a strategic management process; the second, the restructuring of the HRM function itself.[11-15]

Thus, it is clear that if the organisation has no process by which to engage in strategic management at the corporate and business level, it will not be possible for the HR function to develop a strategic thrust, since the HR strategy flows from the corporate or business strategy. Also, as the HR function will be evolving from a reactive administrative focus, it will have to be reorganised to address its strategic responsibilities. Thus the HR system must have its operational house in order before it can afford the luxury of concentrating on the formulation and implementation of an HR strategy.[16-17]

As far as the strategic management aspect is concerned, we find numerous descriptions of the concept. Briefly, however, it involves a process that deals with organisational renewal and growth, with the development of strategies, structures and systems necessary to achieve renewal and growth, and with the organisational systems needed to effectively manage the strategy formulation and implementation processes.[18]

For the HR function to operate at the strategic level, it needs to reorganise the existing HR administrative function into three distinct levels – namely strategic, operational and functional.[19-20] At the strategic level, HR professionals fulfil their strategic partner role and are involved in corporate and human resource planning. Casio identifies the following four features of this role:[21]

- Senior human resource professionals meet regularly with their counterparts in line management to formulate and to review broad human resource strategies (those designed to promote innovation, quality enhancement, or cost control).
- Senior human resource professionals participate fully in all top-level business strategy sessions. This permits early evaluation of proposals in terms of their feasibility and desirability from a human resources perspective, as well as an early warning of upcoming human resource management issues.
- Human resource professionals at all levels work closely with line managers on an ongoing basis to assure that all components of the business strategy are implemented adequately.
- The human resource management function itself is managed strategically. It has its own departmental strategy that identifies priorities, directs the allocation of resources, and guides the work of various specialists (e.g. compensation, labour relations).

At the operational level, the HR team develops action plans to meet present labour needs, and at the functional level it will carry out the many activities which ensure that employees are at the right place at the right time and cost. Take, for example, the performance appraisal function. At the strategic level a decision will be made regarding what will be valued in the long term. At the operational level, appraisal systems that relate current conditions and future potential will be set up. At the functional level, the actual appraisal system will be implemented annually and day-to-day control systems will be put in place.

Once the new HR structure has been finalised, it is important that proper communication links are established with line management. This relationship can be enhanced by having regular meetings with line managers, circulating relevant HR reports to them and establishing a computerised HR system that allows access by all stakeholders.[22]

4.3 The relationship between strategic management and SHRM

From the discussion thus far it is clear that if the functioning of an organisation is to be successful, the relationship that must exist between strategic management and SHRM cannot be ignored. However, in many cases, this relationship between the two processes within a company is non-existent for a number of reasons. Rothwell & Kazanas have named a few:[23]

- top managers do not perceive a need for a relationship;
- HR practitioners are perceived as "personnel experts" not "experts in business";
- HR information is sometimes incompatible with other information used in strategy formulation; and
- conflicts may exist between short-term and long-term HR needs.

A model designed by Tichy that indicates the important relationship between strategic management and SHRM will be briefly discussed (see Figure 4.1).[24-25] Although it was developed during the 1980s, we have selected this model, known as the "human resource management cube", because it has several advantages. First, it has been shown to be a relatively powerful model of organisational effectiveness; second, it has important implications for the strategic management of the HR function; and, third, it has been commonly used in the SHRM literature.

According to Tichy, companies are continually confronted by three basic problems that must be managed: a technical problem, a political problem and a cultural problem (see Figure 4.1).[26] As far as the technical problem is concerned, Tichy is of the opinion that, as a result of the external threats and opportunities and the internal strengths and weaknesses of companies, all companies continually face a production problem. In other words, technical

Figure 4.1 The human resource management cube

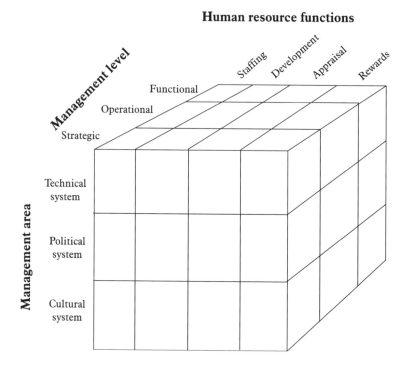

SOURCE: Reprinted from *Organizational Dynamics* (Autumn), p. 75. Copyright © 1982 American Management Association International. Reprinted by permission of American Management Association International, New York, NY. All rights reserved. http://www.amanet.org.

resources must be managed in such a way that the required output is continuously delivered. To solve problems in this area, management is regularly involved in strategy and goal formulation and the design of organisational and management systems.[27]

As far as the political problem is concerned, companies continually have problems with the allocation of power and resources within the organisational structure. Aspects that are important here are the direction in which they are moving, and who will share in the benefits. Decisions in this regard will be reflected in the compensation paid, budget allocations made and the allocation of decision-making power to the different levels within the organisational structure.[28]

Regarding the cultural problem, it is important to remember that companies are held together by their "culture". Culture consists of values, beliefs and views shared by the employees within the company. The organisation must thus continually decide which values, views and beliefs its employees must possess and also which sections within the company must possess which values.[29]

To solve these problems, Tichy suggests that companies design three systems – namely the technical system, the political system and the cultural system. The technical system will include all those aspects that are required to solve the production problem. The political system will contain all the practices, activities and elements that will be involved in the allocation problem, and the cultural system will contain all the symbols, values and elements necessary to address the ideology problem within the organisation.[30]

Tichy suggests that, for these systems to be managed properly, certain aids are required. He identifies the following three as necessary:[31]

• the mission and strategy of the company;
• the structure of the organisation, including the administrative procedures; and
• the HRM systems of the company.

"Mission and strategy" refer to the setting of goals and the development of a strategy. The structure will include the tasks, the manner in which workers are grouped and co-ordinated to perform the tasks, and the management processes of control and information to enable the organisation to function properly. The HRM system will include all the activities such as recruitment, selection, performance appraisal, training and development, and compensation. Thus, for the organisation to be managed efficiently and effectively, these issues must be managed as an integrated whole (see Figure 4.1). This process will be briefly discussed.[32]

4.3.1 The technical system

• **Mission and strategy**. Here the traditional tasks of designing a mission and strategy must take place. Through this process the types of products to be manufactured or services to be provided are identified and resources allocated to make this possible.
• **Organisation structure**. The structure of the organisation is designed in such a way as to make the organisation function properly.
• **Human resource management**. The third management aid to support the technical system is that of HRM. This entails the proper placement of individuals in posts, determining performance levels/outputs and the

development of career and development processes/criteria for filling present as well as future posts in the company.[33]

4.3.2 The political system

- **Mission and strategy.** It is important to determine who will be responsible for the mission and strategy or who will be playing the most important role in influencing it – for example, all the heads of departments, or only the vice-presidents of the company. After the mission and strategy have been accepted, the next step is their physical execution. The strategy might involve the establishment of new businesses, the sell-off of present ones or the amalgamation of two businesses. All these decisions can influence the employees and their jobs – either negatively or positively. These decisions entail the allocation of resources and budgets and can even have an effect on the good relationship between employees.
- **Organisation structure.** The second issue in the management of the political system is the organisation structure. At the technical level, we looked at how the organisation will be structured; here we will consider how power will be distributed throughout this structure – in other words, how much power each division or departmental head will receive with regard to control over their budgets and their employees.
- **Human resource management.** The HR system must fit in with the political system within the organisation. Issues like the following will have to be addressed: who will be promoted or not, how will the compensation system be designed, what benefits will be available and who will be evaluated, by whom and on what grounds?[34]

4.3.3 The cultural system

- **Mission and strategy.** Two issues must be addressed here: the impact of the mission and strategy on the culture of the organisation and the type of culture desired by management. This is vital for success.
- **Organisation structure.** The organisation structure must address a number of elements in the cultural system. The first is the development of a management style to fit the technical and political structure developed within the organisation. For example, a company moving from a functional to a matrix structure needs an open management style instead of a closed one. Second, different subcultures must also be developed within the organisation – for example, the production division must have a cost-

effective culture, while the research and development division must have an innovative and creative one. The important issue here is the management of the different cultures within the structure.

- **Human resource management.** The HRM system provides the final aid in the management of the cultural system, and must be used to develop work-orientated cultures within the organisation. For example, these cultures can be enhanced through the company's training and development processes, and nurtured and developed by means of compensation (for example, by promoting those whose culture supports the goals of the organisation).[35]

To summarise, the strategic management task within an organisation involves more than the mere choice of a portfolio of businesses and the design of strategies; it entails the management of all the different issues discussed above. To do this successfully, it must include the SHRM approach as well. Thus, without the effective and efficient management of the HRM system, strategic management will not be successful. The HRM practices, systems and policies must be in line with the strategic initiatives of the company. For example, each of the HRM activities (recruitment, training, compensation, performance appraisal, etc.) must be viewed from a technical, political and cultural perspective, on a strategic, operational and functional level.

Having indicated the important and vital role to be played by the HRM function within the organisation, the next question that can be asked is: how can we design the individual HRM strategies to make this success possible? In the next section this aspect will be discussed.

4.4   The design of an HR strategy

To implement the SHRM process, one needs HR strategies. Dyer & Holder make the following remarks regarding HR strategies:[36-37]

> While a wide variety of issues are addressed in such strategies, at a minimum they include four components:
> - mission statement or a set of prioritized goals for the function and the major subfunctions (e.g. training, compensation)
> - a proposed organisation structure
> - a programme portfolio to outline priorities and policies and
> - ultimately, a budget to address the issue of resource allocation.

A human resource strategy is described by Labelle as "a set of important decisions an organisation makes about the management of human resources that define an adaptation to both internal and external environments in the pursuit of its objectives".[38] Hax, another researcher, continues with the remark that "a human resource strategy is a critical component of the firm's corporate and business strategies comprising a set of well coordinated objectives and action programmes aimed at securing a long-term sustainable competitive advantage over the firm's competitors".[39]

In other words, in view of the above, a strategy can thus be seen as a plan of action which includes both means and ends. HR goals can, for example, include quality of performance (productivity goals), quantity of employees (HR quantity goals) and costs goals.[40] On the other hand, the means can include, for example, HR practices and HR policies. As far as the use of HR practices is concerned, Schuler has provided an HRM practice menu from which a selection can be made to support a particular company strategy (see Table 4.1).[41]

However, the use of these HR practices can be successful only if the management of a company has in its mission statement made a commitment to its employees. According to Nininger, this component could be compiled as follows:[42]

The people in the organisation will be managed in such a manner as to generate a climate of opportunity and challenge for each employee within which the individual can most effectively contribute to the fulfilment of his/her goals and those of the organisation. This will be accomplished by:

- having a clear understanding of all the qualities of each employee such as skills, knowledge, potential, aspirations and limitations
- setting standards of performance that challenge each employee and by ensuring that this performance is attained
- rewarding excellent employee performance in both material and non-material terms
- planning properly for manpower needs
- providing employees throughout the organisation with opportunities for promotion and for developing their job knowledge, skills and satisfaction
- practising a form of management that allows decision-making authority to be as decentralised as is practical, and
- being alert and receptive to new and productive developments in the field of human resource management.

Table 4.1 HRM practice menu

Planning choices

Informal	....	Formal
Short term	....	Long term
Explicit job analysis	....	Implicit job analysis
Job simplification	....	Job enrichment
Low employee involvement	....	High employee involvement

Staffing choices

Internal sources	....	External sources
Narrow paths	....	Broad paths
Single ladder	....	Multiple ladders
Explicit criteria	....	Implicit criteria
Limited socialisation	....	Extensive socialisation
Closed procedures	....	Open procedures

Appraising choices

Behavioural criteria	....	Results criteria
Purposes: development, remedial, maintenance		
Low employee participation	....	High employee participation
Short-term criteria	....	Long-term criteria
Individual criteria	....	Group criteria

Compensating choices

Low base salaries	....	High base salaries
Internal equity	....	External equity
Few perks	....	Many perks
Standard, fixed package	....	Flexible package
Low participation	....	High participation
No incentives	....	Many incentives
Short-term incentives	....	Long-term incentives
No employment security	....	High employment security
Hierarchical	....	High participation

Training and development

Short term	....	Long term
Narrow application	....	Broad application
Productivity emphasis	....	Quality of work life emphasis
Spontaneous, unplanned	....	Planned, systematic
Individual orientation	....	Group orientation
Low participation	....	High participation

SOURCE: From *Managing Human Resources*, 7th ed., by S.E. Jackson and R.S. Schuler. © 2000 Reprinted with permission of South-Western College Publishing, a Division of Thomson Learning.

Thus an HR strategy will express the intentions of an organisation about how it should manage its human resources. These intentions provide the basis for plans, developments and programmes for managing change. Typical questions to be asked by the HR professional when participating in the strategy process would be: what sort of people do we need in the business to achieve our mission? How can the required changes to our culture and value system be achieved? What are the implications of those plans for the future structure, HR systems and resource requirements?

It is important to note that a number of issues besides the company strategy can influence the formulation of an HR strategy. As indicated earlier in the chapter, this does not take place in isolation but is influenced by both external and internal issues. Externally we think of issues in the economic, technological, social, political, legal, geographical, cultural and labour market environments. Internally, issues such as employee demographics, employee skills, productivity, organisation structure, potential of employees, organisational culture and turnover can all play important roles.

In conclusion, please note that two types of HR strategies can be distinguished, namely organisational strategies and functional strategies. Organisational strategies can be seen as part of the organisational or company strategy and have a major impact throughout the organisation. On the other hand, functional strategies are seen as more narrowly focused and are involved only with the strategic management of HR divisions or departments.[43]

It was inevitable that, with the emergence of SHRM as a field of study and practice, "how to" models also started appearing. In the next section a brief overview of the major types of models found in the SHRM literature will be given.

4.5   Models of SHRM

Several SHRM models have been developed in recent years which describe how the company strategy and HRM should be linked.[44-52] However, two dominant approaches to integration can be found. The first is the reactive role of HRM, in which strategy dictates HR policies, and the second is a proactive role in which HRM is involved in the strategy formulation process itself.

In order to understand the SHRM models found in the literature a classification method designed by Dyer will be applied. Dyer suggests in his four-quadrant model that two dichotomies are important to consider. The first is to separate the organisational- from the functional-level HR concerns, and the second, to differentiate between content and process elements.[53]

According to Lengnick-Hall *et al.*, content concerns specific choices such as policies and practices in SHRM, whereas process focuses on the means by which these policies and practices are derived and implemented.[54] In the literature studied it is clear that content versus process distinctions have prevailed throughout. The different models will consequently be discussed according to their specific classification.

4.5.1 Organisational SHRM content models

Two important models are found here – namely those of Labelle and Wils. In his investigation, Labelle[55] found that company strategy was the determining factor for the content of the organisational HR strategy and that both the content of the organisational HR strategy and the company strategy were influenced by internal and external environmental factors. Various types of HRM practices and goals to fit company strategies were identified by Labelle. Unfortunately, however, the investigation was limited to only 11 companies from diverse sectors. A similar investigation was carried out by Wils[56] in the US. He identified a strong correlation between the content of the company strategy and the content of the organisational HR strategy. However, his investigation was limited to only one company consisting of 22 business units. Although both studies made an important contribution to the content theory of organisational HR strategy, they did not explore the relationship between companies with stable and unstable strategies, to determine whether company strategy is a stronger contributing factor in the content of organisational HR strategy in turbulent or normal times. There is also a need to investigate companies with the same company strategy but different organisational HR strategies.

4.5.2 Functional SHRM content models

A number of diverse models are found in this group. As the purpose of this chapter is not to discuss each model in detail, only a representative number will be evaluated.

In their model, Baird & Meshoulam[57] are of the opinion that two strategic fits must be managed. The first is an external fit, where HRM practices fit the development stage of the organisation; the other is an internal fit, where the components of HRM complement and support each other. The content of the HRM practices is thus determined by the developmental stage of the organisation. Shortcomings of this approach are the fact that Baird & Meshoulam see the classification of an organisation into a specific phase as too simplistic, and the fact that the determination of a specific phase is also largely based on subjectivity.

Miles & Snow,[58] in their model, identify three company strategies which according to them can be found in every company – namely "defender", "prospector" and "analyser". By using these strategies, Miles & Snow identify various types of HRM practices that could support them (see Table 4.2). These practices were based on information gathered throughout various types of companies in Canada. One of the biggest drawbacks of this approach is the idea that strategies are rigid and that the only flexible aspect is human resources.

The last group of models found in this category are those based on the life-cycle concept. Here development occurs in relatively predictable discrete building blocks of birth, maturity, decline and death. Authors like Smith[59] and Stybel[60] have used these building blocks to identify the content of various HRM practices (see Table 4.3).

One of the drawbacks of these models is the fact that organisations do not follow a cycle which includes death, but constantly reform and renew themselves to fit the environment.

4.5.3 Organisational SHRM process models

A very large number of models can be found in this category.[61-71] However, a noticeable limitation of work in this area has been the failure to take a more comprehensive view, matching the HRM function to strategic or organisational conditions.

Nininger's[72] model, for example, provides a framework to enhance organisational effectiveness by integrating the strategic planning and management function with human resources. Golden & Ramanuyum[73] adopt a similar view. Apart from these and a few other studies (an example of Nkomo's[74] model appears in Figure 4.2), little work has been done that takes a comprehensive view of the HRM function at the strategic level. Although these authors provide steps for the integration and implementation of HRM in the organisation, one of the major drawbacks of these models is that they do little to overcome the problems of identifying and analysing the appropriate information, either to characterise the strategic situation or to clarify the HR manager's role under a specific set of conditions. Nor do they consider the inevitable need for change as new products and technologies enter the marketplace.

Table 4.2 The composition of three functional HR strategies

HRM system	Type A (Defender)	Type B (Prospector)	Type AB (Analyser)
Basic strategy	Building human resources	Acquiring human resources	Allocating human resources
Recruitment, selection and placement	Emphasis: "make" Little recruiting above entry level Selection based on weeding out undesirable employees	Emphasis: "buy" Sophisticated recruiting at all levels Selection may involve pre-employment psychological testing	Emphasis: "make" and "buy" Mixed recruiting and selection approaches
Staff planning Training and development	Formal, extensive Skill building Extensive training programmes	Informal, limited Skill identification and acquisition Limited training programmes	Formal, extensive Skill building and acquisition Extensive training programmes Limited outside recruitment
Performance appraisal	Process-orientated procedure (for example, based on critical incidents or production targets) Identification of training needs Individual/group performance evaluations Time-series comparisons (for example, previous years' performance)	Results-orientated procedure (e.g. management by objectives or profit targets) Identification of staffing needs Division/corporate performance evaluations Cross-sectional comparisons (for example, other companies during same period)	Mostly process-orientated procedure Identification of training and staffing needs Individual/group/ division performance evaluations Mostly time-series, some cross-sectional comparisons
Compensation	Orientated towards position in organisation hierarchy Internal consistency Total compensation heavily orientated towards cash and driven by superior/ subordinate differentials	Orientated towards performance External competitiveness Total compensation heavily orientated towards incentives and driven by recruitment needs	Mostly orientated towards hierarchy, some performance considerations Internal consistency and external competitiveness Cash and incentive compensation

SOURCE: Miles, R.E. & Snow, C.C. 1984. Designing strategic human resources systems. *Organisational Dynamics*, vol. 13 no. 1 (Summer), p. 49. (Originally adapted from Canadian Pacific Ltd.) Used with permission.

Table 4.3 Characteristics of HR programmes by maturity stages

HR programmes		Development stages			
		Embryonic	**High growth**	**Mature**	**Ageing**
Compensation	Fixed vs. variable	High variable; low fixed; non-predictable	High variable; low fixed; big carrot	Less variable relative to fixed; predictable	High fixed, lower variable; security
	Central vs. local control of compensation	Local control; immediate response	Policy centralised; administration local	Policy centralised; consistent administration	All control centralised
	Policy line vs. market	High pay for high risk	High pay for excellence	Median pay; high security	Higher pay; higher risk
	Basis of variable compensation	Sales growth; risk; innovation; survival	Growth of sales and profits; new products; share	Control systems; consistency; cost reduction; hold share	Cash generation; cost control; consistency
	Time focus	Short-term, rapidly changing goals	Short-term for operations; longer for strategy	Stronger focus on long-term optimisation	Short-term
Manpower planning	Forecasing of organisational needs	Not used; future totally unpredictable	Forecasting critical to adequate staffing	Forecasting limited to retirements, major reorganisation	Forecasts only to identify excess
	Individual career planning	Not used	Directional use only; opportunities outnumber qualified people	Need employee retention; optimisation of human resources	Needed; optimise fewer opportunities
Management style (selection)	Entrepreneurial vs. bureaucratic	Entrepreneurial; rapid response; directive	Entrepreneurial for growth, but building systems to preserve gains	Bureaucratic; economy of scale; repetitive quality	Entrepreneurial-directive; cuts, reorganises; survives
Employee development	Hiring vs. training	All skills hired; no training	Much hiring needed but training becomes important	Emphasis on internal development and promotion; little hiring	No hiring, no training
Benefits	Profit sharing pension	Profit sharing or nothing; cash or deferred cash	Profit sharing; some guaranteed benefit like savings	Defined benefit pension; also savings	Pension; security

SOURCE: Strategic Business Planning and Human Resources: Part I, by Eddie C. Smith, copyright August 1982. Used with permission of ACC Communications/*Personnel Journal* (now known as *Workforce*), Costa Mesa, CA. All rights reserved.

Figure 4.2 A conceptual model of strategic HR planning

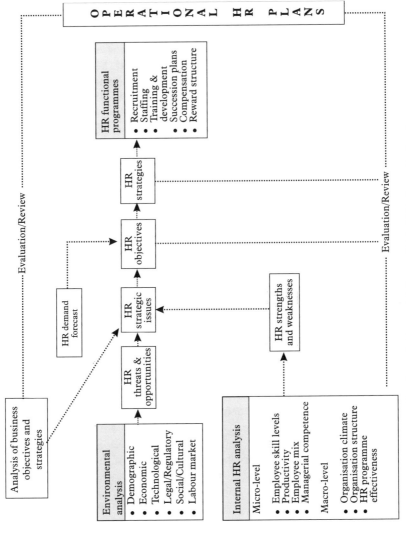

SOURCE: Reprinted from *Long Range Planning*, vol. 21, no. 1, Nkomo, S.M. 1988. Strategic planning for human resources – let's get started, p. 67. Copyright (1988), with permission from Elsevier Science.

4.5.4 Functional SHRM process models

While the research regarding the organisational SHRM process models concentrated on the wider organisation, the emphasis in this category is narrowed down specifically to the HR function. Odiorne's[75] model was the only one found in this category. It seems that no large-scale systematic attempts have thus far been made to study ways in which HR functions determine their strategies, the factors to which they respond during this process or the quality of results obtained. In his model, Odiorne recommends a process by which the company's human resources can be evaluated and classified into four different groups: "stars", "problem children", "cash cows" and "dogs". To classify the workforce, use is made of a matrix whose vertical axis indicates performance and whose horizontal axis indicates potential.

The performance capability of an individual is determined by a management-by-objectives (MBO) approach and the potential by assessment centres.[76] The matrix is then used as a basis for the development of various HRM practices. One of the drawbacks of this approach is that an average individual cannot easily be classified into one of the categories. Subjectivity also plays an important role in the process, and the impression is created that it is a very static and rigid short-term model, so it is not very future-orientated.[77]

When examining the various groups of models as classified according to Dyer's framework, it appears that not much attention is given to content models. Process models, on the other hand – especially the organisational SHRM models – have reached a more advanced stage of development. This is a logical development, as the process of any system must first be implemented before the content can be identified.

4.5.5 General SHRM models

Besides the different types of models already discussed, a number of general models which contain elements of the four different categories of models are also found in the literature. The models of authors such as Dyer & Holder,[78] Rothwell & Kazanas,[79] Lengnick-Hall & Lengnick-Hall[80] and Schuler's 5 P model[81] are of importance here. An example of the model of Rothwell & Kazanas – one of the most comprehensive in the field of SHRM – appears in Figure 4.3.

4.5.6 Models of "fit" versus "flexibility"

In the traditional SHRM models discussed thus far in this chapter, the focus has been on two types of congruence or fit. One is a vertical fit, which involves

Figure 4.3 The SHRM model of Rothwell & Kazanas

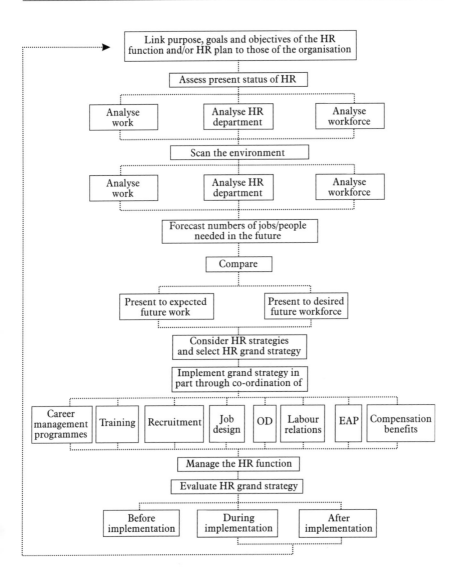

SOURCE: Reprinted from *Planning & Managing Human Resources,* written by Rothwell & Kazanas, copyright 1994. Reprinted by permission of the publisher, HRD Press, Amherst, MA, (413) 253 3488.

the alignment of HRM practices and the strategic management process; the other is a horizontal fit, which implies a congruence or fit among the various HRM practices.[82-83] The vertical fit involves directing human resources towards the main initiatives of the organisation, whereas the horizontal fit is viewed as being instrumental in efficiently allocating the resources needed by the horizontal fit.

In addition to the so-called "fit" approach, a number of articles have also been found in which the emphasis has been on the so-called "flexibility" in SHRM.[84-85] The authors in this area are of the opinion that organisations are faced with a complex and dynamic environment which requires them to adapt to changing requirements by means of being flexible. Thus they see "fit" as a snapshot of a particular short period of time.

The question that can be asked is: can the two types of models exist next to each other, or are they in conflict with one another? Nadler & Tushman,[86] as quoted by Wright & Snell, define congruence or fit as "the degree to which the needs, demands, goals, objectives and/or structure of one component are consistent with the needs, demands, goals, objectives and/or structure of another component". Thus, it can be deduced that organisations should be more effective when they achieve fit than when they do not.

In contrast to this, Sanchez,[87] as quoted by Wright et al., defines flexibility as "a firm's abilities to respond to various demands from dynamic competitive environments". Thus flexibility provides an organisation with the ability to modify current practices in response to changes in the environment. By consistently scanning the environment and detecting changes, organisations will have to have a pool of alternatives available to accommodate these changes.

Wright et al.[88] indicate that, as a result of the existence of "fit versus flexibility", two opposing groups of researchers can be found: those that see the two alternatives as opposites – the so-called "orthogonal" group – and those that are of the opinion that the two approaches are independent of one another – the so-called "complementary" group. The complementary group is of the opinion that both concepts are essential for organisational effectiveness, since the strategic management challenge is to cope with change (requiring flexibility) by continually adapting to achieve fit between the firm and its external environment.

We find that the "orthogonal" group is thus concerned with companies at one point in time, while the complementary group sees fit over a longer time frame while exploring adaptation processes. The first group sees what firms actually do, while the complementary group sees what firms ought to do.[89]

Wright & Snell designed a SHRM model in which they included both views (see Figure 4.4).[90] These authors see "fit" as an interface between an external and internal variable, while "flexibility" is seen as only focusing internally. According to Wright, a company is required to increasingly promote organisational flexibility, in order to achieve a dynamic fit. A brief discussion of the HR model as it appears in Figure 4.4 follows.

In the model, the top half depicts the "fit" component and the lower half the "flexibility" part.

Like other SHRM models, this model starts with the mission and goals of the organisation, followed by an examination of internal resources (strengths and weaknesses) and external developments (opportunities and threats). These make up the basic components of the model that lead to the choice of a given strategy. At the same time, input is also received from the HRM function regarding the strengths and weaknesses, opportunities and threats, as seen from the point of view of the company's human resources.[91] As in previous models, the model also uses the company's strategy to dictate the skills and behaviours required from employees to successfully implement the strategy. This subsequently drives the HRM practices. These desired HRM practices are then operationalised into actual HRM practices which influence the actual skills and behaviours of human resources impacting on the company's performance. Finally, the company's performance is fed back into the strategy formulation process that will affect future strategies. This concludes the "fit" process of the model. It is interesting to note that a number of assumptions are made here – that decision makers are able to identify all the skills and behaviours required for a specific strategy, that decision makers can specify and control all HRM practices, and lastly that the environment stays stable enough to achieve fit.[92]

However, these assumptions cannot always be accepted in an ever-changing environment. Hence the lower part of the model, where flexibility plays an important role. The authors view this part as important in that achieving fit over time may depend upon the extent to which flexibility exists in the system. The flexibility component expands upon the fit component in a number of ways – namely that it is accepted that HR practices can focus on more than just fit, that a broader range of skills than those needed to implement the current strategy exists and that the employees possess a broader repertoire of behaviours than simply those relevant to the strategy.[93] These various skills and behaviours make it possible to implement different strategies that can respond to a variety of different competitive demands. Finally, the model also highlights the role of the participative infrastructure in developing, identifying and exploiting emergent strategies.[94] This model is an interesting development within the SHRM theory and reflects the future trend in the flexible firm.

Figure 4.4 A fit/flexibility model of SHRM

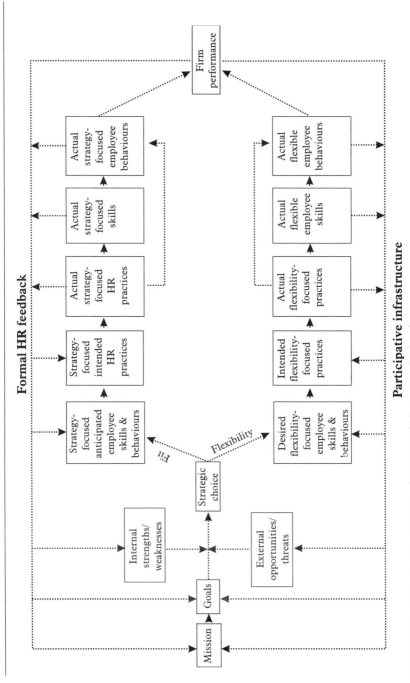

SOURCE: Republished with permission of *Academy of Management Review*, from Toward a unifying framework for exploring fit and flexibility in strategic human resource management, Wright, P.M. & Snell, S.A., vol. 23, no. 4, p. 760. 1998. Permission conveyed through Copyright Clearance Center, Inc.

4.6 Summary

From the discussion it is clear that SHRM plays a critical role in the superior achievement of the company's strategic goals. This, however, is only possible with the availability of a strategic management process and the restructuring of the traditional HRM function into strategic, operational and functional levels. The strong relationship that exists between strategic management and strategic human resource management also received attention, as did the important link between the HR professional and line management.

To operationalise the process, HR strategies need to be designed to support company strategies. These consist of means (e.g. HR practices, policies) and ends (e.g. productivity goals). Many models have also been developed to help with the implementation process, but only a few present a total integrated process. With the existence of firm flexibility the rigid tight fit approach has been supplemented by a flexible arrangement whereby numerous alternatives are generated to address the challenges from an ever-changing environment.

References

1 Lundy, O. & Cowling A. 1996. *Strategic human resource management*. London, International Thomson Business Press, pp. 1–6.

2 Martell, K. & Carroll, S.J. 1995. How strategic is HRM? *Human Resource Management*, vol. 34, no. 2 (Summer), p. 253.

3 *Ibid.*

4 Boxall, P.F. 1992. Strategic human resource management: Beginnings of a new theoretical sophistication? *Human Resource Management Journal*, vol. 2, no. 3, pp. 60–79.

5 Ackermann, K.F. 1989. Strategic human resource management: concepts and applications for managing people at work in turbulent times. Lecture, University of South Africa, Pretoria (July).

6 Ackermann, K.F. 1986. A contingency model of HRM strategy. *Management Forum*, vol. 6, pp. 65–83.

7 Huselid, M.A., Jackson, S.E. & Schuler, R.S. 1997. Technical and strategic human resource management effectiveness as determinants of firm performance.

Academy of Management Journal, vol. 40, no. 1, pp. 171–188.

8 Tsui, A.S. 1987. Defining the activities and effectiveness of the human resource department: A multiple constituency approach. *Human Resource Management*, vol. 26, no. 1, p. 36.

9 McKinlay, A. & Starkey, K. 1992. Strategy and human resource management. The *International Journal of Human Resource Management*, vol. 3, no. 3, pp. 435–449.

10 Dyer, L. & Holder, G.W. 1988. A strategic perspective of human resource management. In Dyer, L. (ed.) *Human resource management: evolving roles and responsibilities*. Washington, The Bureau of National Affairs.

11 Anthony, W.P., Perrewé, P.L. & Kacmar, K.M. 1996. *Strategic human resource management* (second edition). Fort Worth, The Dryden Press, Harcourt Brace College Publishers, pp. 3–30.

12 Walker, J.W. 1992. *Human resource strategy*. Singapore, McGraw-Hill.

13 Greer, C.R. 1995. *Strategy and human resources – a general management perspective.* Englewood Cliffs, NJ, Prentice-Hall.

14 Tyson, S. 1995. *Human resource strategy: Towards a general theory of human resource management.* London, Pitman Publishing.

15 Butler, J.E., Ferris, G.R. & Napier, N.K. 1991. *Strategy and human resources management.* Cincinnati, OH, South Western Publishing.

16 Anthony *et al.*, pp. 3–30.

17 Huselid *et al.*, pp. 171–188.

18 Pearce II, J.A. & Robinson Jr, R.B. 1991. *Strategic management: Formulation, implementation and control* (fourth edition). Homewood, Il, Irwin, pp. 2–19.

19 Anthony *et al.* pp. 3–30.

20 Fombrun, C.J. Tichy, N.M. & Devanna, M.A. 1984. *Strategic human resource management.* New York, Wiley, p. 43.

21 Casio, W.F. 1989. Gaining and sustaining a competitive advantage: challenges for human resource management. In Nedd, A., Ferris, G.R. & Rowland, K.R. (eds), *Research in personnel and human resource management,* supplement I. Connecticut, JA Press.

22 Kavanagh, M.J., Gueutal, H.G. & Tannenbaum, S.I. 1990. *Human resource information systems: Development and application.* Boston, PWS-Kent, p. 2.

23 Rothwell, W.J. & Kazanas, H.C. 1988. *Strategic human resources planning and management.* Englewood Cliffs, NJ, Prentice Hall, pp. 15–17.

24 Tichy, N.M. 1983(a). Managing organizational transformations. *Human Resource Management,* vol. 22, no. 1, pp. 45–60.

25 Tichy, N.M. 1983(b). The essentials of strategic change management. *Journal of Business Strategy,* vol. 3, no. 4, pp. 55–67.

26 Tichy 1983(a), p. 48.

27 *Ibid.,* pp. 48–49.

28 *Ibid.,* p. 49.

29 *Ibid.,* p. 50.

30 Tichy 1983(b), p. 60.

31 Tichy, N.M. 1982. Managing change strategically: The technical, political and cultural keys. *Organisational Dynamics,* vol. 10, no. 2, pp. 59–80.

32 *Ibid.,* p. 68.

33 *Ibid.,* pp. 67–69.

34 *Ibid.,* p. 70.

35 *Ibid.,* p. 72.

36 Dyer *et al.* 1988, p. 32.

37 Cooke, R. 1992. Human resources strategies for business success. In Armstrong, M. (ed.), *Strategies for human resource management: A total business approach.* London, Kogan Page, pp. 25–44.

38 Labelle, C.M. 1984. Human resource strategic decisions as responses to environmental challenges. Unpublished Masters thesis. Cornell University, Ithaca, New York.

39 Hax, A.C. 1985. A new competitive weapon: the human resource strategy. *Training and Development Journal,* vol. 39, no. 5, p. 76.

40 Labelle, 1984, p. 141.

41 Schuler, R.S. 1988. Human resource management practice choices. In Schuler, R.S., Youngblood, S.A. & Huber, V.L. (eds), *Readings in personnel and human resource management* (third edition). St Paul, MN, West Publishing.

42 Nininger, J.R., 1982. *Managing human resources: A strategic perspective.* The Conference Board of Canada. Study No. 71, p. 113.

43 Dyer, L. 1985. Strategic human resource management and planning. In Rowland, K.M. & Ferris, G.R. (eds), *Research in personnel and human resources management* (vol. 3). Connecticut, JAI Press.

44 Baird, L., Meshoulam, I. & De Give, D. 1983. Meshing human resources planning with strategic business planning: A model approach. *Personnel,* vol. 60, pp. 14–25.

45 Dyer, L. 1983. Bringing human resources into the strategy formulation process. *Human Resource Management,* vol. 22, no. 3, pp. 257–271.

46 Dyer & Holder, 1988.

47 Kelleher, E.J. & Cotter, K.L. 1982. An integrative model for human resource planning and strategic planning. *Human Resource Planning,* vol. 5, pp. 15–27.

48 Nkomo, S.M. 1988. Strategic planning for human resources – let's get started.

Long Range Planning, vol. 21, no. 1, pp. 66–72.

49 Rothwell *et al.*, 1988.

50 Schuler, R.S. 1992. Strategic human resource management: linking the people with the strategic needs of the business. *Organizational Dynamics* (Summer), pp. 18–32.

51 Grobler, P.A. 1993. Strategic human resource management models: A review and a proposal for South African companies. *Management dynamics: contemporary research*, vol. 2, no. 3 (Winter), pp. 1–21.

52 Kane, B. & Palmer, I. 1995. Strategic HRM or managing the employment relationship? *International Journal of Manpower*, vol. 16, no. 5/6, pp. 6–21.

53 Dyer, L. 1985, pp. 3–4.

54 Lengnick-Hall, C.A. & Lengnick-Hall, M.L. 1988. Strategic human resources management: a review of the literature and a proposed typology. *Academy of Management Review*, vol. 13, no. 3, p. 456.

55 Labelle, C.M. 1984.

56 Wils, T. 1984. Business strategy and human resource strategy. Unpublished doctoral dissertation, Cornell University, Ithaca, New York.

57 Baird, L. & Meshoulam, I. 1988. Managing two fits of strategic human resource management. *Academy of Management Review*, vol. 13, no. 1, pp. 116–128.

58 Miles, R.E. & Snow, C.C. 1984. Designing strategic human resources systems. *Organisational Dynamics*, vol. 13, no. 1, pp. 36–52.

59 Smith, E.C. 1982. Strategic business planning and human resources (part I). *Personnel Journal*, vol. 61, no. 8, pp. 606–610.

60 Stybel, L.J. 1982. Linking strategic planning and manpower planning. *California Management Review*, vol. 25, no. 1, pp. 48–56.

61 Baird *et al.* 1983.

62 Cassell, F.H., Hervey, A. & Roomkin, J. 1985. Strategic human resources planning: An orientation to the bottom line.

Management Decision, vol. 23, no. 3, pp. 16–28.

63 Dyer, L. 1983. Bringing human resources into the strategy formulation process. *Human Resource Management*, vol. 22, no. 3, pp. 257–271.

64 Galosy, J.R. 1983. Meshing human resources planning with strategic business planning one company's experience. *Personnel*, vol. 60, pp. 26–35.

65 Gould, R, 1984. Gaining a competitive edge through human resource strategies. *Human Resource Planning*, vol. 7, no. 1, pp. 31–38.

66 Kelleher *et al.* 1982, pp. 15–27.

67 Manzini, A.O. & Grindley, J.D. 1986. *Integrating human resources and strategic business planning*. New York, American Management Association.

68 Nkomo, S.M. 1988.

69 Rothwell *et al.* 1988.

70 Schuler, R.S. 1992.

71 Deleny, J.E. & Doty, D.H. 1996. Modes of theorizing in strategic human resource management: Tests of universalistic, contingency, and configurational performance predictions. *Academy of Management Journal*, vol. 39, no. 4, pp. 802–835.

72 Nininger, J.R. 1982. *Managing human resources: a strategic perspective*. Study no. 71. The Conference Board of Canada.

73 Golden, K.A. & Ramanuyam, V. 1984. Between a dream and a nightmare: On the integration of the human resource management and strategic business planning process. *Human Resource Management*, vol. 24, pp. 429–452.

74 Nkomo, S.M. 1988.

75 Odiorne, G.S. 1984. *Strategic management of human resources: A portfolio approach*. San Francisco, Jossey Bass.

76 *Ibid.*, p. 66.

77 *Ibid.*, p. 66–67.

78 Dyer *et al.* 1988, pp. 1–31.

79 Rothwell *et al.* 1988.

80 Lengnick-Hall *et al.* 1988, pp. 454–470.

81 Schuler, R.S. 1992.

82 Wright, P.M. & Snell, S.A. 1998. Toward a unifying framework for exploring fit and flexibility in strategic human resource

management. *Academy of Management Review*, vol. 23, no. 4, p. 756.

83 Myne, L., Tregaskis, O. & Brewster, C, 1996. A comparative analysis of the link between flexibility and HRM strategy. *Employee Relations*, vol. 18, no. 3, pp. 5–24.

84 Kerr, J.L. & Jackofsky, E.F. 1989. Aligning managers with strategies: management development versus selection. *Strategic Management Journal*, vol. 10, pp. 157–170.

85 Milliman, J., Von Glinow, M.A. & Nathan, M., 1991. Organisational life cycles and strategic international human resource management in multinational companies. Implications for congruence

theory. *Academy of Management Review*, vol. 16, pp. 318–339.

86 Nadler, D. & Tushman, M. 1980. A diagnostic model for organisational behaviour. In Hackman, J.R., Lawler, E.E. & Porter, L.W. (eds), *Perspectives on behaviour in organisations*. New York, McGraw-Hill, pp. 83–100.

87 Sanchez, R., 1995. Strategic flexibility in product competition. *Strategic Management Journal*, vol. 16, pp. 135–159.

88 Wright *et al.* 1998, p. 757.

89 *Ibid.*

90 *Ibid.*, pp. 759–761.

91 *Ibid*, p. 759.

92 *Ibid.*

93 *Ibid.*, pp. 757–761.

94 *Ibid.*, p. 761.

5

Managing flexible patterns of work for competitive advantage

5.1 Introduction

In recent years a variety of factors – such as increasing economic volatility, competitiveness and new technology – have led many organisations to actively seek more efficient and effective ways of utilising their resources.[1-2] In addition, the "internationalisation" of the marketplace has shifted competitive advantage from the traditional areas of capital and technology to the management of an organisation's human resources.[3] A key aspect in the development of competitive advantage through human resources is the ability of management to flexibly adjust the available internal and external labour market resources in line with the supply and demand of the market, with minimal disruption to the production process.[4-12] As Ursell[13] notes:

> A major goal implicit in the idea of flexible labour is to render HRM as a strategic, rather than merely a tactical activity. . . . By this is meant a multi-fold process involving one or many of the following:
>
> (i) for any individual worker, a wider range of tasks and abilities and a willingness to employ them on behalf of the organisation which purchases them;
>
> (ii) a greater variety in the time periods of employment;
>
> (iii) a greater ability by the employer to dispense with certain workers when not strictly essential to the production process (an ability which may be grounded in the replacement of traditional contracts of employment by franchise and subcontractor relations, and/or the greater use of part-time and temporary employees); and
>
> (iv) a greater capacity among workers (in both internal and external labour markets) to be so deployed, necessitating changed attitudes for all, and skill and time-management change for some.

The development of these work patterns and practices indicates a new-found strategic focus by management, integrating both the 'hard' or quantitative approach to human resources (which emphasises the link to organisational strategy) and the 'soft' or qualitative approach (which focuses on the developmental aspects of managing human resources).[14-15] In this chapter we will thus consider the following issues:

- What is flexibility?
- The growth of global flexibility.
- Flexibility and organisational design.
- Advantages and disadvantages of flexible patterns of work.

5.2   What is flexibility?

Difficulty in defining "flexibility" occurs because the term has been applied to a wide range of issues and levels of analysis.[16-17] At a national level the debate is focused on rigidities in the regulation of the labour markets.[18] At an organisational level flexibility is concerned with the integrative use of employment practices and organisational structures to create a capacity to adapt and manage innovation.[19-23] In the context of these dimensions the following forms of flexibility have been identified.

Functional flexibility refers to management's ability to deploy and re-deploy particular sections of the workforce to a wide range of tasks, in response to market demand, as and when required. To ensure that this can be achieved efficiently, employees are trained in a wide range of skills. As Atkinson notes:[24]

> This might mean the deployment of multi-skilled craftsmen from mechanical, electrical and pneumatic jobs; it might mean moving workers between indirect and direct production jobs or it might mean a complete change of career. . . . As products and production methods change, functional flexibility implies that the same labour force changes with them, in both short and medium term.

The volatility of product markets and the blurring of skill boundaries as a result of technological change provide the continuing environment for the development of this form of flexibility. Central to the development of functional flexibility is the reversal of the Taylorist (or scientific management) practices of fragmentation and de-skilling.[25]

Numerical flexibility is a quantitative approach to the utilisation of the workforce, and is based on the principle of relating the size of the workforce easily and at short notice to the levels of economic activity.[26] As the workload fluctuates, management has the option to adjust or redeploy its human resources accordingly.[27-28] The use of casual, part-time and subcontracted workers typically provides this form of flexibility.

The pressures of unpredictable short-term fluctuations in demand, combined with increased competitiveness, make these work patterns efficient and effective to sustain, as organisations are relieved of the cost of a fixed labour force.[29] While these patterns of work organisation have been traditional aspects of some segments of the labour market (for example the service and retail sectors), the use of these work practices to externalise traditional core organisational activities is the major factor in increasing enterprise efficiency through numerical flexibility.[30-31]

Work-time flexibility or *internal numerical flexibility* is a further process of adjusting the "quantity and timing of labour input without modifying the number of employees".[32] This has been part of the traditional patterns of work organisation (e.g. overtime and shift working), although it has traditionally incurred financial penalties. The incorporation of these patterns of work into contract hours per week, month or year[33] provides the organisation with the flexibility to arrange and adjust work patterns, and leads to a closer correlation between labour utilisation and production demands, without financial penalty or the additional costs of hiring labour.[34]

Job sharing refers to a situation where one job (often full-time) is split between two (or more) employees. The employees may work a variety of combinations, including split day or split week or alternating weeks. These work patterns can provide both functional and numerical flexibility.

Distancing relates to the outsourcing of activities that may include core and non-core activities. The outsourcing of non-core activities (e.g. cleaning, catering and security) is well established, and the increased outsourcing of traditional core activities, particularly in the human resources area,[35] facilitates the reduction of the core or permanent workforce.

Financial flexibility is a compensation system designed to facilitate the development of flexible patterns of work, in particular numerical and functional flexibility. As Atkinson outlines:[36]

> Financial flexibility is sought for two reasons: first, so that pay and other employment costs reflect the state of supply and demand in the external labour market.... Secondly, and probably of greater importance in the long term, pay flexibility means a shift to new pay and remuneration systems that facilitate numerical or functional flexibility, such as assessment-based pay systems in place of rate-for-the-job systems.

Financial flexibility therefore provides the duality of (a) allowing market forces to dictate relative wage rates, providing cost-efficient numerical flexibility to the organisation, and (b) providing the incentive for the core workforce to increase its skill base by relating pay to skill levels.

Procedural flexibility is the central tenet in the development of flexible patterns of work, particularly in the highly regulated labour markets. Procedural flexibility is concerned with the establishment of consultative mechanisms for introducing changes or negotiating variations in work practices, primarily through changes in both legal and traditional practices covering employment.[37] As Wood notes:[38]

> In most industrialised countries the "flexibility debate", concerned with changing rigidities in labour and employment patterns, has been an important element in industrial policy making and industrial relations ...

At the level of the organisation, the process can range from a directive to a participative framework of negotiation. The substantive aspects of the traditional "Taylorist" relationship between employer and employee and the employee's representative (trade unions) are fundamentally recast for flexible patterns of work to be fully utilised.[39-40] Central to the tenet of procedural flexibility is the acceptance of, and a role in managing and co-operating in, the new relationship for the employees and their representatives.[41] Such procedures are indicative of commitment to joint administration of labour flexibility within the workplace.[42] Procedural flexibility facilitates the combination of work patterns and practices that increase the utilisation of the enterprise's human resources.[43-46]

Regulatory flexibility is a process to encourage and facilitate the establishment, development or relocation of enterprises through the relaxation, amendment or exempting of public policy. This may include changes in labour law restrictions or issues of occupational health and safety.[47]

Mobility, or *location flexibility,* involves a change in the nature of work, or a career change with the same employer.[48] It may also mean a change in work location by means of telecommuting and virtual teams (see Chapter 1), where the location is incidental to the work.

Cognitive flexibility is the mental frame of reference required to effectively perform in the job and at the level of cognitive skill required.[49] The development of new forms of flexibility have significantly changed and continue to modify the psychological contract between the employer and the employee, as indicated earlier in the book. From the development of less secure forms of employment – even to the extent of zero-based contracts (where no hours are actually guaranteed) – through to the implementation of multi-skilling (requiring the development of new skills, knowledge and competencies), employees have had to accept and adjust to the differing demands and expectations that are placed on them by the organisation.[50-52]

Organisational flexibility is a structural response to the development of the flexible patterns of work described above. Despite the increased interest in the development of flexible work practices, there is actually little that is new in any of these patterns of work. What is new, however, is management's explicit desire to seek to develop integrative or multiple forms of flexibility.[53] In this context, the pursuit of multiple flexibilities requires a parallel development in organisational forms to accommodate these changes.[54] The contention is that the traditional hierarchy/bureaucracy organisation cannot adequately handle these changes in work patterns and must therefore be replaced by organisational structures with the capacity to adapt and manage change and innovation.[55-56]

5.3   The growth of global flexibility

There is little doubt that flexible patterns of work have been one of the major areas of research and discussion in management literature over the past two decades, as organisations have sought ways to increase their competitive advantage through better utilisation of one of their most expensive assets – labour. The continuing currency of flexibility can be seen in the globalisation of the issue, the development of national and regional labour market policies, the output of public and private research units and policy makers and the dedication of whole (special) issues of academic journals to the subject.[57-58] To illustrate the global nature and importance of flexible patterns of work, an overview of the research illustrates its centrality in the development of competitive advantage through the deployment and redeployment of human resources.

5.3.1 Flexible work patterns in Europe

Arguably, the origins of the debates on flexibility emerged in Europe,[59-60] where the most extensive research has been undertaken in the development of work patterns associated with flexibility. In particular, the Cranfield Network of European Human Resource Management (Cranet-E) has undertaken an extensive analysis of work patterns across 18 countries and 6 000 organisations employing 200 or more people. The results of this research indicate that aspects of numerical flexibility, in particular part-time and contractual (short-term contracts and subcontracting) flexibility, have been major forms of employment growth in the past decade, with almost one in seven employees working part time.[61] However, despite this upward trend the research does identify considerable variations across countries and regions. In particular, Tregaskis et al.[62] identify a north–south divide with regard to the use of part-time employees. Around 20–30 per cent of the workforce in Nordic countries, the Netherlands and the UK are identified as part time. This contrasts with the Mediterranean countries of Greece, Spain, Italy, and Portugal, with less than 10 per cent of the workforce categorised as part time.[63]

The use of contractual flexibility (which implies a limited contractual relationship between the parties) also indicates strong growth across all European countries. However, this growth varies considerably from country to country. The southern European countries of Greece and Spain show extensive use of these forms of flexibility, with more than 30 per cent of the workforce employed in this way. By contrast, northern European countries such as Luxembourg, Belgium and the UK have less than 7.5 per cent of their workforce engaged under these conditions.[64]

The concept of financial flexibility also varies markedly across Europe, according to the Cranet-E research. However, the use of annual hours is also gaining impetus, with major organisations such as Philips, British Gypsum and Lever Brothers, NatWest Bank and Panasonic taking the opportunity to eliminate the cyclic cost of underutilisation of the workforce and overtime payments in high-demand periods.[65-66]

With regard to functional or task flexibility, Brewster[67] notes a genuine interest in the development of more intrinsically satisfying employment through the use of flexibility. This is also supported by Gunnigle et al.,[68] who note a marked increase in the use of functional, numerical and financial flexibility. They note that the variations across European countries (and industries) identified in research such as the Cranet-E, is contingent upon market pressures, institutional arrangements, local customs and legislation. However, in regard to the changes identified by the Cranet-E research, Brewster notes:[69]

> Taken overall, the evidence is incontrovertible: there has been a substantial change in Europe's labour markets. Employers now have open to them, and are using more extensively, a wider range of means of getting work done.... The evidence shows that there has been a drive to develop different forms of working practices ... across Europe. This drive is created by the requirement to use the most expensive items of operating costs – the labour that organisations use – in the most cost-effective way.

5.3.2 Flexible work patterns in Asia

As if to emphasise the global nature of flexible patterns of work, the newly industrialising economies of Asia, traditionally considered the catalyst for much of the change driving the review of Western work patterns, have also adopted more flexible patterns of work to increase competitiveness as market instability and competition have increased. Hong Kong, for example, has increased its use of non-standard employment as there is little statutory regulation covering (or protecting) employees engaged under these conditions as regards dismissal or redundancy payments.[70] This, combined with increased labour costs and regional instability, provides organisations with the flexibility they need to adjust to market conditions. This philosophy has also infiltrated the public sector, with non-core activities increasingly being subcontracted out.[71]

Malaysia's historical links with Britain and the US, combined with the hosting of organisations from these and other Western countries,[72] have resulted in a hybrid of work patterns and practices. However, the increasingly close ties with countries in its own region – in particular Japan – have seen the increased adoption of techniques such as lean production to increase organisational competitiveness.[73] Finally, the issue of flexibility in South Korea has been of particular interest as this was one of the countries most severely hit by economic turbulence in the Asian market. As organisations seek to restructure, the traditional hierarchical bureaucratic organisational forms (Chaebols) are unable to cope with increased instability and competitiveness. Organisational restructuring and the development of work patterns and practices which increase employees' autonomy are seen as central issues in developing competitive strategies.[74]

5.3.3 Flexible work patterns in Australia, New Zealand and South Africa

The development of flexible patterns of work in Australia has generated considerable interest and research as Australia continues down the road of managed microeconomic reform and deregulation of the labour market.[75-79] Most of this research has been focused at the organisational level and suggests a general adoption of a variety of working practices associated with flexibility, in particular numerical and functional flexibility. The most recent and arguably the most comprehensive analysis of the Australian environment has been undertaken using the Cranet-E survey.[80] The survey of 299 organisations with 200+ employees revealed extensive use of numerical flexibility. The survey found that 59 per cent of organisations were increasing their use of part-time and casual employment, 50 per cent were increasing their use of temporary, casual, subcontracting and outsourcing work practices, and 40 per cent were increasing their use of flexible working hours and job sharing.[81] What is apparent from the survey is that the trends in Australia correspond to those developing in Europe.

Until the early 1990s, New Zealand also had a highly regulated and centralised labour market. However, the Employment Contract Act (1991) replaced the traditional centralised collective system with individual contracts underpinned by a set of minimal (or safety) statutory entitlements.[82] Despite these changes, a comparison with Australia (see Table 5.1) indicates a similar breakdown in workforce characteristics. Interestingly, the major difference is that Australia has twice the proportion of employees whose work is identified as casual.[83] As is the case in Australia, flexible patterns of work in New Zealand are still less common forms of employment.

The South African labour market system has traditionally been far less regulated than either Australia or New Zealand (and reflects in many respects the traditional voluntary system of the UK). Despite this, South Africa displays a highly traditional employment structure, with almost 90 per cent of employees categorised as permanent full-time, and 78 per cent of employees working a standard working week – defined as working between 6 a.m. and 7 p.m., Monday to Friday.[84]

Table 5.1 Distribution of workforce (%)

Employment form	Australia	New Zealand	South Africa
Permanent full-time	67	69	87
Permanent part-time	13	15	1
Apprentice	2	1	1
Fixed term	2	3	3
Temporary	2	3	5
Casual/occasional	10	5	2
Contractor/consultant	4	3	2
Standard	52	62	78

SOURCE: Brosnan *et al.* 1997. *Non-standard employment: Results from a workplace survey in three countries.* Paper presented at the Fifth IIRA European Regional Industrial Relations Congress, Dublin (26–29 August), p. 4. Used with permission.

5.4   Flexibility and organisational design

As is clear from the extensive debate on flexibility, what has emerged from empirical research is the increasing use of multiple forms of flexible patterns of work, to facilitate more timely responses to the competitive forces of the market.[85-87] This has required the parallel development of organisational structures to facilitate these changes.[88-89] Organisational flexibility therefore provides management with the template to adjust and utilise the available human resources in a flexible manner in response to changing demands.[90-91] Two models have attracted particular attention – flexible specialisation and the flexible firm, or core-periphery, model.

5.4.1 Flexible specialisation

Flexible specialisation is based upon the premise of an emerging dynamic economic environment characterised by fragmented and niche markets. In order for an organisation to compete effectively, it requires a workforce with polyvalent skills working on multi-functional machinery and innovative technology, accommodating ceaseless change in the production process – multiple flexibility.[92-95] The focus is on economies of scope rather than scale.[96] To accommodate these new patterns of work requires the redefining of the way the organisation is structured.[97-99] These simultaneous changes are described by Sparrow & Marchington[100] as parallel flexibility.

Evidence of world-competitive organisations applying the flexible specialisation approach to the organisation of resources has been identified in a variety of regions, including Baden-Wurttemberg in Germany and Silicon Valley in the US.[101] However, it is the northern Italian regions of Romagna and Bologna that have generated the most interest.[102-104] These regions support a diverse range of industries, including engineering, textiles, clothing and food processing, using flexible specialisation as the basis of production.[105] They act as integrated and self-contained economic systems,[106] producing varied and customised goods (see "The case of Benetton", p. 91).

The key elements in the labour process are minimal skill differences within organisations and across skill boundaries, as well as between conception and execution.[107] A small core organisation is maintained by continually "splitting" the production process when the organisation reaches a critical mass. At this point, a satellite organisation may be set up under the control of the central core unit. This modern "putting-out" system allows the core organisation to reduce fixed cost investments of production, while maximising labour market flexibility. The focus of production is displaced to the subcontractor, who must contend with market demands and fluctuations.[108]

Figure 5.1 Schematic representation of the decentralisation of production

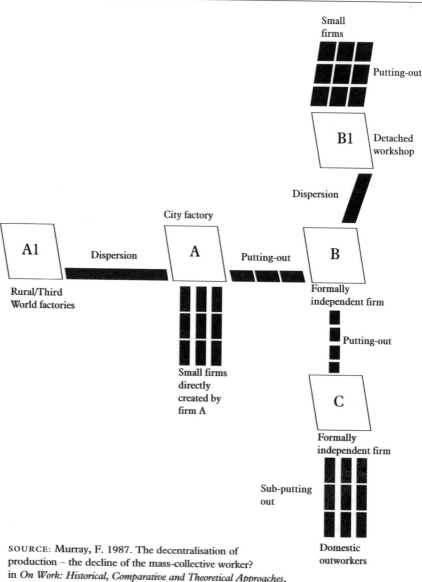

SOURCE: Murray, F. 1987. The decentralisation of production – the decline of the mass-collective worker? in *On Work: Historical, Comparative and Theoretical Approaches,* edited by R.E. Pahl, Blackwell, 1988, p. 268. Used with permission.

The case of Benetton

The major exponent of the flexible specialisation form of production is considered to be the international fashion house Benetton. Benetton's workforce of 11 500 comprises 1 500 direct employees (or 13 per cent of the total workforce), with the remainder employed by subcontractors in factories employing 30–50 workers each.[109] A key aspect of the work patterns and practices at Benetton is the integration of jobs, decision making, conception and execution between the core organisation and the (peripheral) subcontractors. The clothing/fashion industry is a volatile and uncertain market within which to operate. Through the innovative use of information technology, Benetton is in direct contact with its sales points, which provide up-to-date product information for analysis at head office.

Up-to-date sales information allows Benetton to identify which styles and colours are selling and thus place orders for these items with subcontractors.[110] This approach allows production runs to be varied, modified and altered, based on market trends and demands.[111-114] It also allows Benetton to pass on to the subcontractor the cost of holding reserve stock and raw materials, as well as employment and the means of production. This forces subcontractors to be responsive to market variations.[115]

Other global organisations competing in this region developing their own forms of flexible specialisation include Fiat Motor Company, which has introduced flexible robot systems and decentralised work groups, and has outsourced assembly, suspension and electronic systems production.[116] The electronics giant Olivetti has increased the use of flexible technology in the production process, because of the decreasing life cycle and increasing obsolescence of products within the electronics industry.[117] Both Fiat and Olivetti have developed extensive "putting-out" systems on a regional, national and international basis.[118] On a smaller scale, the Morni motorcycle plant in Bologna employs a small "core" workforce. Except for the camshaft and the engine mounting, all the component manufacture is outsourced to subcontractors.

Many of these enterprises have also developed a highly integrated group of co-operatives or associations, which provide administrative services and co-ordinate purchasing, thus providing economies of scale. This integrative network places these small firms at the core of capitalist development.[119]

Despite the success of this model at a regional level,[120-121] several critiques suggest that this is a difficult model to sustain and replicate.[122-124] Pollert,[125] for example, argues that:

The niche company may innovate, but only in the short term; the large retailer and large producer can quickly capture that product and exploit its entrenched advantage in the market.

This is reinforced by evidence indicating that large organisations have fared well in sectors (and regions) where flexible specialisation is predominant as they continue to restructure and invest in new technology.[126-129] Research also indicates that Benetton itself departs from the ideal (multi-skilled) integrative model by exploiting subcontractors, who are poorly paid and take the burden of risk because of the nature of their relationship with the core organisation.[130-132] All variations in market demand and insecure employment are reflected in the secondary or peripheral sector of this model.[133-134] It is also well documented that there is a clear connection between the proliferation of small enterprises and "black" labour, to avoid social welfare, tax and minimum wage levels.[135-138] Tomaney sums up the problems with this model by noting:[139]

> In summary, it is possible to identify three major problem areas emerging from the flexible specialisation theory in its application to changes in the production process. These are: first, the utility of the mass production/flexible specialisation dichotomy itself; second, the inability to account for diverse outcomes to the process of restructuring ... and finally, the fact that even where instances of flexible specialisation can be identified it does not necessarily have the benefits for labour which they assume.

The concept of flexible specialisation appears therefore to be more of a regional phenomenon or variation.[140-141] In this context it appears to be associated with the ability to exploit rather than enhance the available human resources. As Hyman notes, "In this sense the 'second industrial divide' may mean, literally, a growing polarisation in conditions of work."[142]

5.4.2 The flexible firm model

Research by the Institute for Employment Studies (IES) (formerly the Institute of Manpower Studies (IMS)) in the UK identified the development of a distinct organisational structure to accommodate the development of multiple forms of flexibility, in particular functional, numerical and financial flexibility.[143-145] Thompson & McHugh note that the *flexible firm* or *core-periphery model* provides competitive advantage through the restructuring of the employment relationship:[146]

[the flexible firm model] is based on a break with unitary and hierarchical labour markets and organisation of internal means of allocating labour, in order to create a core workforce and a cluster of peripheral employment relations.

In place of the traditional hierarchical structures, the flexible firm model redefines the organisation into two broad segments – the core and the periphery. The make-up of the two segments reflects the different types of flexibility required by the organisation. The core reflects the need for the organisation to develop a permanent, highly skilled group of employees with internal career paths.[147-149] As a result, "core" employees experience a high degree of job security, with resources provided for training in firm-specific skills not readily bought in. This segment of the organisation is characterised by functional forms of flexibility.[150-152] In contrast, the peripheral workforce is associated with the organisation's development of qualitative or numerical flexibility. The key function of this sector for the organisation is the undertaking of day-to-day activities that are important but not vital to the organisation. As Atkinson points out:[153]

In effect they are offered a job not a career. For example, they might be clerical, supervisory, component assembly and testing occupations. The key point is that their jobs are "plug-in" ones, not firm-specific. As a result the firm looks to the external market to fill these jobs, and seeks to achieve numerical flexibility and financial flexibility through more direct and immediate links to the external labour market than is sought for the core group.

Where either the core or peripheral workforce needs supplementing, the secondary peripheral workforce accommodates this through part-time temporary or subcontracting work.[154] This provides increased numerical and functional flexibility with minimal organisational commitment or disruption. The new organisation therefore takes the form of a core with a variety of peripheral activities to serve its changing requirement, as Figure 5.2 illustrates. The focus of the flexible firm model is to closely match organisational (labour) resources with work demand, increasing the efficiency of human resource utilisation while dampening the effects of market volatility and uncertainty, thereby increasing organisational effectiveness.[155-157]

In the UK, empirical research into the emergence of the flexible patterns of work has been extensive (Employer's Labour Use Strategies [ELUS]; Workplace Industrial Relations Surveys; Institute of Personnel Management/

Figure 5.2 The flexible firm model

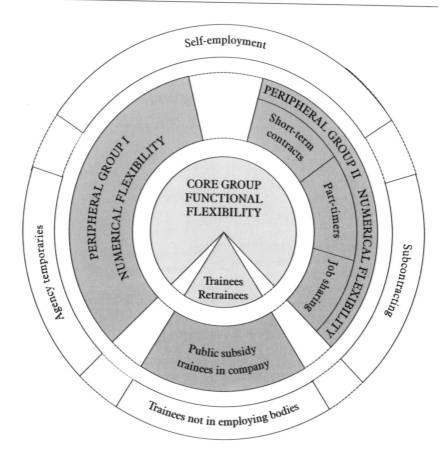

SOURCE: Atkinson, J. 1985. *Flexibility, Uncertainty and Manpower Management,* Institute for Employment Studies (formerly the Institute of Manpower Studies), Brighton, England.

Price Waterhouse Survey of Flexible Work Patterns; and Warwick Company Level Survey). Despite this, however, the evidence is mixed.

Research on the development of the flexible firm model is less well developed outside the UK. However, Burgess[158] has provided a useful summary of the changes in work practices in Australia. His research indicates a growth in non-standard employment, including part-time and casual work,[159-161] although these changes tend to be ad hoc or confined to traditional work patterns and practices in sectors such as retail, rather than a strategic development of numerical flexibility. In terms of developing a core of multi-skilled employees, the evidence is ambiguous.[162] This is supported by case study research which finds little evidence for the flexible firm model.[163-165] Burgess[166] concludes that employment strategies in Australia reflect traditional patterns of work and a reactive approach to the demands of the market, rather than a new-found strategic view of management towards the organisation of its human resources.

Despite the mixed evidence relating to the development of the flexible firm, the model has generated significant debate.[167-176] What is distinctive about the flexible firm model and its approach to the organisation and management of human resources is the extent to which it implies a distinctive strategy on the part of management in developing more efficient and effective labour utilisation.[177-179] Critics of the flexible firm model contend that this is simplistic, and argue that change is far more uneven and complex and that therefore the model is too abstract to represent reality.[180-185]

The flexible firm model is also criticised for its promotion of variation in terms and conditions of employment within organisations,[186-187] the outcome of which is the creation of a (skill) polarised workforce with an elite core workforce and a disenfranchised low-skilled, low-wage peripheral workforce.[188-190] From a management perspective, it can be argued that the flexible firm model incorrectly assumes that organisations have uniformly moved from ad hoc to explicit labour strategies in both the short and the long term.[191-195] In addition, many researchers allude to the lack of empirical evidence to support the uniform development of the flexible firm.[196-202]

Despite these criticisms, the flexible firm model does provide a framework for analysis, insight and explanation with respect to the development of new patterns of work.[203-208]

5.5 Advantages and disadvantages of flexible patterns of work

Much research and debate have surrounded the development of flexible patterns of work; however, there has been less attention paid to the outcomes of these work patterns and practices. Emmott & Hutchinson[209-210] have attempted to address this situation by identifying the advantages and disadvantages (both real and potential) of the development of flexible patterns of work.

5.5.1 The employer perspective on flexible patterns of work

The key advantages flexible patterns of work have for employers are that they:
- enable employers to match organisational resources more closely with customer/product demand;
- reduce fixed costs (for example, homeworkers do not require office space);
- aid recruitment and retention;
- increase productivity – those working for a reduced period of time are likely to be less tired and stressed;
- reduce absence and turnover.

The most important factor for management in the adoption of flexible patterns of work is the ability to respond quickly and with minimal disruption to market demands. This may take the form of moving employees from one job to another, or adjusting the level of human resources in response to fluctuation or changes in demand, as the market dictates. The use of homeworkers or telecommuters (see Chapter 1), in cases where the place of work is incidental to the requirements of the job, and/or where office space is at a premium, can provide substantial cost savings.

Flexible work patterns also allow the employer to cover changes in work requirements as and when required, by integrating the various types of flexibility. Again, the ability to change the structure of the workforce or work patterns with minimal disruption is a key to efficient and effective utilisation of the available human resources. These work patterns can aid recruitment and retention by providing employees with employment opportunities which suit their requirements. These opportunities may have otherwise been unavailable because of other commitments (see below). In terms of productivity, the obvious fatigue problems associated with working long periods have been well documented in the occupational health and safety literature.[211-212] Therefore, the obvious attraction of reduced periods of work is an overall increase in productivity and shorter recovery periods. In jobs that are repetitive and/or require high levels of mental alertness, the advantages are clear.[213]

The main disadvantages for employers of flexible patterns of work include:
- increased training costs;
- higher direct costs – for example, part-timers who receive pro rata benefits;
- a more complex administration;
- communication difficulties;
- management of the flexible workforce.

Development of these work patterns requires significant and long-term investment on the part of the organisation in ongoing training and development, in order to create and maintain the required skills, knowledge, and expertise.[214] These increased costs, combined with the more complex administration associated with managing these work patterns and an increasing requirement for employers to pay pro rata compensation and benefits to part-time employees, may diminish the perceived competitive advantage in developing flexibility, even to the extent that it is no longer a viable option. Where new patterns of work result in changes in work time, managers and employees may not necessarily be working at the same time or during the same shift. This creates the potential for communication difficulties or breakdowns.[215] Equally, the increased use of telecommuting and the use of virtual teams provide their own difficulties.

Finally, management of the "flexible" workforce requires a significant increase in planning and co-ordination and the support of senior management, if these patterns of work are to provide the organisation with a competitive advantage. Management also needs to develop a peripheral labour supply which can be "plugged in" with minimal disruption to the production process, or provide specialist skills. The variable nature of the employment relationship and the changing demands on internal and external labour must also be managed to ensure the retention and maintenance of these resources. For example, temporary employment could be used as an opportunity or prerequisite for a permanent position.[216] For the multi-skilled workforce there must be opportunities to use the skills developed to ensure they are maintained at a satisfactory level.

Where the task requires the bringing together of workers of differing backgrounds and terms and conditions, there is the potential for tension and commitment problems to develop. As Geary identifies in his study of permanent and temporary staff working closely together, frequent problems and animosity between the groups emerged, to the extent that:[217]

> In one instance, the tension between temporary and permanent employees was of such a degree that it compelled the supervisor to stop production for an afternoon so that she could take employees off the shop floor to resolve the differences.

Geary[218] also notes that similar conflict elsewhere in the plant required the supervisors to spend increasing amounts of time in a close supervisory role, distracting them from their other roles and creating an atmosphere of mistrust. In addition, the ad hoc nature of the recruitment of temporary workers caused problems for supervisors, who complained of the quality and attitude of these employees, also citing an increasing sense of diminished control over the workforce. This case illustrates some of the potential difficulties in managing flexibility.

5.5.2 The employee perspective on flexible patterns of work

The main advantages for employees associated with flexible work patterns include:
- the ability to combine work with outside interests, for example career responsibilities or hobbies;
- greater job satisfaction;
- improved motivation; and
- less tiredness.

Flexibility can provide the opportunity to combine work with outside activities (which typically implies family commitments). This allows employees to maintain a presence in the workforce which may not otherwise have been possible.[219] In addition, the increase in part-time work, flexible career paths and the development of portfolio careers allows employees to develop the right balance of work, career development and outside commitments.

Greater job satisfaction and improved motivation are associated with those employees who have the opportunity to develop their skill range (multi-skilling). The intrinsic opportunity to develop skills by undertaking a wider range of tasks and responsibilities fits in with the theories that underpin the motivational aspects of job design. It may also provide satisfaction for peripheral employees, as it provides them with the appropriate mix of work commitments and outside interests (see above).

The major negative implications of flexible patterns of work for the employee include:
- unequal treatment in terms of pay and benefits;
- reduced career opportunities;
- limited training opportunities;
- threatening of the "psychological contract";
- increased job insecurity; and
- increased stress.

To facilitate the development and the advantages of flexible patterns of work, the employment relationship is likely to be based upon a variation in terms and conditions, as the workforce becomes less uniform. The minimal obligation of the organisation to the peripheral workforce may mean that their terms, conditions and employment opportunities are significantly less favourable than the full-time "core" workforce, despite the fact they may be engaged in work of a similar skill demand. These employees provide qualitative flexibility, and therefore the very nature of this relationship places less obligation on the employer to invest in their training or development. They are therefore likely to be caught in a permanent labour pool of low-skilled work with little opportunity to acquire new skills. For those on fixed-term contracts, casual or part-time work, the lack of entitlements, job insecurity and increased stress go hand-in-hand with the almost non-existent career prospects.

For multi-skilled employees, flexibility is generally interpreted as a skill formation and enhancement process, which provides the employee with relevant and up-to-date skills and therefore increased opportunity to progress within the organisation.[220] Critics of this approach to work organisation point to the de-skilling and work intensification aspects of the downward enlargement of job profiles which fall within the umbrella term of multi-skilling.[221-225] Employees in this context provide efficiencies through cost cutting rather than skill development.

The development of multi-skilling, which by its nature requires employees to increase their range of tasks, combined with the elimination of work restrictions, offers the employer the opportunity to do more with fewer employees, thereby increasing the potential for job insecurity. In addition, the constant change in work demands requires a continual reassessment and renegotiation of the employment relationship. This redefining of the role or position of an employee within the organisation can undermine the relationship between the employee and employer. Combined with the increase in stress and potential for job insecurity, these patterns of work can threaten the security of the very employees for whom flexibility was intended as an enhancement.[226]

5.6   Summary

The development of flexible work patterns requires a shift in approach in the management of human resources to ensure that these work patterns are used and maintained to their full potential. The variable nature of the employment relationship with regard to terms and conditions, as well as the changing demands, requires human resource managers to have the prerequisite skills and understanding to balance the changing requirements quickly and with minimal disruption. For example, where an organisation is seeking to develop internal flexibility it must ensure that it provides the training and development required to facilitate such changes. Where a team is brought together from the internal and external environment, management should ensure that terms and conditions are not so variant that they create tension or motivation and commitment problems.

The development of these various forms of flexibility requires management to plan and be able to use these different work patterns on demand – this requires management to develop a strategic approach to its labour requirements. This may mean the development of a pool of subcontractors or part-time employees, who are available as and when required to maximise the utilisation of organisational resources. In addition, the development of such work practices requires the development of a participative/consensual management style to support rather than direct an increasingly skilled workforce in a complex and dynamic environment.

From a senior management perspective, Pettinger has identified several key themes to ensure the successful implementation, development and maintenance of flexible patterns of work:[227]

- a long-term commitment to creating the necessary environment and conditions supported and resourced by top management;
- a long-term view of the results desired. These do not happen overnight, and the benefits may not be apparent for months, or even years; and
- a long-term commitment to creating the required skills, knowledge, attitudes, behaviour and expertise, including training programmes.

The key model developed in this area is the Institute for Employment Studies' core-periphery or flexible firm model, which has attracted wide attention and criticism. It has been acknowledged as a framework and a benchmark upon which organisations can draw to develop their own particular "flexible firm" suited to localised products, markets and workforces. To facilitate this approach to labour utilisation, there is a need for procedural changes in work practices – particularly in the restrictions associated with lines of demarcation, a (re)combination of jobs and the provision of mechanisms to support and encourage these changes, such as training and development.

Despite the controversy and criticism which surround the area of flexibility, the growing literature on the subject cannot be dismissed. In the same vein, Harvey notes:[228]

> The evidence for increased flexibility throughout the capitalist world is simply overwhelming. .... The argument that there is an acute danger of exaggerating the significance of any trend towards flexibility ... stares most workers in the face.

The emerging patterns of flexibility are wide and varied. However, despite this, research suggests that the integrative development of multiple forms of flexible patterns of work is increasingly being adopted by organisations to enhance their effectiveness through more efficient utilisation of resources in response to an increasingly turbulent and competitive environment.

References

1 Sengenberger, W. 1992. Intensified competition, industrial restructuring and industrial relations. *International Labour Review*, vol. 131, no. 2, pp. 139–154.

2 Liemt, G.V. 1992. Economic globalisation: Labour options and business strategies in high labour cost countries. *International Labour Review*, vol. 131, nos. 4-5, pp. 453–470.

3 Pfeffer, J. 1994. Competitive advantage through people. *California Management Review*, vol. 36, no. 3, pp. 9–28.

4 Atkinson, J. 1984. Manpower strategies for flexible organisations. *Personnel Management*, nos. 28–31 (August).

5 Atkinson, J. 1987. Flexibility or fragmentation? The United Kingdom labour market in the eighties. *Labour and Society*, vol. 12, no. 1, pp. 87–105.

6 Hakim, C. 1987. Trends in flexible workforce. *Employment Gazette*, no. 95 (November), pp. 549–560.

7 Hakim, C. 1990. Core and periphery in employers' workforce strategies: Evidence from the 1987 ELUS survey. *Work, Employment and Society*, vol. 4, no. 2, pp. 157–188.

8 Blyton, P. 1992. Flexible times?: Recent trends in temporal flexibility. *Industrial Relations Journal*, vol. 23, no. 1, pp. 26–36.

9 Blyton, P. & Morris, J. 1991. *A flexible future? Prospects for employment and organization*. Berlin, De Gruyter.

10 Blyton, P. & Morris, J. 1992. HRM and the limits of flexibility. In Blyton, P. & Turnbull, P. (eds.), *Reassessing human resource management*. London, Sage, pp. 116–130.

11 Procter, S.J., Rowlinson, M., McArdle, L., Hassard, J. & Forrester, P. 1994. Flexibility, politics and strategy: In defence of the model of the flexible firm. *Work, Employment and Society*, vol. 8, no. 2, pp. 221–242.

12 Legge, K. 1995. *Human resource management: Rhetorics and realities*. London, Macmillan.

13 Ursell, G.D. 1991. Human resource management and labour flexibility: Some reflections based on cross-national and sectoral studies in Canada and the UK. In Blyton, P. & Morris, J. (eds.), *A flexible future? Prospects for employment and organisation*. Berlin: De Gruyter, pp. 311–327, on p. 312.

14 Storey, J. 1991. Introduction: from personnel management to human resource management. In Storey, J. (ed.), *New perspectives on human resource management*. London: Routledge, pp. 1–18.

15 McGraw, P. 1997. *HRM – history, models, process and directions*. In Kramar, R., McGraw, P. & Schuler, R., *Human resource management in Australia* (third edition). Melbourne, Longman, pp. 44–86.

16 Hakim, C. 1990. Core and periphery in employers' workforce strategies: Evidence from the 1987 ELUS survey. *Work, Employment and Society*, vol. 4, no. 2, pp. 157–188.

17 Blyton & Morris, 1991.

18 Wood, S. 1989. *The transformation of work: Skill, flexibility and the labour process*. London, Unwin-Hyman.

19 Atkinson, J. 1984.

20 Organisation For Economic Co-operation and Development (OECD). 1986. *Labour market flexibility*. Report by a high-level group of experts to the Secretary-General. Paris, OECD.

21 Organisation For Economic Co-operation and Development (OECD). 1990. *Labour market policies for the 1990s*. Paris, OECD.

22 Guest, D. 1991. Human resource management: Its implications for industrial relations and trade unions. In Storey, J. (ed.), *New perspectives on human resource management*. London, Routledge, pp. 41–55.

23 Bamber, G. 1990. Flexible work organisation: Inferences from Britain and Australia. *Asia Pacific Human Resource Management*, vol. 28, no. 3, pp. 28–44.

24 Atkinson, J. 1984, p. 28.

25   Treu, T. 1992. Labour market flexibility in Europe. *International Labour Review*, vol. 131, no. 4, pp. 497–512.
26   Atkinson, J. 1984.
27   *Ibid.*
28   Rimmer, M. & Zappala, J. 1988. Labour market flexibility and the second tier. *Australian Bulletin of Labour*, vol. 14, no. 4, pp. 564–591.
29   National Economic Development Office (NEDO) 1986. *Changing work patterns.* Brighton, Institute of Manpower Studies/ National Economic Development Office.
30   *Ibid.*
31   OECD, 1986.
32   Rimmer & Zappala, 1988, p. 567.
33   Blyton, P. 1992.
34   Nelson, L. & Holland, P. 1999. The impact of 12 hour shifts: The views of managers and unions. *Asia Pacific Journal of Human Resources (forthcoming).*
35   Herriot, P. 1998. The role of the HRM function in building a new proposition for staff. In Sparrow, P. & Marchington, M. (eds.), *Human resource management: The new agenda.* London: Financial Times/ Pitmans, pp. 106–114.
36   Atkinson, J. 1984, p. 29.
37   Boyer, R. 1988. *The search for labour market flexibility: The European economies in transition.* Oxford, Clarendon Press.
38   Wood, S. 1989, p. 1.
39   Mathews, J. 1989. *Tools of change: New technology and the democratisation of work.* Sydney, Pluto Press.
40   Bamber, G. 1990.
41   Grint, K. 1991. *The sociology of work.* Cambridge, Polity Press.
42   Rimmer & Zappala, 1988, p. 537.
43   Atkinson, J. 1984.
44   Hakim, C. 1987.
45   Mathews, J. 1989.
46   Procter *et al.* 1994.
47   Bamber, G. 1990.
48   *Ibid.*
49   Sparrow, P. & Marchington, M. 1998. Introduction: Is HRM in crisis? In Sparrow, P. & Marchington, M. (eds.), *Human resource management: The new*

agenda. London. Financial Times/ Pitmans, pp. 3–20, on p. 19.
50   Morrison, D. 1994. Psychological contracts and change. *Human Resource Management*, vol. 33, no. 3, pp. 353–372.
51   Greenhaus, J.H. & Callanan, G.A. 1994. *Career management* (second edition). Fort Worth, Dryden Press.
52   Rosseau, D.M. 1995. *Psychological contracts in organisations: Understanding written and unwritten agreements.* Thousand Oaks, California, Sage.
53   Atkinson, J. 1984.
54   Sparrow & Marchington, 1998.
55   Guest, D. 1991. Human resource management: Its implications for industrial relations and trade unions. In Storey, J. (ed.), *New perspectives on human resource management.* London: Routledge, pp. 41–55.
56   Hassard, J. & Parker, D. 1993. *Postmodernism and organisations.* London, Sage.
57   See for example *International Journal of Human Resource Management*, vol. 9, no. 3, 1998.
58   See also *Employee Relations*, vol. 19, no. 6, 1997.
59   Atkinson, J. 1984.
60   Kern, H. & Schumann, M. 1984. *End of the division of labour?* Munich, Verlag.
61   Brewster, C. 1998. Flexible working in Europe: Extent, growth and the challenge for HRM. In Sparrow & Marchington, 1998.
62   Tregaskis, O., Brewster, C., Mayne, L. & Hegewisch, A. 1998. Flexible working in Europe: The evidence and the implications. *European Journal of Work and Organizational Psychology*, vol. 7, no. 1, pp. 61–78.
63   Brewster, C. 1998.
64   *Ibid.*
65   Gall, G. 1996. All year round: The growth of the annual hours in Britain. *Personnel Review*, vol. 25, no. 3, pp. 35–52.
66   Brewster, C. 1997. *Flexible employment in Europe.* Paper presented to the IPD. South West London Branch. Kingston Business School (March).
67   *Ibid.*

68 Gunnigle, P., Turner, T. &. Morley, M. 1998. Employment flexibility and industrial relations arrangements at organisation level: A comparison of five European countries. *Employee Relations*, vol. 20, no. 5, pp. 430–442.

69 Brewster, C. 1998, pp. 252–254.

70 Chow, I. 1998. The impact of workforce regulation on workforce flexibility in Hong Kong. *International Journal of Human Resource Management*, vol. 9, no. 3, pp. 494–505.

71 *Ibid.*

72 Mansor, N. & Ali, M.A.M. 1998. An exploratory study of organizational flexibility in Malaysia: A research note. *International Journal of Human Resource Management*, vol. 9, no. 3, pp. 506–515.

73 *Ibid.*

74 Lee, S. 1998. Organisational flexibility in Korean companies: Rules and procedures on managerial discretion and employee behaviour. *International Journal of Human Resource Management*, vol. 9, no. 3, pp. 478–493.

75 Bamber, G. 1990.

76 Bamber, G., Boreham, P. & Harley, B. 1992. Economic and industrial relations outcomes of different forms of flexibility in Australian industry: An analysis of the AWIRS data. In *Exploring Industrial Relations Further Analysis of AWIRS No.4.* Industrial Relations Research Series (ed.). Canberra: AGPS Press, pp. 1–70.

77 Holland, P.J. & Dowling, P.J. 1998. *Achieving competitive advantage through new patterns of work: The Australian experience.* Paper presented at the Sixth International Human Resource Management Conference. Paderborn, Germany, 22–25 June.

78 Reed, K. & Blunsdon, B. 1998. Organizational flexibility in Australia. *International Journal of Human Resource Management*, vol. 9, no. 3, pp. 457–477.

79 Nelson, L. & Holland, P. 1999.

80 Kramar, R. & Lake, N. 1997. *International strategic human resource management.* Sydney, Macquarie University.

81 Kramar, R. 1998. Flexibility in Australia: Implications for employees and managers. *Employee Relations*, vol. 20, no. 5, pp. 453–460.

82 Brosnan, P., Horwitz, F. & Walsh, P. 1997. *Non-standard employment: Results from a workplace survey in three countries.* Paper presented at the Fifth IIRA European Regional Industrial Relations Congress. Dublin (26-29 August).

83 *Ibid.*

84 *Ibid.*

85 NEDO, 1986.

86 Hakim, C. 1987.

87 Bamber *et al.* 1992.

88 Thompson, P. & McHugh, D. 1995. *Work organisation: A critical introduction* (second edition). London, Macmillan Business.

89 Sparrow & Marchington, 1998.

90 Atkinson, J. 1984.

91 Procter *et al.* 1994.

92 Piore, M. & Sabel, C. 1984. *The second industrial divide: Possibilities for prosperity.* New York, Basic Books.

93 Smith, C. 1989. Flexible specialisation, Automation and mass production. *Work, Employment and Society*, vol. 3, no. 2, pp. 203–220.

94 Amin, A. 1991. Flexible specialisation and small firms in Italy: Myths and realities. In Pollert, A. *Farewell to flexibility?* Oxford: Blackwell, pp. 119–137.

95 Amin, A. 1994. Post-Fordism: Models, fantasies and phantoms of transition. In Amin, A. (ed.), *Post Fordism: A reader.* Oxford, Blackwell.

96 Harvey, D. 1989. *The conditions of post modernity.* Oxford, Blackwell.

97 Wood, S. 1989.

98 Mathews, J. 1989.

99 Thompson & McHugh, 1995.

100 Sparrow & Marchington, 1998.

101 Sabel, C. 1994. Flexible specialisation and the re-emergence of regional economies. In Amin, A. (ed.), *Post Fordism: A reader.* Oxford, Blackwell, pp. 101-156.

102 Piore & Sabel, 1984.

103 Amin, A. 1989. Specialisation without growth: Small footwear firms in an inner-

city area of Naples. In Goodmann, E. (ed.), *Small firms and industrial districts in Italy*. London, Routledge.

104 Amin, A. 1994.

105 Murray, F. (1987) Flexible specialisation in the "Third Italy". *Capital & Class*, no. 33 (Winter), pp. 84–95.

106 Amin, A. 1991.

107 Murray, F. 1987.

108 *Ibid.*

109 Murray, R. 1985. Bennetton Britain: The new economic order. *Marxism Today* (November), pp. 28–32.

110 *Ibid.*

111 Sabel, C. 1982. *Work and Politics*. Cambridge, Cambridge University Press.

112 Sabel, C. 1994.

113 Murray, R. 1985.

114 Murray, F. 1987.

115 Amin, A. 1991.

116 Murray, F. 1987.

117 *Ibid.*

118 Murray, R. 1985.

119 Amin, A. 1991.

120 Piore & Sabel, 1984.

121 Sabel, C. 1994.

122 Wood, S. 1989.

123 Amin, A. 1991.

124 Tomaney, J. 1994. A new paradigm of work organization and technology? In Amin, A. (ed.), *Post Fordism: A reader*. Oxford, Blackwell, pp. 157–194.

125 Pollert, A. 1991. The orthodoxy of flexibility. In Pollert, A. (ed.), *Farewell to Flexibility?* Oxford: Blackwell, pp. 3–31, on pp. 18–19.

126 Murray, F. 1987.

127 Tolomelli, C. 1988. *Policies to support innovation processes: Experiences and prospects in Emilia Romagna*. Paper presented to the Regional Science Association's European Summer Institute. Trento (July).

128 Rey, G. 1989. Small firms: A profile of their evolution 1981–1985. In Goodmann, E. (ed.), *Small firms and industrial districts in Italy*. London, Routledge.

129 Amin, A. 1991.

130 Murray, F. 1987.

131 Rainnie, A. & Kraithman, D. 1992. Labour market change and the organisation of work. In Gilbert, N., Burrows, R. and Pollert, A. (ed.), *Fordism and Flexibility*. London: Macmillan, pp. 49–65.

132 Legge, K. 1995.

133 Brusco, S. 1982. The Emilian model: Productive decentralisation and social integration. *Cambridge Journal of Economics*, vol. 6, no. 2, pp. 167–184.

134 Amin, A. 1991.

135 Brusco, S. 1982.

136 Bluestone, B. & Harrison, B. 1986. *The great American jobs machine: The proliferation of low wage employment in the US economy*. A study prepared for the Joint Economic Committee of the US Congress, Washington DC.

137 Amin, A. 1991.

138 Legge, K. 1995.

139 Tomaney, J. 1994.

140 Amin, A. 1991.

141 Burrows, R., Gilbert, N. & Pollert, A. 1992. Introduction: Fordism, post-Fordism and economic flexibility. In Gilbert, N., Burrows, R. & Pollert, A. (eds.), *Fordism and flexibility*. London, Macmillan, pp. 1–12.

142 Hyman, R. 1991. Plus ca change? The theory of production and the production of theory. In Pollert, A. (ed.), *Farewell to flexibility?* Oxford, Blackwell, pp. 259–283.

143 Atkinson, J. 1984.

144 Atkinson, J. & Meager, N. 1986. *New forms of work organisation*, Report 121. Brighton, Institute of Manpower Studies.

145 Atkinson, J. & Gregory, D. 1986. Is flexibility just a flash in the pan? *Personnel Management* (September), pp. 26–29.

146 Thompson & McHugh 1995, pp. 174–175.

147 Atkinson, J. 1984.

148 NEDO, 1986.

149 Wood, S. 1989.

150 Atkinson, J. 1984.

151 Hakim, C. 1987.

152 Wood, S. 1989.

153 Atkinson, J. 1984, p. 20.

154 Morris, J. & Imrie, R. 1991. *Transforming buyer-supplier relations: Japanese style industrial practices in a Western context.* London, Macmillan.

155 Atkinson, J. 1984.

156 Atkinson, J. 1987.

157 Blyton & Morris, 1991.

158 Burgess, J. 1997. The flexible firm and the growth of non-standard employment. *Labour & Industry*, vol. 7, no. 3, pp. 85–102.

159 Lewis, H. 1990. *Part-time work: Trends and issues.* Canberra, AGPS.

160 Romeyn, J. 1992. *Flexible working time: Part-time and casual employment.* Industrial Relations Research Monograph, No 1. Canberra, Department of Industrial Relations.

161 Brosnan, P. & Campbell, I. 1995. Labour market deregulation in Australia: Towards new forms of workforce division? Paper presented at the 17th meeting of the International Working Party on Labour Markets, Siena (July).

162 Mylett, T. 1995. Labour market polarisation: Evidence of a solidifying core? In Pullin, L. & Fastenau, M. (eds.), *Employment relations theory and practice: Current research.* International Employment Relations Association, University of Western Sydney, pp. 381–406.

163 Jamieson, N. & Webber, M. 1991. Flexibility and part-time employment in retailing. *Labour & Industry*, vol. 4, no. 1, pp. 55–70.

164 Deery, S. & Mahony, A. 1994. Temporal flexibility: Management strategies and employee preferences in the retail industry. *Journal of Industrial Relations*, vol. 36, no. 3, pp. 332–352.

165 Probert, B. 1995. *Part-time work and managerial strategy: Flexibility in the new industrial relations framework.* Department of Employment Education and Training, Canberra, AGPS.

166 Burgess, J. 1997.

167 Atkinson, J. 1984.

168 Atkinson, J. 1985. The changing corporation. In Clutterbuck, D. (ed.), *New*

patterns of work. Aldershot, Gowers, pp. 13–34.

169 Pollert, A. 1988. Dismantling flexibility. *Capital and Class*, no. 34, pp. 42–75.

170 Pollert, A. 1991. The orthodoxy of flexibility. In Pollert, A. (ed.), *Farewell to flexibility?* Oxford, Blackwell, pp. 3–31.

171 MacInnes, J. 1988. The question of flexibility. *Personnel Review*, vol. 17, no. 1, pp. 12–15.

172 Horstman, B. 1988. Labour flexibility strategies and management style. *Journal of Industrial Relations*, vol. 30, no. 3, pp. 412–431.

173 Hunter, L., McGregor, A., MacInnes, J. & Sproull, A. 1993. The flexible firm: Strategy and segmentation. *British Journal of Industrial Relations*, vol. 31, no. 3, pp. 383–407.

174 Procter *et al.* 1994.

175 Legge, K. 1995.

176 Burgess, J. 1997.

177 NEDO, 1986.

178 Wood, S. 1989.

179 Procter *et al.* 1994.

180 MacInnes, J. 1988.

181 Pollert, A. 1988.

182 Pollert, A. 1991.

183 Burrows *et al.* 1992.

184 Horstman, B. 1988.

185 Hunter *et al.* 1993.

186 Trade Union Council (TUC). 1986. *Flexibility: A trade union response.* London, TUC.

187 Brookes, B. 1990. Labour flexibility and employment law: The new order. *The Economics and Labour Relations Review*, no. 1 (June), pp. 107–120.

188 TUC 1986.

189 Grint, K. 1991.

190 Hyman, R. 1991.

191 MacInnes, J. 1988.

192 Pollert, A. 1991.

193 Penn, R. 1992. Flexibility in Britain during the 1980s: Recent empirical evidence. In Gilbert, N. Burrows, R. & Pollert, A. (ed.), *Fordism and Flexibility.* London, Macmillan, pp. 66-86.

194 Hunter *et al.* 1993.

195 Legge, K. 1995.

196 Hakim, C. 1987.
197 Pollert, A. 1988.
198 Pollert, A. 1991.
199 Horstman, B. 1988.
200 Hunter *et al.* 1993.
201 Wilkinson, F. & White, M. 1994. Product market pressures and employer responses. In Rubery, J. & Wilkinson, F. (eds.), *Employer strategies and the labour market.* Oxford, Oxford University Press, pp. 111–137.
202 Legge, K. 1995.
203 NEDO, 1986.
204 Wood, S. 1989.
205 Bamber, G. 1990.
206 Garrahan, P. & Stewart, P. 1992. *The Nissan enigma: Flexibility at work in a local economy.* London, Mansell.
207 Procter *et al.* 1994.
208 Burgess, J. 1997.
209 Emmott, M. & Hutchinson, S. 1998. Employment flexibility: Threat or promise? In Sparrow & Marchington 1998.
210 See also Evans, J. S. 1991. Strategic flexibility for high technology man-oeuvres: A conceptual framework. *Journal of Management Studies,* vol. 28, no. 1, pp. 69–89.
211 Bent, S. 1998. The psychological effects of extended working hours. In Heiler, K. (ed.), *The 12 hour workday: Emerging issues.* ACCIRT Working Paper No. 51. Sydney: University of Sydney, pp. 27–33.
212 Spurgeon, A., Harrington, J.M. & Cooper, C.L. 1997. Health and safety problems associated with long working hours: A review of the current position. *Occupational and environmental medicine,* vol. 54, no. 6, pp. 367–375.
213 Baker, K., Olsen, J. & Morisseau, D. 1994. Work practices, fatigue and nuclear power plant safety performance. *Human Factors,* vol. 36, no. 2, pp. 244–257.
214 Pettinger, R. 1998. *Managing the flexible workforce.* London, Cassell.
215 Nelson & Holland, 1999.
216 Atkinson, J. & Rick, J. 1996. *Temporary work and the labour market,* Report 311. Brighton, Institute of Employment Studies.
217 Geary, J. 1992. Employment flexibility and human resource management. *Work, Employment and Society,* vol. 6, no. 2, pp. 251–270, on p. 259.
218 *Ibid.*
219 Legge, K. 1995.
220 Atkinson, J. 1984.
221 Pollert, A. 1988.
222 Pollert, A. 1991.
223 TUC, 1986.
224 Garrahan & Stewart, 1992.
225 Legge, K. 1998.
226 Herriot, P. & Anderson, N. 1997. Selecting for change: How will personnel and selection psychology survive? In Anderson, N. & Herriot, P. (eds.), *International handbook of selection and assessment.* Chichester, John Wiley.
227 Pettinger, R. 1998, pp. 3–4.
228 Harvey, D. 1989, p. 191.

6

Integrating total quality management and human resource management

6.1 Introduction

Total quality management (TQM) practices have spread widely in recent years.[1] Once thought to be the sole responsibility of specialists such as quality engineers, product designers and process engineers, the development of quality across the entire organisation has become an important function of the HR department.[2] In this chapter the following issues will be addressed:

- What is quality?
- The emergence of quality as a management issue.
- The evolution of quality management.
- Total quality management and HRM.
- Problems and paradoxes of TQM.

6.2 What is quality?

Despite the wide interest and debate on the issue of quality as a source of competitive advantage, a review of the literature in this area illustrates the diverse nature of the concept. As Reeves & Bednar identify:[3]

A search for the definition of quality has yielded inconsistent results. Quality has been variously defined as value (Abbot, 1955; Feigenbaum, 1951), conformance to specifications (Gilmore, 1974; Levitt, 1972), conformance to requirements (Crosby, 1979), fitness for use (Juran, 1974; 1988), loss avoidance (Taguchi, cited in Ross, 1989), and meeting and/or exceeding customer expectations (Gronroos, 1983; Parasuraman, Zeithaml & Berry, 1985). Regardless of the time period or context in which quality is examined, the concept has had multiple and often muddled definitions and has been used to describe a wide variety of phenomena.

However, Dale & Plunkett,[4-5] rather than seeing this as a weakness, suggest this is a virtue, as it provides a degree of flexibility in appropriating the concept of quality to different uses and circumstances. This is reinforced by Munro,[6] who suggests that "quality's elusiveness to definition appears to be part of its resource". This therefore allows organisations in differing industries and markets to utilise quality to enhance competitive advantage in differing forms and differing ways.[7] Despite this divergence, there are a number of common elements in establishing organisational commitment to quality, including senior management support, employee involvement and a focus on customer relations.[8] Ross[9] notes that a commitment to quality has a number of demonstrable outputs which are likely to include:

- customer satisfaction that results in customer loyalty and repeat business;
- lower cost of production and higher productivity;
- improved cash flow and return on investment;
- ability to charge a higher price;
- higher stock price; and
- reduced service calls.

While the concept of quality has manifested itself in a variety of ways, attempts to draw distinctions between the various aspects have focused on what have been described as the "hard" and "soft" approaches to quality.[10-11] The "hard" aspects of quality focus on the quantitative approach of statistical analysis and systematic measuring and monitoring of the processes of production.[12] The "soft" concept of quality focuses on qualitative aspects of quality management, and includes internal customer orientation and employee empowerment linked to a change in the organisation's culture.[13-15] These perspectives of quality are developed further in the following sections.

6.3   The emergence of quality as a management issue

The emergence of quality as an issue in the management literature in the late 1970s and early 1980s can be linked to the success and increasing dominance of Japanese organisations in all the major world markets. Underpinning the competitiveness of these organisations was the high value placed on the management of quality as a key feature of the production process. The irony in the increasing attention given in the West to quality as a means of competitive advantage was the fact that the concept of quality had its origins in the US in the 1920s and was imported to Japan after the Second World War, under the guidance of luminaries such as Dr E.W. Deming and, later, Dr Joseph Juran.

With the application of techniques of mass production in the early part of the twentieth century, the ability to standardise production and quality became an important issue. The major developments during this time came from research at Bell Telephone Laboratories, which was attempting to develop uniformity across its telephone network. The recognition that variability was a fact of production, and the ability to differentiate between acceptable and unacceptable variation, constituted a paradigm shift in understanding and managing quality.[16] This was the catalyst for the emergence of control charts and sampling techniques, which laid the foundation for the modern quality movement.[17]

In the 1950s, as Japan was reconstructing its industrial base, the Union of Japanese Scientists and Engineers (UJSE) invited Dr E.W. Deming to lecture on quality management to engineers and senior managers of companies including Mitsubishi, Nissan and Toyota.[18] Dr Deming had acquired his reputation in the area of quality as an advisor on statistical process control to the US government during the war. This was considered a key factor in the US armament industry, reducing poor-quality work and reworking of limited resources, and ensuring acceptable standards from multiple high-volume contractors.[19-21] However, after the war, quality control departments were disbanded as a perceived unnecessary cost in a demand-driven economy, where the US in particular had a virtual monopoly on mass production and anything produced had a ready market of consumers.[22-23] This was reinforced by the dominant mode of production, mass production, whereby competitive advantage was achieved by means of economies of scale and cost minimisation, marketing, and financial performance.[24] Where any quality control did take place, it was limited to basic quality assurance, despite the persuasive arguments and results that supported the management of quality.[25]

While Dr Deming and Dr Juran emphasised the use of statistical quality control applications to the management of quality assurance and quality control,[26] they saw quality as an integral part of everyone's job, which would develop into a proactive approach of prevention rather than the traditional reactive detection and inspection model.[27] This approach was reinforced by Feigenbaum,[28] who considered quality a cross-functional activity not simply limited to quality assurance alone. Only with this shift to "total" quality could a proactive approach to the management of quality be made.[29]

As a country with limited natural resources, Japan identified the manage-
ment of quality as a central feature in developing a competitive advantage.
The importance placed on this aspect of management was illustrated in the
development of the *Journal of Quality Control* in 1950,[30] the Deming Prize for
Quality in 1951, and the establishment of the first Quality Control Circles
(QCC) by 1957.[31] As Tuckman notes:[32]

> ... the role of QCC was to educate foremen in the techniques of quality
> control. For the Japanese, the attraction of this method of training
> shopfloor workers in methods of detecting defects was that it saved the
> cost of inspection.

The Quality Control Circles (or Quality Circles) provided a two-way
communication forum in which the foreman's role was to educate the
workforce in quality control, while the employee could provide management
with ideas and information on production and how to build quality in rather
than inspect it out.[33-34] Throughout this period, as Dean & Evans[35] note,
"While the Japanese were improving quality at an unprecedented rate, quality
levels in the West remained stagnant." As noted above, the first Quality
Circles in Japan were established in 1957, the ten-thousandth in 1966 and the
hundred-thousandth in 1977. By comparison, the first QCC in the US was
established in 1974.[36]

The instability created by the economic "shocks" of the 1970s in many
mature markets, combined with the increasing competition from newly
industrialised countries such as Japan and South Korea, made it difficult for
established organisations simply to lift economies of scale and volume of
production to increase profits.[37] In this context, organisations in the West
were forced to seek alternative approaches to achieving competitive
advantage. Most of these organisations did not have far to look, with the
establishment of Japanese manufacturing plants in Western countries
replicating the efficiency and effectiveness of their parent organisations. As
a recent study in the UK indicates, British employees in Japanese trans-
planted companies still make fewer mistakes than their compatriots in UK-
owned firms.[38] In analysing Japanese practices, the management of quality
was identified as a central element in the production process. The competitive
advantage emanating from the management of quality was also seen to be
diverse, in that it could differentiate on quality of service and delivery, allowed
organisations to respond quickly to customer needs, eliminated poor-quality
goods, and therefore reduced the cost of scrapping and rework, thus
increasing bottom line profits and organisational efficiency. In combination,
these aspects of quality management put tremendous pressure on those
organisations which had not taken up the issue of quality management.[39]

6.4   The evolution of quality management

The statistical background of the early practitioners of quality management and its application to mass production during the Second World War produced a range of statistical tools to monitor and manage the quality aspects of the production process.[40] This is described as the "hard" side of quality, as it focuses on data and figures to monitor performance.[41] The seven major "tools" associated with the "hard" side of quality are: pareto analysis, fishbone diagrams (or cause and effect analysis), scatter diagrams, flow charts, histograms, control charts and run charts. More recently these techniques have been supported by what are often described as the seven new tools of quality control: affinity diagrams, interrelationship digraphs, tree diagrams, matrix charts, matrix data analysis, process decision programme charts and arrow diagrams.[42] This approach to controlling the process of production emphasises improvement through final inspection by a quality control department.[43] This therefore results in reactive or preventative maintenance in the management of quality. It was only through the adoption and application of the concept of TQM that a move to a proactive approach to the management of quality would take place. TQM builds on previous forms of quality management processes, but takes a holistic approach which includes the "soft" aspects of quality and includes all members of the organisation.[44] As Hill states:[45]

> It [TQM] seeks to involve employees from shopfloor to senior management, in a quality improvement culture. It is not just tacked on, so the argument runs, but promises a fundamental overhaul of the labour process.

Dale & Plunkett[46] concede that there appear to be as many definitions of TQM as there are writers on the subject. This is probably due to the variety of forms and procedures that TQM can take.[47-50] However, the fundamental change that TQM brings to organisations is cultural, in that each process or production point learns to recognise that the next person down the line in the labour process is their customer, as shown in Figure 6.1. In other words, customers are constructed where none existed previously.[51] This is a key principle which Tuckman[52] asserts can be achieved only with a fundamental review of work patterns and practices.

From a workforce perspective, Legge[53] illustrates the central role of the organisation's human resources in developing TQM:

> TQM requires the involvement of all. This includes the continuous support of senior management to drive a culture of quality; their

delegation of major responsibilities to inter-departmental and cross-functional middle management project teams; the enlisting of the commitment of "empowered" workers, organised into teams and participating in decision-making, to take responsibility as "suppliers" of zero-defect goods to internal customers. It also involves developing high trust relationships with external suppliers, based on long-term commitment, cooperation and mutual obligation.

Figure 6.1 The quality chains

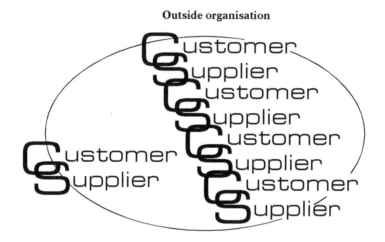

Outside organisation

SOURCE: Oakland, J.S. 1993. *Total quality management: The route to improving performance* (second edition). London, Butterworth-Heinemann, p. 17. Used with permission.

TQM therefore focuses on the organisational culture and structure, management of production and management of human resources, supported by techniques of control and monitoring.[54] At an organisational level, management must re-evaluate its attitude, behaviour and organisational structures and processes in order to facilitate the development of TQM. With regard to structures and processes, change in the organisational structure needs to focus on de-layering and simplifying the organisation's process, to enable decision making to be pushed down the organisation, to facilitate the development of team-based work and more open communication.[55] These tenets are central to empowering employees to become responsible for the quality of their work.

Thus TQM has major implications for the management and organisation of labour.[56] Supporting these changes is the need to develop a participative management style based on a relationship of consensus and trust through increased autonomy and self-direction if employees are to embrace these organisational goals. Therefore, central to the success of TQM is the management of the organisation's human resources.[57-61]

6.5   Total quality management and HRM

Quality has become a key issue for organisations seeking a competitive advantage. Research increasingly identifies that the HR implications of these quality initiatives, although a frequently neglected dimension, are critical to the successful implementation of TQM.[62-66] Central to the importance placed on HRM in the implementation, development and management of TQM is the identification of an organisation's employees as a source of competitive advantage.[67-70] Underlying this is the emphasis on utilising labour to its full capacity through the development of policies which focus on developing high commitment, quality and flexibility.[71-72]

In this context, HRM facilitates the development of initiatives such as TQM as well as providing sophisticated and integrative policies to support these initiatives.[73-75] Of particular importance is the opportunity to develop the type of work patterns and practices management requires,[76] in an environment characterised by continuous change and increased competition. To ensure a fit between HR policies, practices and new techniques requires the development of sophisticated recruitment, selection and socialisation techniques, supported by company-specific training and a remuneration and appraisal system that rewards flexibility, commitment and quality.[77-81]

In this respect, there is a convergence between the management of quality (in particular the "soft" aspects) and HRM, as both concepts view the workforce as an asset in enhancing organisational flexibility, efficiency, quality and performance.[82-88] Indeed, it has been suggested that TQM and HRM are in pursuit of the same goals.[89] This point is reinforced by Guest,[90] who comments:

> The empirical evidence also indicates that the driving force behind the introduction of HRM . . . is the pursuit of competitive advantage in the market place through the provision of high-quality goods and services, through competitive pricing linked to high productivity, through the capacity swiftly to innovate and manage change in response to changes in the market place or to breakthroughs in research and development.

In identifying employees as a source of competitive advantage, the culture of the organisation needs to be managed[91-92] to ensure the development of a relationship of high trust and commitment between employees and management. Underpinning this relationship is the development of shared mutual interest in ensuring that organisational goals are achieved.[93] The implementation of such a culture provides the prerequisite conditions for establishing a high degree of flexibility, adaptability and quality within the workforce. As Guest points out, "To ensure high quality is maintained, considerable attention must be given to recruitment and selection, training, appraisal and goal-setting".[94] In this context, research by Williams *et al.* has identified four key aspects of HRM:[95]

1 Changing the people in the organisation, through selective recruitment and redundancy programmes, with greater emphasis on selecting people with the desired attitudes, as well as technical skills and experience. This may involve the use of sophisticated selection techniques, for example psychometric testing, assessment centres, and biodata.
2 Moving people into new jobs to break up old subcultures.
3 Providing employees with training and role models appropriate to the desired culture. This may involve getting supervisors and managers at all levels to act as role models and demonstrate personal commitment to new goals.
4 Training employees in new skills, and thus influencing their job attitudes. An example here is the training of operators in quality monitoring and improvement techniques, in a bid to win commitment to quality.

6.5.1 Linking HRM and TQM

In order for the relationship between TQM and HRM to be mutually supportive and to provide the organisation with a competitive advantage, HRM policies need to be aligned and integrated. In particular, the establishment of a well-trained, motivated workforce is a prerequisite to developing a culture of quality.[96-97] In order to develop this culture of quality, the recruitment and development of a high-calibre workforce with the requisite skills and behavioural characteristics (flexible and adaptable), combined with an ability to internalise the organisational goals and the values of TQM, is seen as directly affecting the product or service.[98-100] Bowen & Lawler[101] suggest the development of appropriate selection criteria to identify candidates with aptitude for problem solving, teamwork and decision making. This is supported by Snape *et al.*[102] and Redman & Mathews,[103] who advocate effective job advertising to facilitate self-screening, and using realistic job previews. The time and effort taken at this stage are also likely to have a positive impact on retention rates.

The induction process is the next phase in which the established values and culture of the organisation and the individual's role and relationship can be developed.[104] The induction process can instil an understanding of the importance of various techniques, such as TQM, in ensuring the organisation's competitive advantage and continuous improvement in service and quality.[105]

Training is an essential element in the development of job-related skills and the implementation of TQM.[106-108] Indeed, Oakland[109] describes training as "the single most important factor in actually improving quality". It is also seen as providing the prerequisite skills to empower the workforce by providing greater capacity for decision making and responsibility at the shopfloor level. This concurs with TQM, where empowerment, decision making and a commitment to the organisation's goals are essential for its development.[110-113] However, as Simmons et al. note, these changes impact on management development and management style:[114]

> TQM requires alterations in the required skills of employees and managers. In the context of teams and greater functional integration, employees must be provided with a broad base of skills that cover several different jobs. The devolution of authority is placing demands on supervisors and middle managers as they find themselves in the role of facilitator and coach. The transition to this role may place increased stress on mid-level managers (Shadur & Bamber, 1994). Leadership and management training should be provided to these managers to ease the transition.

Given the fact that TQM requires a fundamental change in work patterns and practices, management style and organisational relationships, Snape et al. also point out that the de-layered, flexible organisation also reduces traditional hierarchical career paths, thus increasing the need for career planning. "Horizontal career development is thus likely to become more significant, and career paths may become more complex and diverse. This suggests that there will be a need for individual career counselling".[115]

Middle management can potentially become the strongest advocate of TQM.[116] However, the changes which TQM brings to work patterns and practices require significant resources to be focused on management training and development, to ensure a successful transition from controller to coach or facilitator. As Wilkinson et al. note:[117]

> Removal of expert power is perceived as a significant threat by many middle managers and they may therefore resist the introduction of TQM – or alternatively go along with it, but emphasize the "hard"

controlling aspects of TQM as a way of maintaining the existing power relationship.

Research indicates that this is one of the key issues in the failure of TQM programmes.[118-121] As Roth points out:[122]

> They [managers] realise the need to get employees involved, but there are limits beyond which they are unwilling to go. The most important of these limits is that managers insist on maintaining a degree of control traditionally inherent in their position.... managers have been unwilling to give up much of [their] control and truly to empower their employees.

While the response of managers will vary, resisting the introduction of TQM or only allowing partial rather than full empowerment of the workforce will at the most only slow down its implementation. This is reinforced by Marchington,[123] whose review of the research in the area identifies managerial philosophical resistance to these new employment practices and the use of partial empowerment as key problems in the successful implementation of TQM.

Performance appraisal is seen by many writers as central to the development of TQM, as it provides a two-way vehicle for managers and employees to develop, monitor and assess individual and organisational performance.[124-125] However, Deming[126] and others[127-128] argue that performance appraisal focuses the attention of employees and managers on individual short-term performance, which nurtures an environment of rivalry, politics and risk avoidance. This detracts from the central goals of TQM – long-term planning, teamwork, co-operation and organisational goals. Deming[129] and Waldman[130] argue that variations in performance are attributable to work systems rather than individual performance. This is supported by research[131] which estimates that 85 per cent of TQM failures and faults are the result of inadequate management systems. Therefore, quality improvements are likely to be achieved by adjusting the processes rather than the people.[132] However, Western organisations have been reluctant to restructure performance appraisal systems.[133] In this context, Simmons et al. [134] argue that performance appraisal can have a positive effect on performance and quality when the system is designed with TQM in mind:

> We argue that a well designed system that is compatible with TQM would contain the following elements:
> - identify and recognise the quality of inputs and process and not just outputs;
> - focus on the achievement of the individual, team and enterprise;

- improve future performance through performance planning, coaching and counselling;
- rate personal improvements and not just rate performance relative to peers;
- provide qualitative feedback for employees.

Others have suggested removing the hierarchical framework from the appraisal process and focusing on peer review,[135-136] internal and/or external customer evaluations,[137] and manager/supervisor appraisal by subordinates.[138] These aspects of performance appraisal can make the system more effective, but the issue still remains that performance appraisal focuses on the individual, and an arbitrary judgement at a point in time, which can create a climate of blame, fear and risk avoidance.[139] Therefore, management must be aware of the potential problems and attempt to place itself in the position of a coach rather than a judge.[140] This is supported by Fletcher,[141] who argues for a process built on personal objectives linked to training and development, thus focusing on developmental or continuous improvement.

The area of remuneration or reward is closely linked to performance appraisal – and, as with performance appraisal, there are differing views as to its applicability to the development of TQM. As Wilkinson points out:[142]

> ... although companies have tried to foster a quality culture, not many have tried to embody this in their payment systems. The quality management literature assumes employees are keen to participate in the pursuit of quality improvements with little concern for extrinsic rewards.

It is generally acknowledged that incentive schemes and performance-based pay put people in competition with each other and concentrate on output, generally militating against the development ideals of teamwork, co-operation, customer focus and commitment to quality, espoused by advocates of TQM.[143-145] As Snape et al. point out:[146]

> A key element in HR strategy is to retain and motivate employees through the rewards system. The retention of high quality employees will require an innovative approach to rewards, particularly in competitive labour markets.

Therefore, the reward system needs to be linked to TQM, through the appraisal system. At an individual level, Drummond & Chell,[147] Hackman & Wageman[148] and Simmons et al.[149] see TQM as implying new and shared responsibilities for employees. In this context, a reward system such as gain-sharing or profit-sharing, which rewards collective achievement and can reinforce teamwork, co-operation and skill development, can be implemented.[150] The combination of intrinsic and extrinsic rewards can provide strong and mutual reinforcement of organisational goals.[151] Alternatively, employees may become disillusioned if they do not receive their share of the benefits for implementing these new work practices. Evidence from the US[152] indicates that this is the case, with many TQM programmes breaking down after three to five years. As Wilkinson *et al.*[153] put it, "It seems that praise and a pat on the back may go only so far in a society where cash has traditionally been regarded as the true measure of value." In this context, Redman & Mathews argue:[154]

> It thus seems that reward strategies have a key role in sustaining employee motivation to maintain quality improvement when the excitement of TQM's introduction and managerial exhortations to improve quality begin to wane.

TQM is consistent with the key elements of job design, as both emphasise the development of meaningful work which incorporates autonomy, control, discretion and control over a whole job or task, and knowledge of results.[155-156] In addition, there needs to be enough delegation of power and knowledge for the work to be carried out autonomously or independently of direct managerial control or discretion.[157] The wider range of tasks, combined with increased flexibility in work practice, team-based work organisations and responsibility for quality assurance, requires job analysis to encompass broader job categories and to be continually updated to ensure it is in alignment with human resource availability and the evolving nature of work practices and TQM.[158] Simmons *et al.* comment:[159]

> Future orientated job analysis involves gathering information regarding jobs so that decision makers can be better informed on how work will be arranged in the future. This process is essentially the same as process analysis within TQM. The aim is to scrutinize job content and work systems to identify where improvements can be made.

However, as Hackman & Wageman point out, TQM is continually looking for the "best work practices",[160] which can limit employee discretion and can lead to work patterns and practices more reminiscent of scientific management job design. In this context, TQM may actually lead to work intensification as non-productive practices are continually eliminated from the work environment,[161] in the search for the "one best way". It may also create rigidity and prevent changes, as the focus on eliminating waste from the current process may preclude seeking alternative processes or methods of production. Simmons *et al.* dispute this point, arguing for a balanced approach:[162]

> ... it is not essential that jobs be completely standardised in order for improvements to be made. The tension between measurement and control on the one hand and flexibility and autonomy on the other can be alleviated. In service sector jobs, for instance, there can be flexibility and variation in how jobs are performed, but process analysis can still play an important role. One example is work flow analysis. Careful examination of work processes can reveal that certain tasks or procedures are unnecessary and should be abandoned. This might reduce the workload of employees without removing flexibility which is present in their work activities. It may even give them greater freedom over their work since less time is needed to be spent on unnecessary components of their work.

6.5.2 Trade unions and TQM

The role of trade unions is one of the more contentious areas of debate in the field of TQM, yet one of the less considered and discussed.[163] As Wilkinson *et al.* point out:[164]

> ... the industrial relations aspects of TQM are often neglected by employers. TQM, like much of the prescriptive writing on HRM, is unitarist and is regarded as essentially a management policy that is outside the union sphere of influence. However, because TQM involves changes in work practices and job control – traditional areas of union concern – industrial relations issues become increasingly important.

From a positive perspective, TQM can offer trade unions a strategic role and partnership in the development of new patterns of work, by providing unions with an alternative avenue to influence the decision-making process.[165-166] In this context, unions can "keep management honest",[167] for example by ensuring that work practices associated with TQM do not lead to work intensification and/or job loss, as well as ensuring that the contribution of the workforce is equitably rewarded.[168] Indeed, in the UK, the Trade Union Council (TUC) has endorsed this co-operative partnership approach to organisational change[169] and the potential such opportunities offer for building relationships between management and union representatives.[170] In this context, Kochan *et al.*[171] argue that this approach can enhance the union role and power base. Research indicates that trade union involvement in the development and implementation of new work practices is generally positive.[172-173] As Wilkinson *et al.* suggest:[174]

> The union can also use management needs for union support and employee commitment to push for improvements in working conditions and human resource practices. These gains give the impression of union effectiveness, so strengthening their position and standing.

However, the alternative, or negative, perspective argues that the increased direct communication between management and employees through flatter organisational structures can threaten the legitimacy and role of the trade unions. The development of TQM can establish alternative channels of communication between the workforce and management which bypass the unions.[175] Secondly, the flexibility and adaptability of work patterns and practices which are central to the development and implementation of TQM can threaten job security and the union power base. Thirdly, the development of such a partnership may in fact be nothing more than management reinforcing its right to manage and a strategy to marginalise the countervailing power of the unions, making their role ineffective, while simultaneously increasing managerial control.[176]

Research suggests that TQM has been used in this context as a tool to marginalise the role of the trade union within the workplace. In the US, Fucini & Fucini,[177] in their research at Mazda's automotive plant at Flat Rock, Michigan, note that in agreeing to management's "right to manage", which took the form of management developing its own work rules, the unions were then unable to prevent the development of work practices that resembled scientific management rather than TQM. This resulted in the union representatives being voted out of office, and the emergence of an alternative union power base. As Sashkin & Kiser note on this point:[178]

> Trying to get around the union, reduce its power, and perhaps even eliminate it are actions inconsistent with TQM. Such actions make it impossible to create a climate of trust and may actively promote a climate of fear.... Eventually all TQM elements will be undermined.

Research in the UK[179] also suggests that under conditions of high unemployment and weakened trade unions, management has taken the opportunity to exclude unions from a role in the implementation and development of TQM, despite the changes TQM brings to the management of labour relations – a key area for management and trade unions to address jointly.[180] As Snape et al.[181] point out, "management would do well to recognise the industrial relations implications of TQM and avoid falling in the trap of simply ignoring it". Sashkin & Kiser[182] suggest that the development of union–management committees with equal membership and the right of veto is central to ensuring that the development of the relationship between management and unions is one based on mutual respect and trust.

6.5.3 Linking HRM and TQM in practice

The implications of the issues described above indicate the central role of HRM in the successful development, implementation and integration of TQM. In this context, Wilkinson[183] has identified key HRM issues in each of the phases of development, implementation, maintenance and review of TQM, which are outlined as a general set of objectives below:

- **Developmental phase.** The following are typical examples of areas in which intervention may take place:
  - Preparing and synthesising reports from other organisations which have experience of TQM.
  - Assisting with the choice of TQM approach to be adopted.
  - Influencing the type of improvement in infrastructure to be adopted.
  - Shaping the type of organisation structure and culture appropriate for the introduction of TQM.
  - Designing and delivering senior management development courses which create the right climate for TQM.
- **Implementation phase.** The following activities are likely to be undertaken:
  - Training of middle managers and supervisors in how to develop the TQM process with the staff.
  - Training of facilitators, mentors and team members in interpersonal skills and how to manage the improvement process.
  - Designing communication events to publicise the launch of TQM.
  - Consulting with employees and trade union representatives about the introduction and development of TQM.
  - Assisting the board of directors to adapt mission statements and prepare quality objectives for dissemination to staff and customers.
- **Maintenance phase.** This can be undertaken in the following ways:

- Introducing or upgrading the TQM component within induction courses.
- Ensuring that training in quality management tools, techniques and processes continues to be provided within the organisation.
- Redesigning appraisal procedures so that they contain criteria relating to specific TQM objectives.
- Preparing/overseeing special newsletters or team briefs on TQM.
- Assisting quality improvement teams or suggestion schemes to work effectively and produce ideas.

- **Review phase.** The review of procedures may include:
  - Contributing to/leading the preparation of an annual TQM report.
  - Assessing the effectiveness of the improved infrastructure, steering committees, quality service teams, improvement groups, etc.
  - Preparing and administering employee attitude surveys on TQM.
  - Benchmarking the effectiveness of the organisation's TQM with that of competitors or employees in other sectors/countries.
  - Facilitating the operation of internal reviews using criteria such as the European Quality Award or the Malcolm Baldridge National Quality Award.

In the true spirit of TQM, Wilkinson suggests that the personnel/HR function should also review its own activities using the processes identified above. As Wilkinson notes, the areas of activity, like the business as a whole, will depend on the structure and function, but might include:[184]

- preparing offer and contract letters within a specified time;
- advising staff on their terms and conditions;
- evaluating training provisions on an annual basis;
- preparing and disseminating absence and labour turnover data to line managers on a monthly basis; and
- providing advice on disciplinary matters within a specified and agreed time period.

The fundamental changes that TQM brings to an organisation and the subsequent changes to all aspects of work patterns and practices mean that HR issues are an important aspect in the successful implementation, development and maintenance of TQM. Only with a close integration of TQM and HRM can TQM achieve its potential.[185] HRM is therefore central to the implementation of TQM at a variety of stages. Simply trying to impose such changes on the workforce without taking into account the issues and potential problems that surround such fundamental change is unlikely to achieve the aims of TQM.[186-187]

6.6   The problems and paradoxes of TQM

A central feature of the successful implementation and development of TQM is the increasing control, monitoring and standardisation of production it brings through continual improvement. However, where full empowerment is not concomitant with such approaches to work patterns, these concepts may be more reflective of scientific management. From an HRM perspective, this can result in the development of management styles which emphasise monitoring and control.[188-189] However, the terminology of TQM abounds with discussion on "participation", "empowerment" and "teamwork", which imply increased autonomy, accountability and decision making as employees assume increasing responsibility – which is the very antithesis of scientific management.[190-192] Therefore, as Wilkinson points out:[193]

> ... there is a considerable degree of ambiguity about TQM in practice
> – while the language is about increased involvement, there is also a
> strong emphasis on reinforcing management control.... There are
> thus potential contradictions between increased decision-making, and
> the limited impact of employee involvement upon underlying
> organisational structures.

These contradictions are further reinforced when TQM is "tacked on" to highly bureaucratic and hierarchical organisational structures[194-196] which reinforce the traditional lines of communication, power and control. Equally, where techniques such as TQM are "introduced on an ad-hoc basis with little analysis of what they will contribute, or schemes bought off-the-shelf without adaptation for specific requirements",[197] the effectiveness of such techniques is likely to be undermined. A further paradox is that the degree of participation offered under TQM is linked to and is strictly within an agenda set by management. As Godfrey *et al.* note, "It does not extend to power sharing and offers involvement that is normally confined to the production process ..."[198] Wilkinson & Wilmott illustrate this point with the following proposition:[199]

> It is, however, also worth asking whether employees are empowered to
> remove incompetent or recalcitrant management.... Does quality
> management facilitate the development of participation on key issues
> of resource allocation and accountability? Or does it use participation
> primarily as a stratagem for reducing managerial overheads and for
> promoting self-discipline, including the continuous identification and
> consenting introduction of efficiency gains at the point of production?

The problem inherent in this approach to TQM in practice is that it may be seen as a way of legitimising the alignment of the interests and goals of employees and management, with little opportunity or empowerment to discuss these issues.[200] As McArdle *et al.* [201] have pointed out, this approach stems from the unitarist approach from which TQM (and HRM) have emerged, which assumes that individual values and interests are uniform and can be aligned with those of the organisation. This underlying assumption in the quality literature overlooks issues such as conflict and diverse culture. Where problems occur they can simply be attributed to poor implementation of quality programmes or systems.

Marchington[202] and Redman & Mathews[203] note the lack of reference to superficial acknowledgement of trade unions in this context, which reinforces this problem. This is despite the evidence confirming the positive impact that trade unions can have on the development of such programmes.[204-205] Indeed, where trade unions are acknowledged in the literature, they are seen only as playing a marginal or superficial role in relation to low-level decision making.[206] Also in this context, Redman & Mathews[207] note that no account is made of the variations across the spectrum from high-commitment consensus employee relations to low-trust adversarial relations found within and across many industries and organisations. This is supported by the work of Dawson,[208] who notes that many TQM programmes are doomed to failure because management fails to take account of "the rich diversity of sub-cultures" within an organisation. A further issue in the successful integration of TQM programmes is the assumed uniform and co-ordinated nature of their introduction and development. As Cruise-O'Brien has identified:[209]

> In several firms, the multiple uncoordinated introduction of performance improvement initiatives (including just-in-time, business process re-engineering as well as TQM) made people increasingly sceptical and in some firms cynical about management strategy and consistency.

6.6.1 The role of middle managers

With regard to the implementation of TQM, the role of supervisors and middle managers is central to its success or failure. As employees become empowered and teams undertake responsibility for checking and making decisions about their own work, so they become increasingly responsible and accountable.[210] The literature sees the removal of the need for close supervision as liberating for employees and first-line managers alike. It also suggests first-line managers uncritically move from a supervisory position to one of facilitator. This change in role (and, by inference, the removal of institutional or legitimate power and managerial prerogative) is perceived to be uniformly accepted by managers. However, as McArdle *et al.* point out:[211]

> Among advocates of TQM, the political and organisational implications of the process of "disempowerment" are often simply not considered (Wilkinson, 1992). In particular the disempowerment of supervisors and line managers is often seen as unproblematic, as the TQM literature regards managers as resources upon which to draw, rather than as a set of political actors.

Research indicates that managers are often unwilling to relinquish their power.[212-214] Klein[215] identifies the issues of job security and the loss of status as central to supervisor opposition to change, and, to a lesser extent, a lack of training, resources and belief in their own ability to undertake such a culture change programme. These findings are supported by the research of Marchington *et al.*[216-217] and Denham *et al.*,[218] who also point out that in an environment where job insecurity is increasing while promotion opportunities are decreasing, the development of empowerment can lead to what Jackson *et al.*[219] describe as "career defence" on the part of lower and middle management. Research by Denham *et al.*[220] identifies the issue of changing channels of communication as TQM matures and increasingly bypasses lower-level management. As Wilkinson points out, "Placing responsibility for implementing TQM in the hands of those whose future is threatened by TQM is likely to shape the manner and enthusiasm in which they perform."[221]

A further paradox and problem associated with the implementation of TQM is that it is often undertaken during a time of restructuring and de-layering. Considering that TQM is based on the development of high-trust relationships, the introduction of such techniques during a period of restructuring can often result in disappointing outcomes, if not outright failure of such programmes.[222] Redman & Mathews make the point that:[223]

> Redundancies produce feelings of mistrust and fear among the workforce and are a poor foundation for an effective TQM program. Why should employees strive for continuous improvement, if it only leads to the dole queue for either themselves or their colleagues? It is very difficult for a management team, in the words of Deming, to "drive out fear", when employees see jobs disappearing around them and experience work intensification and increased stress levels.

This point is reinforced by research which identifies lack of commitment by employees and lower and middle management as a central factor in the failure of many TQM programmes.[224-227]

Research in the UK also identifies the role of senior management as the major issue in the success or otherwise of TQM,[228] particularly where the rhetoric of support is replaced by the need to invest resources and commitment to the development of quality programmes. As Wilkinson *et al.*[229] illustrate in Table 6.1, the control management imposes on resource allocation, cost constraints and a short-term focus upon return on investment are identified as the major difficulties in the development of quality programmes. These findings are supported by Marchington,[230] who identifies a short-term attitude to the results expected from TQM programmes and changing of priorities as key criteria in the difficulties in sustaining these programmes. These points are reinforced by further research by Wilkinson *et al.*,[231] which identifies senior management as the major problem in terms of support for these programmes (see Table 6.2). Interestingly, trade unions provide the fewest problems.

Table 6.1 Difficulties faced by organisations in the improvement of quality

	(% of respondents) Major difficulties
Lack of resources	42
Cost constraints	38
Emphasis on short-term goals	34
Measuring quality	27
Communication	25
Lack of training	23
Clash with other initiatives	22
Recession	21
Quality of management	17
Lack of quality infrastructure	12
Seen as production operations' concern only	11
Quality of employees	7
Other	4

SOURCE: Adapted from Wilkinson, A., Redman, T., Snape, E. & Marchington, M. 1998. *Managing with total quality management: Theory and practice.* London, Macmillan Business, p. 83. Used with permission.

Table 6.2 To what extent has lack of commitment from the following groups caused difficulty in implementing quality management?

	(% of respondents) Major difficulties
Top management	18
Middle management	11
Supervisors	7
Employees	11
Trade unions	4

SOURCE: Adapted from Wilkinson , A., Redman, T., Snape, E. & Marchington, M. 1998. *Managing with total quality management: Theory and practice.* London, Macmillan Business, p. 81. Used with permission.

The tendency to marginalise the role of interested third parties such as trade unions, and the superficial empowerment of employees, lead several researchers to suggest that TQM can result in a form of emasculation and exploitation rather than empowerment.[232-236] These problems and paradoxes in implementing TQM gain greater significance when seen in the context of the success rate of TQM programmes. Surveys show that the proportion of successful TQM programmes is within the range of 20–30 per cent.[237] Wright[238] reports success rates of 25 per cent in the US and 20 per cent in the UK. This is supported by additional studies in the UK – Kearney,[239] who reports an 80 per cent failure rate, and an Institute of Management Study,[240] with a failure rate of over 90 per cent.[241]

6.7 Summary

There is no doubt that quality management has become a key aspect of an organisation's competitive strategy, and that central to the implementation of programmes such as TQM is the development of the requisite HRM policies and practices to ensure that TQM and labour policies are aligned to utilise their full capacity and potential. However, it should be noted that the TQM literature takes little account of the fundamental impact of these changes on the organisation of work and on the relationships between management and employees – in particular, the fundamental change TQM brings to the traditional supervisory role, from one based upon directing and monitoring to one of facilitator or coach. Only when these changes are understood and the resources are provided to facilitate the development of a new culture and organisational framework can such techniques develop and eventually prosper.

References

1 Hill, S. & Wilkinson, A. 1995. In search of TQM. Reassessing total quality management. *Employee Relations*, vol. 17, no. 3, pp. 8–25.

2 Clinton, R.J., Williamson, S. & Bethke, A.L. 1994. Implementing total quality management: The role of human resource management. *SAM Advanced Management Journal*, vol. 59, no. 2, pp. 10–16.

3 Reeves, C. & Bednar, D. 1994. Defining quality: Alternatives and implications. *Academy of Management Review*, vol. 19, no. 3, pp. 419–445, on p. 419.

4 Dale, B. & Plunkett, J.J. 1990. *Managing quality*. Herts, Philip Allan.

5 Dale, B. & Cooper, C. 1992. *Total quality and human resources: An executive guide*. Oxford, Blackwell.

6 Munro, R. 1995. Governing the new province of quality: Autonomy, accounting and the dissemination of accountability. In Wilkinson, A. & Wilmott, H. (eds.), *Making quality critical: Studies in organisational change*. London, Routledge, pp. 127–155, on p. 130.

7 Wilkinson, A., Redman, T., Snape, E. & Marchington, M. 1998. *Managing with total quality management: Theory and practice*. London, Macmillan Business.

8 Martinez-Lorente, A.R., Dewhurst, F. & Dale, B. 1998. Total quality management: Origins and evolution of the term. *The TQM Magazine*, vol. 10, no. 5, pp. 378–386.

9 Ross, J.E. 1993. *Total quality management: Text, cases and readings*. Florida, St. Lucie Press.

10 Oakland, J. S. 1989. *Total quality management: The route to improving performance*. London, Butterworth-Heinemann.

11 McArdle, L., Rowlinson, M., Procter, S., Hassard, J. & Forrester, P. 1995. Total quality management and participation:

Employee empowerment or exploitation? In Wilkinson, A. & Wilmott, H. (eds.) *Making quality critical: Studies in organisational change*. London, Routledge, pp. 156–177.

12 Wilkinson, A., Marchington, M., Goodman, J. & Ackers, P. 1992. Total quality management and employee involvement. *Human Resource Management Journal*, vol. 2, no. 4, pp. 1–20.

13 Hill, S. 1995. From quality circles to total quality management. In Wilkinson, A. & Wilmott, H. (eds.), *Making quality critical: Studies in organisational change*. London, Routledge, pp. 33–35.

14 McArdle *et al.* 1995.

15 Tuckman, A. 1995. Ideology, quality and TQM. In Wilkinson, A. & Wilmott, H. (eds.), *Making quality critical: Studies in organisational change*. London, Routledge, pp. 54–81.

16 Garvin, D. 1994. History and evolution of the quality movement. In Costin, H. (ed.), *Readings in total quality management*. Fort Worth, Dryden Press, pp. 27–44.

17 Dean, J. W. & Evans, J. R. 1994. *Total quality: Management, organization and strategy*. Minneapolis/St.Paul, West.

18 Macdonald, J. 1998. The quality revolution – in retrospect. *The TQM Magazine*, vol. 10, no. 5. pp. 321–333.

19 Costin, H. 1994. *Readings in total quality management*. Fort Worth, Dryden Press.

20 Delavigne, K.T. & Robertson, J.D. 1994. *Deming's profound changes: When will the sleeping giant awaken?* Englewood Cliffs, NJ, Prentice Hall.

21 Garvin, D. 1994.

22 Dean & Evans, 1994.

23 Latzko, W.J. & Saunders, D.M. 1995. *Four days with Dr. Deming: A strategy for modern methods of management*. Massachusetts, Addison-Wesley.

24 Dean & Evans, 1994.

25 Wilkinson *et al.* 1998.

26 Sarlin, R.W. 1991. Through the quality maze. *Business Wise*, no. 1, pp. 5–12.

27 Wilkinson *et al.* 1998.

28 Feigenbaum, A.V. 1951. *Total quality control*. New York, McGraw-Hill.

29 Wilkinson *et al.* 1998.

30 Tuckman, A. 1995.

31 Latzko & Saunders, 1995.

32 Tuckman 1995, p. 62.

33 Crosby, P.B. 1979. *Quality is free: The art of making quality certain*. New York, Mentor.

34 Tuckman, A. 1995.

35 Dean & Evans, 1994, p. 5

36 Bunning, C. 1992. *Total quality management: Applying it in the public sector and to professional services*. Brisbane, EBIS Publishing.

37 Harvey, D. 1989. *The conditions of postmodernity*. Oxford, Blackwell.

38 Murdoch, A. 1998. Eastern promise: Business lessons from the Japanese. *Accountancy*, no. 122 (October), pp. 43–44.

39 Bunning, C. 1992.

40 Tuckman, A. 1995.

41 Wilkinson *et al.* 1992.

42 *Ibid.*

43 Palmer, G. & Saunder, I. 1992. Total quality management and human resource management: Comparisons and contrasts. *Asia Pacific Journal of Human Resources*, vol. 30, no 2, pp. 67–78.

44 Munro, R. 1995.

45 Hill, S. 1991. Why quality circles failed but total quality might succeed. *British Journal of Industrial Relations*, vol. 29, no. 4, pp. 541–569, on p. 565.

46 Dale & Plunkett, 1990.

47 Waldman, D. 1994. The contributions of total quality management to a theory of work performance. *Academy of Management Review*, vol. 19, no. 3, pp. 510–536.

48 Hackman, R. & Wageman, R. 1995. Total quality management: Empirical, conceptual and practical issues. *Administrative Science Quarterly*, vol. 40, no. 2, pp. 317–342.

49 Wilkinson, A. & Wilmott, H. 1995. Introduction. In Wilkinson, A. & Wilmott, H. (eds.), *Making quality critical: Studies in organisational change*. London, Routledge, pp. 1–32.

50 Tuckman, A. 1995.

51 Atkinson, P. 1990. *Creating cultural change: The key to successful total quality management*. Bedford, IBS.

52 Tuckman, A. 1995.

53 Legge, K. 1995. *Human resource management: Rhetorics and realities*. London, Macmillan, pp. 219–220.

54 Sashkin, M. & Kiser, K.J. 1993. *Putting total quality management to work*. San Francisco, Berrett-Koehler Publishers.

55 Hill, S. 1995.

56 Wilkinson *et al.* 1992.

57 *Ibid.*

58 Hill, S. 1995.

59 Tuckman, A. 1995.

60 Legge, K. 1995.

61 Wilkinson *et al.* 1998.

62 Wilkinson, A. 1994. Managing human resources for quality. In Dale, B., *Managing Quality* (second edition). Hemel Hempstead, Prentice Hall, pp. 273–291.

63 Kochan, T.A., Hoffer-Gittell, J. & Lautsch, B.A. 1995. Total quality management and human resource systems: An international comparison. *The International Journal of Human Resource Management*, vol. 6, no. 2, pp. 201–222.

64 Godfrey, G., Dale, B., Marchington, M. & Wilkinson, A. 1997. Control: A contested concept in TQM research. *International Journal of Operations & Production Management*, vol. 17, nos. 5–6, pp. 588–573.

65 Redman, T. & Mathews, B.P. 1998. Service quality and human resource management: A review and research agenda. *Personnel Review*, vol. 27, no. 1, pp. 57–77.

66 Wilkinson *et al.* 1998.

67 Beer, M., Spector, B., Lawrence, P., Quinn Mills, D. & Walton, R. 1985. *Human resource management: A general manager's perspective*. New York, Free Press.

68 Guest, D. 1991. Human resource management: Its implications for industrial

relations and trade unions. In Storey, J. (ed.), *New perspectives on human resource management*. London: Routledge, pp. 41–55.

69 Legge, K. 1995.

70 Pfeffer, J. 1994. Competitive advantage through people. *California Management Review*, vol. 36, no. 3, pp. 9–28.

71 Storey, J. 1991. Introduction: From personnel management to human resource management. In Storey, J. (ed.), *New perspectives on human resource management*. London: Routledge, pp. 1–18.

72 Guest, D. 1991.

73 Hunter, L. & Beaumont, P. 1993. Implementing TQM: Top down or bottom up? *Industrial Relations Journal*, vol. 24, no. 4, pp. 318–327.

74 Kochan, T.A., Katz, H.C. & McKersie, R.B. 1986. *The transformation of American industrial relations*. New York, Basic Books.

75 Sisson, K. 1994. *Personnel management in Britain* (second edition). Oxford, Blackwell.

76 Guest, D. 1991.

77 Beaumont, P. & Townley, B. 1985. Greenfield sites, new plants and work practices. In Hammond, V. (ed.), *Current research in management*. London, Frances Pinter, pp. 163–179.

78 Townley, B. 1991. Selection and appraisal: Reconstituting "social relations"? In Storey, J. (ed.), *New perspectives on human resource management*. London, Routledge, pp. 92–108.

79 Income Data Service (IDS) 1990. *Flexibility in the 1990s*. Study No 454. London, Income Data Services.

80 Keep, E. 1991. Corporate training strategies: the vital component?. In Storey, J. (ed.), *New perspectives on human resource management*. London: Routledge, pp. 109–125.

81 Guest, D. 1991.

82 Chorn, N.H. 1991. Total quality management: Panacea or pitfall? *International Journal of Physical Distribution & Logistics Management*, vol. 21, no. 8, pp. 31–35.

83 Hunt, V.D. 1993. *Managing quality: Integrating quality and business strategy*. Ilinois, Irwin.

84 Spencer, B. 1994. Models of organization and total quality management: A comparison and critical evaluation. *Academy of Management Review*, vol. 19, no. 3, pp. 446–471.

85 Kerfoot, D. & Knight, D. 1995. Empowering the "quality worker"?: The seduction and contradiction of the total quality phenomenon. In Wilkinson, A. & Wilmott, H. (eds.) *Making quality critical: Studies in organisational change*. London, Routledge, pp. 219–239.

86 Hill, S. 1995.

87 McArdle *et al.* 1995.

88 Wilkinson *et al.* 1998.

89 Herbig, P., Palumbo, F. & O'Hara, B.S. 1994. Total quality and the human resource professional. *The TQM Magazine*, vol. 6, no. 2, pp. 33–36.

90 Guest, D. 1991, p. 43.

91 Legge, K. 1989. Human resource management: A critical analysis. In Storey, J. (ed.), *New perspectives on human resource management*. London: Routledge, pp. 19–40.

92 Armstrong, M. 1987. Human resource management: A case of the emperor's new clothes? *Personnel Management*, vol. 19, no. 5, pp. 30–35.

93 Storey, J. 1991.

94 Guest, D. 1987. Human resource management and industrial relations. *Journal of Management Studies*, vol. 24, no. 5, pp. 503–521, on p. 515.

95 Williams, A. L. 1993. *Teeside works and total quality performance*. Unpublished MBA dissertation, University of Teeside.

96 Wilkinson, A. 1994. Managing human resources for quality. In Dale, B. *Managing Quality* (second edition). Hemel Hempstead: Prentice Hall, pp. 273–291.

97 Hill, S. 1991.

98 Guest, D. 1991.

99 Simmons, D.E., Shadur, M.A. & Preston, A.P. 1995. Integrating TQM and HRM. *Employee Relations*, vol. 17, no. 3, pp. 75–86.

100 Redman & Mathews, 1998.

101 Bowen, D.E. & Lawler, E.E. 1992. Total quality-orientated human resource management. *Organizational Dynamics*, vol. 20, no. 4, pp. 29–41.

102 Snape, E., Wilkinson, A., Marchington, M. & Redman, T. 1995. Managing human resources for TQM: Possibilities and pitfalls. *Employee Relations*, vol. 17, no. 3, pp. 42–51.

103 Redman & Mathews, 1998.

104 Ebel, K.E. 1991. *Achieving excellence in business: A practical guide to the total quality transformation process.* Milwaukee, ASQC Quality Press.

105 Blackburn, R. & Rosen, B. 1995. Does HRM walk the TQM talk? *HR Magazine*, vol. 40, no. 7, pp. 69–71.

106 Snape *et al.* 1995.

107 Redman & Mathews, 1998

108 Oakland, J.S. & Oakland, S. 1998. The links between people management, customer satisfaction and business results. *Total Quality Management*, vol. 9, no. 4–5, pp. 185–190.

109 Oakland, J.S. 1993. *Total quality management: The route to improving performance* (second edition). London, Butterworth-Heinemann, p. 387.

110 Hill, S. 1991.

111 Boynton, A.C., Victor, B. & Pine, B.J. 1993. New competitive strategies: Challenges to organisations and information technology. *IBM Systems Journal* vol. 32, no. 1, pp. 40–64.

112 Wilkinson & Wilmot, 1995.

113 Hackman & Wageman, 1995.

114 Simmons *et al.* 1995, p. 78.

115 Snape *et al.* 1995, p. 46.

116 Roth, W. 1998. Middle management: The missing link. *The TQM Magazine*, vol. 10, no. 1, pp. 6–9.

117 Wilkinson, A., Goffrey, G. & Marchington, M. 1997. Bouquets, brickbats and blinkers: Total quality management and employee involvement in practice. *Organizational Studies*, vol. 18, no. 5, pp. 799–819, on p. 810.

118 Dale, B. & Lightburn, K. 1992. Continuous quality improvement: Why some organisations lack commitment, *Interna-*

tional Journal of Production Economics, no. 27, pp. 57–67.

119 Marsh, S.A. 1993. The key to TQM and world-class competitiveness – Part 1. *Quality*, vol. 32, no. 9, pp. 37–39.

120 Wilkinson, A. 1994.

121 Goffin, K. & Swejczwski, M. 1996. Is management commitment to quality just "a given"? *The TQM Magazine*, vol. 8, no. 2, pp. 26–31.

122 Roth, W. 1998, p. 6.

123 Marchington, M. 1995. Fairy tales and magic wands: New employment practices in perspective. *Employee Relations*, vol. 17, no. 1, pp. 51–66.

124 Deblieux, M. 1991. Performance reviews support the quest for quality. *HR Focus*, nos. 3–4 (November).

125 Snape, E., Wilkinson, A. & Redman, T. 1996. Cashing in on quality? Pay incentives and the quality culture. *Human Resource Management*, vol. 6, no. 4, pp. 4–17.

126 Deming, W.E. 1986. *Out of crisis.* Cambridge, Cambridge University Press.

127 Scherkenbach, W.W. 1986. *The Deming route to quality and productivity.* Rockville, MD, CEE Press.

128 Latzko & Saunders, 1995.

129 Deming, W.E. 1986.

130 Waldman, D. 1994.

131 Wilkinson, A., Allen, P. & Snape, E. 1992. TQM and the management of labour management. *Management Decision*, vol. 30, no. 6, pp. 116–123.

132 Redman & Mathews, 1998.

133 Snape *et al.* 1995.

134 Simmons *et al.* 1995, p. 77.

135 Redman, T. & Snape, E. 1992. Upward and onward: Can staff appraise managers? *Personnel Review*, vol. 21, no. 7, pp. 32–46.

136 Redman, T., Wilkinson, A. & Snape, E. 1996. The long-haul: Sustaining TQM at British Steel Teeside Works. *International Journal of Manpower*, vol. 17, no. 2, pp. 34–51.

137 Wilkinson *et al.* 1998.

138 Redman & Mathews, 1998.

139 *Ibid.*

140 Deming, E. 1986.

141 Fletcher, C. 1993. *Appraisal: Routes to improved performance*. London, Institute of Personnel Management.

142 Wilkinson, A. 1994, p. 285.

143 Hackman & Wageman, 1995.

144 Crosby, P.B. 1979.

145 Wilkinson, A. 1994.

146 Snape *et al.* 1995, p. 46.

147 Drummond, H. & Chell, E. 1992. Should organisations pay for quality? *Personnel Review*, vol. 21, no. 4, pp. 615–633.

148 Hackman & Wageman, 1995.

149 Simmons *et al.* 1995.

150 Wilkinson *et al.* 1998.

151 Sashkin & Kiser, 1993.

152 Walker, T. 1992. Creating quality improvement that lasts. *National Productivity Review* (Autumn), pp. 473–478.

153 Wilkinson *et al.* 1998, p. 44.

154 Redman & Mathews, 1998, pp. 68–69.

155 Saskin & Kiser, 1993.

156 Hackman & Wageman, 1995.

157 Lawler, E. E. III 1994. Total quality management and the employee involvement: Are they compatible. *The Academy of Management Executive*, vol. 8, no. 1, pp. 68–77.

158 Wilkinson, A. 1994.

159 Simmons *et al.* 1995.

160 Hackman & Wageman, 1995, p. 326.

161 Snape *et al.* 1995.

162 Simmons *et al.* 1995, pp. 76–77.

163 Godfrey *et al.* 1997.

164 Wilkinson *et al.* 1997, p. 812.

165 Kochan *et al.* 1995.

166 Kunar, P. 1995. Canadian labour's response to work reorganization. *Economic and Industrial Democracy*, vol. 16, no. 1, pp. 39–78.

167 Sashkin & Kiser, 1993, p. 144.

168 Snape *et al.* 1995.

169 Marchington, 1995.

170 Godfrey, G. & Marchington, M. 1996. Shop stewards in the 1990s. *Industrial Relations Journal*, vol. 27, no. 4, pp. 339–344.

171 Kochan *et al.* 1995.

172 Oakland, J.S. 1993.

173 Mohrman, S., Tenkasi, R., Lawler. E.E. III & Ledford, J. Jnr 1995. Total quality management: Practices and outcomes in the largest USA firms. *Employee Relations*, vol. 17, no. 3, pp. 26-41.

174 Wilkinson & Wilmot, 1995, p. 813.

175 Snape *et al.* 1995.

176 Godfrey *et al.* 1997.

177 Fucini, S. & Fucini, J. 1990. *Working for the Japanese: Inside Mazda's American auto plant*. New York, Free Press.

178 Saskin & Kiser, 1993.

179 McArdle *et al.* 1995.

180 Waxler, R. P. & Higginson, T. 1994. TQM: Labor-management cooperation. In Costin, H. (ed.), *Readings in total quality management*. Fort Worth: Dryden Press, pp. 421–429.

181 Snape *et al.* 1995.

182 Sashkin & Kiser, 1993.

183 Wilkinson, A. 1994.

184 *Ibid*, pp. 286–288.

185 *Ibid*.

186 *Ibid*.

187 Wilkinson, A., Redman, T. & Snape, E. 1995. New patterns of quality management. *Quality Management Journal*, vol. 2, no. 2, pp. 37–51.

188 Dawson, P. 1989. New production arrangements: The totally flexible cage. *Work, Employment and Society*, vol. 3, no. 2, pp. 221–238.

189 Wilkinson, A. 1992. The other side of quality: "Soft" issues and the human resource dimension. *Total Quality Management*, vol. 3, no. 3, pp. 323–329.

190 Legge, 1995.

191 Tuckman, 1995.

192 Wilkinson, A. & Wilmott, H. 1996. Quality management, problems and pitfalls: A critical perspective. *International Journal of Quality & Reliability Management*, vol. 13, no. 2, pp. 55–65, on p. 62.

193 Wilkinson, A. 1994, pp. 281–282.

194 Wilkinson, A. & Witcher, B. 1993. Holistic TQM must take account of political processes. *Total Quality Management*, vol. 4, no. 1, pp. 47–56.

195 Wilkinson, A. 1994

196 Wilkinson. & Wilmott, 1996.

197 Marchington, 1995, p. 63.

198 Godfrey *et al.* 1997.

199 Wilkinson. & Wilmott, 1996, p. 62.

200 Redman & Mathews, 1998.

201 McArdle *et al*. 1995.

202 Marchington, 1995.

203 Redman & Mathews, 1998.

204 Kochan *et al*. 1995.

205 Wilkinson *et al*. 1998.

206 McArdle *et al*. 1995.

207 Redman & Mathews, 1998.

208 Dawson, P. 1998. The rhetoric and bureaucracy of quality management: A Totally questionable method? *Personnel Review*, vol. 27, no. 1, pp. 5–19, on p. 16.

209 Cruise-O'Brien, R. 1995. Employee involvement in performance improvement: A consideration of tacit knowledge, commitment and trust. *Employee Relations*, vol. 17, no. 3, pp. 110–120, on p. 112.

210 Kerfoot & Knight, 1995.

211 McArdle *et al*. 1995.

212 Collard, R. & Dale, B. 1989. Quality circles. In Sisson, K. (ed.), *Personnel Management in Britain*. Oxford, Blackwell, pp. 356–377.

213 Klein, J. A. 1984. Why supervisors resist employee involvement. *Harvard Business Review* (September-October), pp. 87–95.

214 Wilkinson, A. 1994.

215 Klein, J. A. 1984.

216 Marchington, M., Dale, B. & Wilkinson, A. 1993. Who is really taking the lead on quality? *Personnel Management*, vol. 25, no. 4, pp. 30–33.

217 Marchington, 1995.

218 Denham, N., Ackers, P. & Travers, C. 1997. Doing yourself out of a job? How middle managers cope with empowerment. *Employee Relations*, vol. 19, no. 2, pp. 147–159.

219 Jackson, C., Arnold, A., Nicholson, N. & Watts, T. 1996. *Managing careers in the year 2000 and beyond*, Report no. 304. London, Institute of Employment Studies.

220 Denham *et al*. 1997.

221 Wilkinson, A. 1994, p. 282.

222 McCabe, D. & Wilkinson, A. 1995. *If you can keep your "job" whilst all about you are losing theirs: TQM and the politics of orga-*

nisational restructuring. Proceedings of the Strategic Direction of HRM Conference. Nottingham Business School (December).

223 Redman & Mathews, 1998, p. 69.

224 Dale & Lightburn, 1992.

225 Marsh, S.A. 1993.

226 May, C. & Pearson, A.W. 1993. Total quality and R & D. *Journal of General Management*, vol. 18, no. 3 (Spring), pp. 1–22.

227 Goffin & Swejczwski, 1996.

228 Wilkinson, A., Redman, T. & Snape, E. 1993. *Quality management and the manager*. Corby, British Institute of Management.

229 Wilkinson *et al*. 1997.

230 Marchington, M. 1995.

231 Wilkinson *et al*. 1998

232 Delbridge, R., Turnbull, P. & Wilkinson, B. 1992. Pushing back the frontiers: Management control and work intensification under JIT/TQM factory regimes. *New Technology, Work and Employment*, vol. 7, no. 2, pp. 97–106.

233 Marchington, M. 1995

234 Legge, K. 1995.

235 Sewell, G. & Wilkinson, B. 1992. Empowerment or emasculation? Shop-floor surveillance in a total quality organization. In Blyton, P. & Turnbull, P. (eds), *Reassessing human resource management*. London, Sage, pp. 97–115.

236 McArdle *et al*. 1995.

237 Gatachalian, M.M. 1997. People empowerment the key to TQM success. *The TQM Magazine*, vol. 9, no. 6, pp. 429–433.

238 Wright, C. 1993. Introducing TQM - The cultural context. *Quality Australia*, vol. 10, no. 5, pp. 42–46.

239 Kearney, A.T. 1992, in association with *The TQM Magazine. Total quality: Time to take off the rose tinted spectacles*. Kempston: IFS Publications.

240 Wilkinson, A., Redman, T. & Snape, E. 1993. *Quality of Management and the Manager*. An IM Report. Corby: British Institute of Management.

241 Wilkinson *et al*. 1998.

7

Management of intellectual capital within organisations – the HR challenge

7.1 Introduction

Awareness of knowledge as a distinct factor of production within an organisation is gaining momentum. After maximising production factors such as land, buildings, equipment, inventory and financial resources (the tangible assets), companies have discovered that the so-called intangible (hidden) asset of knowledge can play a vital role in helping them obtain a sustainable competitive advantage. Thus, with the arrival of the knowledge era, the central role of physical capital in organisations has gone forever.

Companies have discovered that what they know, how they use what they know and how fast they can know something new will help them grow and succeed in the 21st century.[1-2] Thus the people who own the knowledge must be treated as important assets and not merely as commodities.[3] The sum of everything everybody knows in a company that gives it a competitive edge is known as intellectual capital (IC).[4]

Intellectual capital has become a critical issue within organisations for a number of reasons:[5-6]

- employees with the most intellectual capital are likely to find work opportunities in a wide variety of companies and will become volunteers;
- most assets depreciate when obtained, while intellectual capital appreciates;
- as the service economy grows, the importance of intellectual capital increases; and
- the globalisation of the economy is putting pressure on companies to increase adaptability and innovation.

Further reasons for the importance of intellectual capital include the numerous benefits that a company can derive from its presence, namely:[7-8]

- improved efficiency of people and operations;
- increased responsiveness to customers;
- improved decision making;
- enhanced employee satisfaction;
- savings in research and development costs;
- reduced duplication of efforts; and
- faster innovation of new products.

In view of the important role that intellectual capital can play within an organisation, the following issues will be addressed in this chapter:
- The origins and nature of intellectual capital.
- Knowledge as the key building block of intellectual capital.
- The components of intellectual capital.
- The measurement of intellectual capital.
- HR's role in obtaining, building and retaining intellectual capital.

7.2 The origins and nature of intellectual capital

Having established that intellectual capital is an important intangible asset that can lead to the creation of organisational value, the question is: where does it come from?

First and foremost, it resides in the employees within the organisation. When an employee is employed, the company in a sense rents the intellectual capital from the individual. Only when the individual converts his or her ideas into products, services or work processes does the company take ownership of them.[9] Thus, only once an individual's knowledge is used and shared to create organisational value does that value-added "product" become part of the intellectual capital of the firm.[10]

As intellectual capital is the end result of a process, it is important to establish its origins. It all starts with data (collected facts and figures) that are given structure which then leads to information (logically sorted data). The purposeful consumption and use of information then leads to knowledge. Thus, intellectual capital represents knowledge transformed to something of value to the organisation. Intellectual assets, also known as knowledge assets, are the individual products of this knowledge transformation (e.g. patents, copyrights, trademarks and brands). The key enablers of this dynamic knowledge transformation process are the people, technologies and structures of the organisation.[11]

7.3   Knowledge as the key building block of intellectual capital

As indicated in the previous section, knowledge plays a critical role in the creation of intellectual capital. Other aspects like skills and core competencies, which form the content part of human capital (see section 7.4 below), are also important, but play a lesser role as they are limited in scope.[12] A multi-layered model which demonstrates the means by which the flow of skill development is managed and maintained within a company is illustrated in Figure 7.1. The model identifies six meta-skills, namely skill identification, organisational learning, knowledge embedding, rapid deployment, restructuring and innovation, which combine into an engine of core competence generation. The meta-skills are briefly described in Figure 7.1 and will not be further explored.[13]

As far as the knowledge component is concerned, Pat Clarke defines knowledge as "the understanding of why and how something works, for example, how and why the customer reaches a decision to purchase a good or service".[14]

According to Roos et al.,[15] knowledge is generally related to the level of education of a person. Although it is something that has to be taught, it does not necessarily have to be taught in schools or universities (field training is also acceptable). Thus, knowledge is not inborn but needs some kind of learning from books, teachers or mentors. However, it is important to note that knowledge does not have to be of an academic nature.

7.3.1   Categories of knowledge

Business knowledge can be classified into various categories:[16]
- **Advantaged knowledge** is knowledge that does or can provide competitive advantage for the company.
- **Base knowledge** forms an integral part of the business, e.g. best practices. However, this type of knowledge may provide only a short-term advantage.
- **Trivial knowledge** has no major impact on the company.

It is important to note that knowledge must be unique, valuable, and impossible to imitate, otherwise it will be of no use to the organisation in its attempts to gain the competitive advantage, as rapid imitation by competitors takes place on a daily basis. Thus, not only must companies be able to create new knowledge continuously, but they must also expose themselves to new ideas from outside in order to stay ahead.[17]

Figure 7.1 Core competence as an engine of growth

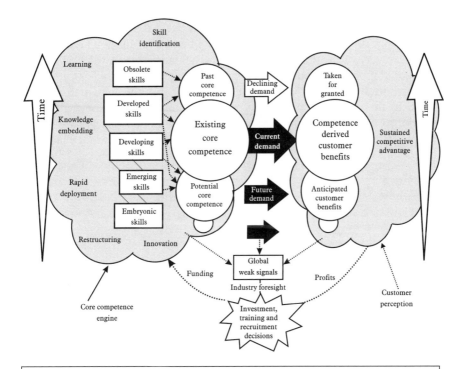

- Skills identification – appreciating which skills are going to be needed in the future.
- Organisational learning – sharing knowledge within and beyond the company's boundaries.
- Knowledge embedding – putting knowledge into the company, e.g. in complex routines, processes.
- Rapid deployment – is concerned with the speed at which an organisation can build and rebuild a core capability.
- Restructuring – the firm will need to re-engineer the processes that are developed from core capability deployment.
- Innovation – involves product design; also relates to business processes.

SOURCE: Reprinted from *Long Range Planning*, vol. 30, no. 4. Petts, N. Building growth on core competencies – a practical approach, pp. 555–557. Copyright 1997. With permission from Elsevier Science.

7.3.2 Types of knowledge

Having established that the individual plays a critical role in the availability of knowledge within the organisation, it is time to look at knowledge within the broader organisational context. To do this effectively, the discussion will focus on the work done by two authors, namely Matusik & Hill.[18] These authors have been very successful in drawing up a schematic structure identifying the different components of organisational knowledge (see Figure 7.2).

When studying Figure 7.2 it is clear that the first major distinction that can be made is that between private (firm-specific) and public knowledge. As mentioned earlier, the knowledge within the organisation (i.e. private knowledge) can be a source of competitive advantage. Private knowledge includes

---

Figure 7.2 Organisational knowledge components

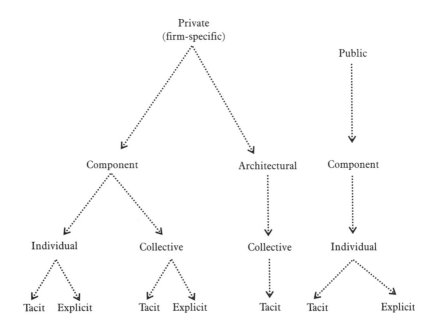

SOURCE: Republished with permission of Academy of Management, from
The utilisation of contingent work, knowledge creation, and competitive advantage,
by S.F. & Hill, C.W.L. 1998. vol. 23, no. 4 (October), p. 684.
Permission conveyed through Copyright Clearance Center, Inc.

items such as a company's unique routines, processes or marketing strategies. On the other hand, public knowledge consists of knowledge not unique to any company and which thus resides in the external environment. Examples of this type of knowledge include just-in-time inventories, team-based incentives and total quality management (TQM). One must bear in mind, however, that at one stage all these "best practices" were classified as private knowledge. The value of applying this type of knowledge (i.e. public knowledge) within the organisation must not be underestimated. These "external best practices" can be a source of competitive disadvantage if ignored by the company.[19]

The next distinction the authors make is that between component and architectural knowledge. Component knowledge, as the name suggests, relates to a sub-routine of an organisation's operations (e.g. the knowledge of a company's new product development process or inventory management process). As indicated in Figure 7.2, this type of knowledge can be held individually as well as collectively and may also contain both a private and a public element.[20]

Architectural knowledge relates to the whole organisation instead of only a component (e.g. the organisation-wide routines of co-ordinating the various components of the organisation and putting them to productive use). Because it covers the whole organisation, this type of knowledge is held collectively. Due to the nature of architectural knowledge, it is understandable that this knowledge will play a major role in influencing component knowledge. In fact, over the long run, it is the architectural knowledge that contributes most to an organisation's competitive position.[21]

The next distinction that can be made (see Figure 7.2) is that between individual and collective knowledge. Individually held knowledge can be seen as the total of an individual's competencies, information and knowledge, whereas collective knowledge consists of routines, practices and past views on goals, missions and competitors held in common by a large number of organisational members.[22]

The last distinction that can be made is that between tacit and explicit knowledge. Tacit knowledge is knowledge learned through experience and is difficult to formalise and communicate. Individual tacit knowledge can be found in individual skills and habits, while collective tacit knowledge can be found in company routines and company culture. Explicit knowledge, on the other hand, is codified and transferable in formal systematic methods such as rules and procedures. Individual explicit knowledge consists of knowledge and skills that can be easily taught or written down, whereas collective explicit knowledge resides in standard operating procedures, documentation and rules.[23]

To be of value to the organisation, it is necessary that the different types of knowledge discussed above be integrated in some form or another (e.g. public as well as private knowledge). This is vital if a sustainable competitive advantage is to be realised.

As far as the internal organisation is concerned, it is important that the integration process not only leads to the transfer of knowledge to the various areas within the organisation, but that it also leads to the creation of new private knowledge. Matusik & Hill have identified a number of internal mechanisms that can be used for this purpose.[24] These include creating teams, establishing feedback mechanisms, rewarding persons for integrating information, and creating advice networks. A company also needs to accumulate knowledge from the external environment in order to survive. In this regard the authors have also identified mechanisms for enhancing external integration.[25] These include funding research to be undertaken on co-operative arrangements such as joint ventures and strategic alliances, developing a formal strategy towards knowledge acquisition, and, as is the case with internal integration, rewarding employees for obtaining information.

7.4   The components of intellectual capital

Before we look at the components of intellectual capital, it is important to have the concept defined.

Klein & Prusak define intellectual capital as "intellectual material that has been formalized, captured and leveraged to produce a higher valued asset".[26] A similar definition is that of Stewart, who defines intellectual capital as "the intellectual material – knowledge, information, intellectual property, experience that can be put to use to create wealth".[27] For knowledge to be created, intellectual action must thus take place, and it would seem that intellectual capital is a means to an end.

A widely used definition of intellectual capital is that of Laurie J. Bassi, who calls it "knowledge that is of value to an organisation".[28] The definition suggests that the management of knowledge (the sum of what is known) creates intellectual capital and contributes to the firm's storehouse of knowledge.

According to Hubert Saint-Onge,[29] and confirmed by many others,[30-32] a company's intellectual capital contains at least three components:

- **Human capital** (also known as employee capital) is the capabilities (usable knowledge, skills and competence) of the individuals in the organisation to solve problems. Hudson[33] indicates that human capital, at an individual level, can be seen as a combination of genetic inheritance, education, experience and attitudes about life and business.

- **Customer capital** (known as relational or external capital) includes knowledge of market channels, customer and supplier relationships and industry associations.
- **Structural capital** (also known as organisational or internal capital) is the capabilities of the organisation to meet market needs (e.g. organisational operating systems, manufacturing processes and all forms of intellectual property owned by the company).

As indicated in section 7.3, there are different types of knowledge held within these components, the most popular being tacit and explicit knowledge. Tacit knowledge has the following characteristics within the three components:[34]

- In **human capital** it is the mindsets of individuals, their assumptions, biases, values and beliefs.
- In **customer capital** it is the individual and collective mindsets of customers, which shape their perceptions of value provided by any given product or service.
- In **structural capital**, it is the collective mindsets of the organisation's members, which shape the culture of that organisation, including the norms and values.

Although there is agreement among the various authors regarding the three main components of intellectual capital, some – like Roos *et al.* – have proposed a number of additional components. The three main components, as well as the additional ones, are included in the model in Figure 7.3, which will be discussed shortly.

As intellectual capital is still a new area of research, it was decided to use the model of the Swedish company Skandia as a basis for the discussion of the different components of intellectual capital. This company was the first to publish an Intellectual Capital Report as a supplement to its Annual Report in 1994.[35] Although a number of other companies have followed its example, it is at present the most advanced in this area.

The adapted model (see Figure 7.3) divides market value, also known as total value, into three groups – physical capital, financial capital and intellectual capital (the focus of this chapter). The intellectual capital component is further divided into human capital (anything that thinks – the source of innovation) and structural capital (defined as what remains in the company when the people go home).[36]

Human capital is further divided into three main areas – competence, attitude and intellectual agility. Competence includes skills and knowledge, while attitude covers the behaviour component of employees' work. Intellectual agility is the ability to innovate and change practices, to think laterally and propose new and innovative solutions to problems. According to

Figure 7.3 A schematic presentation of the components of intellectual capital

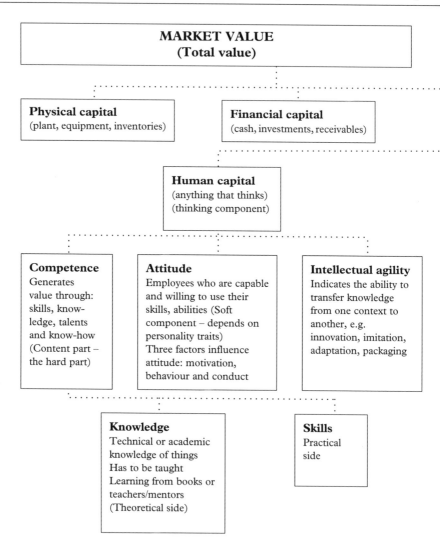

SOURCE: Adapted from Roos *et al.* 1997. *Intellectual capital: Navigating the new business landscape.* Hampshire, Macmillan Business, p. 29 (the Skandia Model). Used with permission from the Skardia Company, Sweden.

Intellectual capital
(all invisible processes and assets)

Structural capital
(remains within the company when employees go home) (non-thinking component)

Customer capital
(External focus)
e.g.
- suppliers
- shareholders
- partners
- customers

Organisational capital
(Internal focus) e.g.
- infrastructure (hardware)
- processes (software)
- culture (wetware)
- strategy

Renewal and development capital
Includes all items that have been built or created and that have an impact on future values

Innovation capital
What creates the success of tomorrow

Process capital
Sum of know-how, manuals, best practices, Internet

Intellectual property
e.g. patents, trademarks, brands

Intangible assets
e.g. planning new plants, new training programmes

Stewart,[37] human capital grows in two ways: (1) when the organisation uses more of what people know, and (2) when more people know more "stuff" that is useful to the organisation. Thus, people generate capital for their company through their competence, attitude and intellectual agility.

Structural capital, on the other hand, includes customer and organisational capital (representing the internal and external focus), as well as renewal and development capital, a component included by Roos *et al.* This component includes all the items that have been built and created and that will have an impact on future value.[38]

Organisational capital (which consists of systems, strategy, structure and culture) can be further divided into innovation and process capital. Process capital is the sum of know-how that is formalised inside the company (e.g. in manuals), while innovation capital is that which creates the success of tomorrow. Innovation capital can also be divided further into intellectual property and intangible assets, which are linked to the renewal and development component in the model. Thus, a company's resources and capabilities include all the physical, financial and intellectual capital assets used by a company to develop, manufacture and deliver products or services to its customers.

From the discussion we can see that intangible assets, as subdivisions within intellectual capital, consist of:[39]

- externally related or customer assets, including brands, customer relationships and reputations;
- internal or structural assets, such as systems, strategies, processes, structures and culture; and
- human assets, the people available to the organisation – their brains, skills, knowledge, experience, and how they are led and motivated.

Human capital matters because it is the source of innovation and renewal. However, to be of value, there needs to be a knowledge flow. Sharing and transporting knowledge requires structural intellectual assets such as information systems. Customer capital is the value of an organisation's relationship with the people with whom it does business.[40]

To be effective, the different components of intellectual capital cannot be seen in isolation, but must be integrated to create added value for the organisation. The question, however, is: *how is this possible?*

According to Stewart,[41] closer co-operation between human capital and structural capital is possible when a company develops a shared sense of purpose, combined with an entrepreneurial spirit. Management must also place a high value on agility and govern more by carrot than by stick. Regarding human capital and customer capital, Stewart sees growth between them as possible when individuals feel responsible for their part in the organisation, interact directly with customers, and know what knowledge and skills the customers expect and value. The growth between customer capital and structural capital is possible when the company and its customers learn more from each other and also strive to make their interactions more informal.

7.5 The measurement of intellectual capital

The famous saying "what you manage you must be able to measure, and what you measure you must be able to manage" also applies to intellectual capital.[42] Researchers, consultants, accountants and managers soon discovered, however, that the traditional financial accounting measures, such as return on investments and earnings per share, could not be adequately utilised for intellectual capital, as they were out of step with the skills and competencies companies were trying to master.[43]

Numerous suggestions were made to solve this problem. For example, some wanted to adjust the traditional financial measures to make them more relevant, while others suggested adapting operational measures like cycle times and defect rates.[44] Some even suggested a combination of the two approaches. However, researchers soon realised that, because of the nature of intellectual capital, new measures had to be developed to determine the value-creating potential of the workforce.[45]

A number of measures became available, and are summarised in Table 7.1. The measures contain many suggestions and ideas for management to consider and use. Here we will examine the most popular one, namely the balanced scorecard approach. This approach, which is used by companies like Sears and American Express, was developed by Robert S. Kaplan and David P. Norton.[46] A brief discussion of this approach follows.

Table 7.1 Twelve ways to measure intellectual capital

The Montague Institute has identified several approaches for measuring intellectual capital.

1 **Relative value.** Bob Buckman of Buckman Laboratories and Lief Edvinsson of Skandia Insurance are proponents of this approach, in which the ultimate goal is progress, not a quantitative target. Example: have 80 per cent of employees involved with customers in a meaningful way.

2   **Balanced scorecard.** Supplements traditional financial measures with these additional perspectives: customers, internal business processes, and learning or growth. The term was coined by several Harvard Business School professors.

3   **Competency models.** By observing and classifying the behaviours of successful employees and calculating the market value of their output, it is possible to assign a monetary value to the intellectual capital they create and use in their work.

4   **Subsystem performance.** It can be relatively easy to quantify success or progress in a particular aspect of intellectual capital. For example, Dow Chemical was able to measure an increase in licensing revenues from better control of its patented assets.

5   **Benchmarking.** Involves identifying companies that are recognised leaders in leveraging their intellectual assets, determining how well they score on relevant criteria, and comparing your own company's performance against their performance. Example of a relevant criterion: leaders systematically identify knowledge gaps and use well-defined processes to close them.

6   **Business worth.** This approach centres on these questions: What would happen if the information we use now disappeared? What would happen if we doubled the amount of key information available? How does the value of that information change after a day, a week, or a year? Evaluation focuses on the cost of missed or underutilised business opportunities.

7   **Business-process auditing.** Measures how information enhances the value of a business process, such as accounting, production or marketing.

8   **Knowledge bank.** Treats capital spending as an expense instead of an asset and treats a portion of salaries (normally a 100 per cent expense) as an asset because it creates cash flow.

9   **Brand-equity valuation.** Measures the economic impact of a brand (or other intangible asset) on such factors as pricing power, distribution reach, and ability to launch new products as line extensions.

10   **Calculated intangible value.** Compares a company's return-on-assets with a published average ROA for the industry.

11   **Micro-lending.** A new type of lending that replaces tangible assets with such intangible collateral as peer group support and training. Used primarily to spur economic development in poor areas.

12   **Colourised reporting.** Suggested by SEC commissioner Steven Wallman, this approach supplements traditional financial statements (which give a "black and white" picture) with additional information

that adds "colour". Examples: brand values and customer satisfaction measures.

SOURCE: Reprinted by courtesy of The Montague Institute, http://www.montague.com/le/le1096.html. Reprinted with permission. Copyright Jean L. Greaf 1997.

In their balanced scorecard approach, Kaplan & Norton allow managers to look at the business from four important perspectives, namely:[47]

- a customer perspective – how do customers see us?
- an internal perspective – what must we excel at?
- an innovation and learning perspective – can we continue to improve and create value?
- a financial perspective – how do we look to shareholders?

These issues correlate with the different intellectual capital components as identified earlier in Figure 7.3. The advantages of using the balanced scorecard approach include the following:[48]

- it brings together many of the competitive elements – e.g. becoming customer-orientated, improving quality and teamwork; and
- it guards against the underutilisation of assets by allowing management to see whether the improvement in one area has taken place at the expense of another area.

To activate the scorecard, managers must translate the company goals relating to the four perspectives (these are normally generic issues which form part of any mission statement) into specific measures that reflect the factors that really matter.[49] See Figure 7.4, in which such a process has been completed, as well as Figure 7.5, in which examples generated by a number of companies and placed under the different components of intellectual capital are indicated.

By making use of information technology and its measures, managers can quickly determine where an imbalance occurs on the scorecard. For example, if the measure for on-time delivery gives trouble, the exact problem, by day, by plant and by division, can be identified.

From the foregoing it is clear that the balanced scorecard places the strategy of the company – and not control efforts – at the centre of the process.[50] The measures are thus designed to pull the employees towards the overall mission of the company. The strength of the scorecard is that it provides a simple conceptual and diagnostic tool to ensure that companies utilise the right processes and people to drive customer and business

Figure 7.4 Balanced business scorecard

Financial perspective	
GOALS	MEASURES
Survive	Cash flow
Succeed	Quarterly sales growth and operating income by division
Prosper	Increased market share and ROE

Customer perspective	
GOALS	MEASURES
New products	Percentage of sales from new products
	Percentage of sales from proprietary products
Responsive supply	On-time delivery (defined by customer)
Preferred supplier	Share of key accounts' purchases
	Ranking by key accounts
Customer partnership	Number of co-operative engineering profits

Internal business perspective	
GOALS	MEASURES
Technology capability	Manufacturing geometry vs. competition
Manufacturing excellence	Cycle time Unit cost Yield
Design productivity	Silicon efficiency Engineering efficiency
New product introduction	Actual introduction schedule vs. plan

Innovation and learning perspective	
GOALS	MEASURES
Technology leadership	Time to develop next generation
Manufacturing learning	Process time to maturity
Product focus	Percentage of products that equal 80% of sales
Time to market	New product introduction vs. competition

SOURCE: Reprinted by permission of *Harvard Business Review* from The balanced scorecard – measures that drive performance, by Kaplan R.S. & Norton, D.P., January/February 1992, p. 76. Copyright 1992 by the President and Fellows of Harvard College. All rights reserved.

Figure 7.5 Examples of intellectual capital measures generated by a number of companies

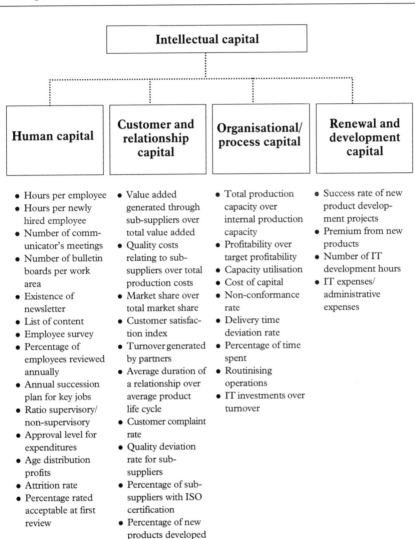

Intellectual capital

| Human capital | Customer and relationship capital | Organisational/ process capital | Renewal and development capital |

Human capital
- Hours per employee
- Hours per newly hired employee
- Number of communicator's meetings
- Number of bulletin boards per work area
- Existence of newsletter
- List of content
- Employee survey
- Percentage of employees reviewed annually
- Annual succession plan for key jobs
- Ratio supervisory/ non-supervisory
- Approval level for expenditures
- Age distribution profits
- Attrition rate
- Percentage rated acceptable at first review

Customer and relationship capital
- Value added generated through sub-suppliers over total value added
- Quality costs relating to sub-suppliers over total production costs
- Market share over total market share
- Customer satisfaction index
- Turnover generated by partners
- Average duration of a relationship over average product life cycle
- Customer complaint rate
- Quality deviation rate for sub-suppliers
- Percentage of sub-suppliers with ISO certification
- Percentage of new products developed with partners

Organisational/ process capital
- Total production capacity over internal production capacity
- Profitability over target profitability
- Capacity utilisation
- Cost of capital
- Non-conformance rate
- Delivery time deviation rate
- Percentage of time spent
- Routinising operations
- IT investments over turnover

Renewal and development capital
- Success rate of new product development projects
- Premium from new products
- Number of IT development hours
- IT expenses/ administrative expenses

SOURCE: Adapted from Roos et al. 1997. *Intellectual Capital: Navigating the new business landscape*. Hampshire: Macmillan Business. (The Skandialink Navigator, p. 72, MEC Track's IC Base, p. 74 and Battery's Intellectual Capital System, p. 76). Used with permission.

performance – the goal of any company striving towards gaining a sustained competitive advantage.[51]

7.6   HR's role in obtaining, building and retaining intellectual capital

It is clear that the ultimate goal of any organisation striving towards obtaining and retaining a sustained competitive advantage is to have a workforce which possesses a unique knowledge base. This type of workforce would, however, be difficult to buy because it must be built to retain its uniqueness.[52] The question that can be asked is: *how can a company obtain, build and retain a world-class workforce with the potential to create a competitive advantage?* The answer to this question poses a big challenge for the HR function as well as the HR professional, especially with the new strategic role it has to play within the organisation.[53] A number of suggestions have been proposed by Richard W. Beatty, James R. Beatty and Dennis J. O'Neill which will be used as a basis for this discussion.[54]

7.6.1 Obtaining intellectual capital

One of the most critical issues in fulfilling the intellectual capital requirement of the company is to obtain the right people. In the traditional way, this can take place by means of recruitment, when the HR professional goes outside the organisation to replace current talent with higher-quality talent or to obtain additional talent required by the organisation.[55]

To be successful, the recruiting effort must attract those individuals who possess a broad competency base as well as having the ambition to expand that base further. Developing and unleashing the human capital already resident within the organisation can also be a further option.[56] In many cases employees have been underutilised by companies due to their lack of an intellectual capital focus. To be successful under these conditions, organisations need to minimise mindless tasks performed by employees, reduce meaningless paperwork and reduce unproductive infighting by creating a culture of learning and teaching.[57] Thus a major educational effort is necessary in most organisations, both private and public.

To encourage and support this process the HR function can also design a reward system whereby individuals are paid for collecting, sharing, creating and distributing new ideas within the organisation. Some major advantages of developing knowledge-sharing initiatives within the organisation include the following:[58]

- information hoarding is discouraged;
- star performers can rise to the top;
- great importance is placed on expertise;
- increasing competitiveness is made possible;
- it avoids wasting time reinventing the wheel; and
- it encourages employees who are not natural networkers to engage in conversation and knowledge sharing.

A further tool that can be used to create more knowledge within the organisation is better use of the information technology available within the company. For example, by updating present systems, information can be distributed to different groups by means of the intranet as well as the World Wide Web. The goal is thus to get the right people communicating at the right time across the entire organisation by breaking down the silos within the company.[59] One important proviso, however, is that the information that becomes available through this process must be exploited, and new information must be created. The organisation must thus become a learning organisation.

Other newer methods of obtaining intellectual capital include mergers and acquisitions. Through this process, which has gained momentum over the past few years, companies can obtain a significant source of intellectual capital. Thus, for companies needing specific expertise, it might be cheaper and quicker to acquire an existing system. HR's challenge in this process is thus to establish the core competencies database of the possible merger/ acquisition.

7.6.2 Building intellectual capital

The process of creating intellectual capital within an organisation does not end when individuals are recruited/obtained from the outside and better communication networks are established inside the company. The workforce must continue to provide unique ways of responding to changes, and this can happen only when a continuous effort is made to improve and build the workforce. For this process to be successful a number of important issues must be addressed. These include:[60]

- re-engineering the organisational structures and taking a long-term view of the potential benefits of building a knowledge-leveraging strategy;
- developing a culture where everyone becomes a knowledge leader;
- making a commitment by management to communicate clearly and to share knowledge;

- developing a framework for capturing knowledge to avoid losing it;
- making information systems accessible and easy to use;
- building technology that is human-centred and focused on solving business problems;
- creating, capturing and transferring knowledge across internal boundaries in order to increase the pace of innovation; and
- providing time and resources for knowledge sharing – tearing down internal barriers to knowledge sharing.

The process of building intellectual capital may also require what is becoming known as a chief knowledge officer (CKO) or chief learning officer (CLO). General Electric and Coca-Cola, two of the world's major companies, were the first to hire such individuals.[61] These individuals are normally part of the HR departmental structure and report directly to the head of HR and the CEO of the company.[62] Recent studies have identified a number of characteristics that are most prevalent among these individuals, for example:[63]

- knowledge officers must have circulated through the company and must have developed a holistic perspective;
- they must be able to energise the organisation and function as cheerleaders to build momentum behind the knowledge initiatives;
- they must be able to withstand a multitude of pressures;
- they must feel rewarded by the accomplishments of other people; and
- they must have a good relationship with the head of HR.

The CLO can influence the organisation in several ways. One is to rapidly generate new knowledge, ideas and solutions to problems throughout the organisation by means of the information technology mentioned earlier. However, before starting such a process, it would be advisable to conduct an intellectual capital audit. Such an examination may consist of a survey.[64] To enhance this process, Stewart[65] suggests using his four-quadrant grid to first classify the workforce within the company. This grid appears in Figure 7.6.

Using the grid, companies can continuously cull their workforces to ensure that they are investing in and retaining the appropriate employees and encouraging those who are no longer growing or contributing. A brief discussion of the grid follows.[66]

- **Lower left quadrant of the grid.** According to Stewart, the first group of individuals that can be identified within any organisation are the unskilled and semi-skilled workers. These are placed in the lower left quadrant of the grid. Although the organisation needs these workers, they can easily be replaced, as the company's success does not depend on them. They thus have low value and their functions may be replaced by machines doing their jobs.

Figure 7.6 Stewart's grid for classifying employees within the organisation

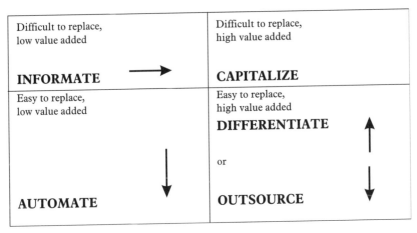

SOURCE: From *Intellectual capital – the new wealth of organisations* by Thomas A Stewart. Nicholas Brealey Publishing, London, 1998, p 91. Tel: 0044171 4300224; Fax: 0044171 4048311.

- **Upper left quadrant of the grid.** In this corner go people who have mastered complicated activities but do not play any further role within the company except performing their duties. Skilled factory workers or experienced secretaries can be typical examples of this group. They may be hard to replace and may be doing important work, but it is not work that customers care about. However, some challenges for the company exist regarding these workers. The company can informate their work – that is, change it to add more information value so that it starts to benefit the customers. For example, auditors can be made competitive assets instead of merely remaining inspectors.
- **Lower right quadrant of the grid.** Although workers in this category are valued highly by customers, they can easily be replaced. For example, their jobs can be outsourced. Workers that fall into this category are those such as design artists. The alternative for the company is differentiation, finding ways to turn generic job knowledge into something the company will be able to exploit – for example, providing job seminars on graphic design for the community.
- **Upper right quadrant of the grid.** Here employees who play irreplaceable roles in the company are placed. Examples include research chemists, top sales representatives, project managers and research engineers. According to Stewart, a company's human capital is embodied,

in this quadrant, in the people whose talents and experience create the products and services that attract customers to it instead of the competitors. He sees the other three quadrants merely as labour costs and not as directly creating customer value.

Thus, by using this model the company can be better focused on building human resources in those areas that are contributing to the economic value of the company. It is also in a better position not to lose critical knowledge when the company downsizes, reorganises or reduces its workforce, by categorising all people within these four quadrants.[67]

Having classified the workforce by means of the grid, the company can proceed to assess the strength of its intellectual capital. This can be done by questioning what the workforce knows in terms of work to be accomplished, and how to do it. Better yet, do they know why – and most critically, do they care why?[68] According to Beatty et al., the acquisition of basic knowledge may be a lower-level intellectual capital challenge, whereas enabling a workforce to know why and ultimately to care why, which can significantly extend the expansion of intellectual capital, is a much greater challenge.[69]

Much of the effort of addressing the challenge of building intellectual capital within organisations will take the shape of formal instruction.[70] However, HR managers must be aware that recent research has indicated that most of the competency acquisition experienced by professionals now comes from work experiences and rotational assignments (70 per cent), while only 10 per cent comes from formal instruction.[71] Thus, the direct challenge facing the HR function is to design jobs that provide employees with the necessary growth opportunities, and to use information technology as an integrated part thereof. Having made substantial investments in building intellectual capital, it is essential that the organisation retain that which is created. In today's highly competitive global environment, the organisation needs knowledge workers more than knowledge workers need the organisation.[72]

7.6.3 Retaining intellectual capital

Having satisfied the initial goal of establishing a workforce with a unique knowledge base, companies are faced with the dilemma of how to prevent these knowledge workers from leaving their organisations. This is an important challenge and one that can become an expanded role for the HR function. One of the underlying issues in this area is how to obtain a commitment from employees. According to Dave Ulrich, this can be achieved by doing the following:[73]

Empower – enable employees to control decisions on how they do their work.

Strategy or vision – offer employees a vision and direction that commits them to working hard.

Challenging work – provide employees with stimulating work that develops new skills.

Work culture – establish an environment of celebration, fun, excitement and openness.

Shared gains – compensate employees for work accomplished; it is important that this compensation is equitable in terms of external market pay.

Communication – candidly and frequently share information with employees.

Concern for people – ensure that each individual is treated with dignity and that differences are openly shared.

Technology – give employees the technology to make their work easier.

Training and development – ensure that employees have the skills to do their work well.

An important issue not addressed by Ulrich is that of having a clear understanding of the organisation's customer constituency, and especially the customers' needs. Employees must understand that for the company to be successful it must make the customers successful too. However, satisfying customers will be very difficult, if not impossible, if the workforce is highly dissatisfied.[74] Therefore, the HR role in effectively satisfying the workforce requires considerable effort – such as becoming an employee advocate, especially for the core competency workers.[75] Thus, if efforts are devoted to the aspects mentioned earlier, the organisation will be successful in retaining its knowledge workforce and also strengthening its competitive position.

7.7   Summary

This chapter has reviewed the important role that intellectual capital can play in helping organisations obtain a competitive advantage. Because of its strategic importance, the origins and nature of intellectual capital were also discussed. It was found that it resides within the employees of the organisation and that knowledge plays a critical role in its creation. Various categories and types of knowledge were found and discussed by means of a model developed by Matusik & Hill.

Following this discussion, various components of intellectual capital were considered in detail. It was determined that a company's intellectual capital contains at least three components, namely human capital, customer capital and structural capital. Suggestions were offered on how to measure intellectual capital, focusing specifically on the balanced scorecard approach. Also discussed was the role of the HR function in obtaining, building and retaining intellectual capital for the company.

References

1   Prusak, L. 1996. The knowledge advantage. *Strategy & Leadership*, vol. 24, no. 2 (March/April), p. 6.
2   Klein, D.A. 1998. *The strategic management of intellectual capital*. Woburn, Massachusets, Butterworth Heinemann, p. x.
3   Hathcock, B.C. 1996. The new breed approach to 21st century human resources. *Human Resource Management*, vol. 35, no. 2 (Summer), p. 246.
4   Sveiby, K.E. 1997. *The new organisational wealth: managing & measuring knowledge-based assets*. San Francisco, Berrett-Koehler Publishers.
5   Ulrich, D. 1998. Intellectual capital = competence x commitment. *Sloan Management Review*, vol. 39, no. 2 (Winter), p. 15.
6   Klein, D.A. 1998, p. ix.
7   Hubeler, R.J. 1996. Benchmarking knowledge management. *Strategy & Leadership*, vol. 24, no. 2 (March/April), p. 22.
8   Mayo, A. 1998. Memory bankers. *People Management* (22 January), p. 36.
9   Miller, W.C. 1998. Fostering intellectual capital. *HR Focus* (January), p. 9.
10 Lynn, B. 1998. Intellectual capital. *Cost & Management*, vol. 72, no. 1 (February), pp. 10–15. Page 3 of Internet article (from webman@localhost, ABI/Inform database).
11 *Ibid.*
12 Roos, J., Roos, G., Dragonetti, N.C. & Edvinsson, L. 1997. *Intellectual capital: navigating the new business landscape*. Hampshire, Macmillan Business, pp. 25–26.
13 Petts, N. 1997. Building growth on core competencies – a practical approach. *Long Range Planning*, vol. 30, no. 4, pp. 555–557.
14 Clarke, P. 1998. Implementing a knowledge strategy for your firm. *Research/Technology Management*, vol. 41, no. 2 (March/April), pp. 28–31. Page 2 of online text: http://gateway.ovid.com/server3/ovidweb.
15 Roos *et al.* 1997, pp. 35–36.
16 Clarke, P. 1998, p. 2.
17 Matusik, S.F. & Hill, C.W.L. 1998. The utilisation of contingent work, knowledge creation, and competitive advantage. *The Academy of Management Review*, vol. 23, no. 4 (October), pp. 682–683.
18 *Ibid.*, pp. 683–685.
19 *Ibid.*, p. 683.
20 *Ibid.*, p. 684.
21 *Ibid.*, pp. 684–685.
22 *Ibid.*, p. 683.
23 *Ibid.*
24 *Ibid.*, p. 685.
25 *Ibid.*
26 Klein, D.A. & Prusak, L. 1994. *Characterizing intellectual capital*. Centre for Business Innovation Working Paper (March), Ernst & Young.
27 Stewart, T.A. 1998. *Intellectual capital – the new wealth of organisations*. London, Nicholas Brealey Publishing.
28 Bassi, L.J. 1997. Harnessing the power of intellectual capital. *Training and Development*, vol. 51, no. 12 (December), p. 26. Page 3 of Internet article: http://gateway.ovid.com/server3/ovidweb.

29 Saint-Onge, H. 1996. Tacit knowledge the key to strategic alignment of intellectual capital. *Strategy & Leadership*, vol. 24, no. 2 (March/April). Pages 1–2 of Internet article: http://gateway.ovid.com/server3/ovidweb

30 Bontis, N. 1996. There's a price on your head: Managing intellectual capital strategically. *Business Quarterly*, vol. 60, no. 4 (Summer), pp. 40–47.

31 Lynn, B. 1998, pp. 10–15.

32 Sveiby, K. 1997. *The new organisational wealth*. San Francisco, Berrett-Koehler Publishers.

33 Hudson, W. 1993. *Intellectual capital: How to build it, enhance it, use it*. New York, NY, John Wiley & Sons.

34 Saint-Onge, H. 1996, p. 12.

35 Roos *et al.* 1997, p. 30.

36 Roos *et al.* 1997, p. 32.

37 Stewart, T.A. 1998, p. 87.

38 Roos *et al.* 1997, p. 51.

39 Mayo, A. 1998. Memory bankers. *People Management*, (22 January) p. 34.

40 Stewart, T.A. 1998, p. 165.

41 *Ibid.*

42 Ulrich, D. 1997. Measuring human resources. An overview of practice and a prescription for results. *Human Resource Management*, vol. 36, no. 3 (Fall), p. 303.

43 Kaplan, R.S. & Norton, D.P. 1992. The balanced scorecard – measures that drive performance. *Harvard Business Review* (January/February), p. 71.

44 *Ibid.*

45 Roos *et al.* 1997, p. 59.

46 Yeung, A.K. & Berman, B. 1997. Adding value through human resources: reorienting human resource measurement to drive business performance. *Human Resource Management*, vol. 36, no. 3 (Fall), p. 322.

47 Kaplan *et al.* 1992, p. 72.

48 *Ibid.*, p. 73.

49 *Ibid.*

50 *Ibid.*, p. 79.

51 Yeung *et al.* 1997, p. 325.

52 Beatty, R.W., Beatty, J.R. & O'Neill, D.J. 1997. HR's next challenge: building and retaining intellectual capital. *Employment Relations Today*, vol. 34, no. 3 (Autumn), p. 33.

53 *Ibid.*

54 *Ibid.*, pp. 33–48.

55 Ulrich, D. 1998, p. 17.

56 Stewart, T.A. 1998, p. 87.

57 *Ibid.*

58 Martinez, M.N. 1998. The collective power. *HR Magazine* (February), p. 91.

59 Lynn, B. 1998, p. 9.

60 Hubeler, R.J. 1996, p. 22.

61 Martinez, M.N. 1998, p. 88.

62 *Ibid.*, p. 90.

63 Daintry, D. 1998. Knowledge champions. *UMI article*, vol. 12, no. 4 (November), clearinghouse number 1639500, p. 1.

64 Bontis, N. 1996. There's a price on your head: managing intellectual capital strategically. *Business Quarterly*, vol. 60, no. 4 (Summer). Page 1 of Internet article: http://gateway.ovid.com/server3/ovidweb

65 Stewart, T.A. 1998, p. 90.

66 *Ibid.*, pp. 90–92.

67 Lynn, B. 1998, p. 5.

68 Beatty *et al.* 1997, p. 38.

69 *Ibid.*

70 *Ibid.*

71 *Ibid.*

72 *Ibid.*, p. 43.

73 Ulrich, D. 1998, p. 21.

74 Beatty *et al.* 1997, p. 44.

75 *Ibid.*

8

International
human resource management

8.1 Introduction

The growing importance of the internationalisation of organisations both large and small is beyond dispute. In line with this, international human resource management (IHRM) is becoming ever more popular. In some cases, perhaps, the world of international business may not involve IHRM: it is not relevant in, for example, the spread of franchising operations and the growth of conglomerates which have no strategic objective of maximising their international operations. But there has been substantial growth in the numbers of internationally operating organisations and internationally operating employees, and for most enterprises, increasing internationalisation equates with the increasingly important role of IHRM.

This chapter addresses these critical issues. It starts with an initial review of the leading theorists in the field, then examines the issue of what can be strategically directed from the centre and what needs to be held at local level. The next section examines the circumstances in which international transfers of individuals may be appropriate, and the subsequent sections consider how the substantial costs involved may be reduced and how the process may be managed in a more effective manner, thus improving the competitive advantage of a company. Finally, some key strategic issues are considered.

8.2 What's special about "international"?

Our understanding of IHRM has not developed in line with its growth. There is still much room for better understanding of successful HRM practices in an international context, as many researchers have argued.[1-12] While it is recognised that the international HRM issues that have been researched are of practical importance to HR managers, this work has been criticised by

Kochan *et al.*[13] for focusing too narrowly on functional activities and lacking appropriate theoretical structures. The essence of their critique is that the current literature on international HRM defines the field too narrowly and is influenced by a discussion of concepts and issues with little backing in systematic research; and they argue that a new field of IHRM studies should be built around a broader set of questions.

This chapter attempts to assess what we mean by the term IHRM, how we conceptualise it, what areas and activities it includes, and how it relates to international business strategy. The majority of studies in this area have traditionally focused on expatriation: cross-border assignments of employees that last for a significant period of time.[14-16] Indeed, for many organisations and many commentators, IHRM and expatriate management are virtually synonymous. This is understandable. Expatriates are among the most expensive human resources in any internationally operating organisation and they are almost invariably in positions of crucial importance for the organisation. They have, and their management involves, issues and problems which go beyond those of most other employees. And yet our understanding of expatriates and the management of expatriates is markedly less than that we have of other employees – and expatriates are often far from being the best-managed employees.

IHRM, however, covers a far broader spectrum than the management of expatriates. It involves the worldwide management of people. Several researchers have proposed detailed models of how IHRM fits into the overall globalisation strategy of organisations. Adler & Ghadar[17] suggest that organisations will need to follow very different IHRM policies and practices according to the relevant stage of international corporate evolution, which they identify as domestic, international, multinational and global. Linking these with the attitudes and values of top management at headquarters (classified by Heenan & Perlmutter[18] as ethnocentric, polycentric, regiocentric and geocentric), they outline how organisations could adapt their HRM approaches and practices to fit the firm's external environment and its strategic intent.

Evans & Lorange[19] developed two logics for shaping HRM policy: *product-market logic* and *social-cultural logic*. Under the product-market logic, different types of managers are seen to be needed for the various phases of the product life cycle. Categories of managers are also split into "corporate", "divisional" and "business unit" levels, with different duties attributed to each category. Under the social-cultural logic, Evans & Lorange use Perlmutter's categories and propose two strategies for dealing with cultural and social diversity. The first strategy is labelled the *global* approach, and relates to Perlmutter's ethnocentrism or geocentrism. In this the company's own specific culture predominates and HRM is relatively centralised and standardised. Under the second strategy, the *polycentric* approach, responsibility for HRM is decentralised and devolved to the subsidiaries. These categories have been critiqued on the grounds that they imply a development from earlier to later categories which may not be the case; that they imply, without evidence, that the earlier stages are less appropriate or effective; and that they give equal weight to the various categories when in practice the vast majority of organisations are clearly ethnocentric.[20]

Schuler *et al.*[21] offer an integrative framework for the study and understanding of strategic international human resource management (SIHRM) which goes beyond theories of strategic HRM based in the domestic context and incorporates features unique to the international context.[22-23] SIHRM is defined as:

> human resource management issues, functions and policies and practices that result from the strategic activities of multinational enterprises and that impact on the international concerns and goals of those enterprises.[24]

The breadth of issues is illustrated by a framework, which links SIHRM orientations and activities to the strategic components of multinational enterprises (MNEs) comprising inter-unit linkages and internal operations. (We have preferred the terminology of multinational enterprise (MNE) to the perhaps more familiar term multinational corporation (MNC) because we want to include intergovernmental, public sector and not-for-profit organisations in our analysis.) Punnet & Ricks, Ghoshal and Galbraith argue that the key determinant of effectiveness for MNEs is the extent to which their various operating units across the world are to be differentiated and at the same time integrated, controlled and co-ordinated.[25-27] Evidence of different solutions adopted by MNEs to the tension between differentiation and integration, otherwise termed the "global vs. local" dilemma, are seen to result from the influence of a wide variety of exogenous and endogenous factors. Exogenous factors include industry characteristics (such as the type of business and technology available, the nature of competitors and the extent of change) and country/regional characteristics (such as political, economic and socio-cultural conditions and legal requirements). Endogenous factors include the structure of international operations, the international orientation of the organisation's headquarters, the competitive strategy being used, and the MNE's experience in managing international operations.

This discussion of SIHRM demonstrates the complexity of HR decisions in the international sphere and the broad scope of its remit, going far beyond the issue of expatriation, to an overall concern for managing people effectively on a global scale. By attempting to adopt an SIHRM perspective, HR practitioners in MNEs can make a contribution to every aspect of international business strategy by attempting to adopt HR policies and practices aimed at the most effective use of the human resource in the firm. A key aspect is the acknowledgment of the influence of the many factors which influence the choice of "global vs. local" HR practices and policies; and perhaps a recognition that, in this immensely complex area, there may be no "right solutions" but rather an ongoing need to pay careful attention to and to be prepared continually to review organisational policies.

The issue that has received most attention from researchers to date, namely the implications of national culture, is but one aspect of IHRM. Although sensitivity to which aspects of business practices in any particular country are emic (i.e. culture-specific aspects of concepts or behaviour) and etic (i.e. culture-common aspects) is regarded as essential to a strategic choice of HR levers, the influence of institutional factors such as economic, structural and political forms is also critical in shaping SIHRM choices. The Schuler *et al.* framework therefore presents a valuable "map" of the territory of SIHRM. It does not, however, consider SIHRM issues for small to medium-sized organisations, or for organisations operating in the public sector (the international governmental organisations, for example) or in the not-for-profit sector (international charities, churches, etc.). Guidance as to appropriate research design to test the linkages remains problematic.

Kobrin[28] attempts to operationalise and test relationships between a geocentric managerial mindset, geographic scope and the structural and strategic characteristics of firms and industries. The Perlmutter[29] definition of a geocentric mindset is contrasted with multinational strategy, defined as a continuum between firms whose strategy is multidomestic or nationally responsive, and firms which are integrated transnationally. Kobrin argues that a geocentric mindset is not necessarily always linked to a transnationally integrated strategy and/or a global organisational structure. He puts forward a tentative hypothesis that the need to transmit knowledge and information through the global network may lead, through increased interpersonal interaction, to organisational geocentrism in terms of attitudes and IHRM policies.

Attempts have also been made to build on previous work on IHRM by drawing on concepts from the resource-based view of the firm, and resource dependence, to develop a theoretical model of the determinants of SIHRM systems in MNEs.[30] Resource-based theory adds to other models of SIHRM the notion that, in order to provide value to the business, the SIHRM system of global firms should be constructed around specific organisational competencies that are critical for securing competitive advantage in a global environment.[31] The resource-dependence framework helps identify those situations in which MNEs will exercise control over the SIHRM system of their affiliates. Taylor, Beechler & Napier[32] quote Lado & Wilson's[33] definition of the resource-based view of HRM:

> the resource-based view suggests that human resource systems can contribute to sustained competitive advantage through facilitating the development of competencies that are firm specific, produce complex social relationships, are embedded in a firm's history and culture, and generate tacit organisational knowledge.

This approach has three implications. First, it acknowledges the critical role that the HRM competence of the parent firm, as perceived by top management, plays in the transfer of HRM policies to affiliates, and how this can contribute to competitive advantage. Second, it recognises the pivotal role of top management in SIHRM. A key research area, in the opinion of the authors, would be an analysis of the factors that influence the ability of top management to perceive an MNE's HRM competence and those factors that lead management to decide whether the firm's HRM competence is context-specific or context-generalisable and hence transferable. A third implication is the need to reconsider the assumption that the critical groups of employees at affiliate level are expatriates. On a more general level, Taylor *et al.* argue that further research is needed into the determinants of the context-generalisability of a resource and the ways in which managers can judge whether a particular resource is useful beyond the context in which it was created.

Much of the original research in this area reflects a North American influence, although one of the originating texts in the field of IHRM was European.[34] This highlights an important issue in IHRM research in general: the hegemony of the USA. Because of the extensive influence of US multinationals and the power of the US academic tradition in defining the nature of research into HRM in general,[35] US researchers have had a defining influence on research into IHRM. By far the largest amount of research into the topic is conducted in the US and focused on US MNEs, and the US texts have tended to "set the agenda". This is changing as researchers recognise that international organisational experience elsewhere predates even the establishment of the United States of America; and there are now ever-greater numbers of countries with substantial international organisations, and ever more internationally operating organisations which are not based in the US. In some parts of the world, such as the Arab states and the Pacific region, the influence of locally based MNEs is becoming crucially important. And, of course, the European Union experiment adds a different flavour to the concept of internationalisation. One of the key missions of the European

Union, the dismantling of the barriers to the international movement of goods, labour and capital within Europe, has led to a substantial increase in cross-border trade in a region which was already well down that road. It is, therefore, unsurprising to note the extensive growth in the amount of research into IHRM now being conducted in Europe.[36-37]

8.3 Key issues: central or local?

A key question in IHRM concerns the issue of what should be decided for the organisation as a whole and what should be decided locally. At the extremes the arguments are clear: pay issues for locally recruited and employed staff have to be determined locally; management development systems for those selected as future organisational leaders should be international. The central organisation will have little idea of relevant pay rates within the local community; but the organisation needs to retain the right to promote and encourage its best and brightest, beyond the local unit if necessary, wherever they are found. It is between these extremes that the problems arise. Should there be a local performance assessment system, so that performance can be related to the local pay scales and take account of local cultures (the discouragement of open responses to seniors in some societies, or the difficulty in admitting fault or failure in others, for example)? Or should the performance assessment system be international, so that it can identify likely future leaders wherever they are found in the organisation? Rosenzweig & Nohria[38] explore the tension between the pressures for internal consistency and local isomorphism. They argue that, of all functions, HRM tends to adhere most closely to local practices, as these are often mandated by local regulation and shaped by strong local conventions. Within HRM, they see the order in which six key practices will most closely resemble local practices as: (1) Time off, (2) Benefits, (3) Gender composition, (4) Training, (5) Executive bonus and (6) Participation. This order is predicated on the assumption that HRM practices for which there are well-defined local norms, and which affect the rank and file of the affiliate organisation, are likely to conform most to practices of local competitors. Practices for which there are diffuse and poorly defined local norms, or which are seen as being critical to maintaining internal consistency, are less likely to conform to local norms.

Three other factors are seen to be important in determining the extent of internal consistency or local isomorphism. The first is the degree to which an affiliate is *embedded* in the local environment. This refers to its method of founding and its age, as well as its size, its dependence on local inputs and the degree of influence exerted on it by local institutions. The second is the strength of the flow of resources such as capital, information and people between the parent and the affiliate. The third relates to characteristics of the parent, such as the culture of the home country, with a high degree of distance between cultures leading to more internal consistency (i.e. an ethnocentric approach). Two final characteristics relate to the parent organisation's orientation to control and the nature of the industry, with greater local isomorphism in a multi-domestic industry as opposed to a global industry.[39-40]

8.4   When is an expatriate needed?

All international organisations struggle with the problems created by the need to fill and manage key assignments around the world, assignments that are likely to be crucial to the success of the organisation. Expatriates are usually chosen to fill the key positions: country manager, financial controller or technical specialist. These people are invariably expensive to service, perhaps costing three or four times as much as a similar posting at home and often far more than a local appointment would cost. At the same time, assignments in the overseas subsidiaries are rarely more than a very small proportion of the overall organisational staffing. Because the numbers are few, it is difficult for all but the largest international organisations to develop the expertise and the policies that they have in dealing with other employees. The problem has been exacerbated by the increasing pressure to cut costs; many of them have done so by reducing the number of expatriates, only to find later that this has caused very significant problems of communication, co-ordination and control. Smaller and younger organisations face a different situation, but one which leads to the same problem: how to decide which assignments can be localised and which should be filled by expatriates.

In practice, most decisions on whether to use an expatriate are taken with surprisingly little consideration of the alternatives: they tend to be based on history and assumption. It is not difficult to analyse the circumstances in which international assignments are appropriate. This can be done using a simple framework intended to link foreign assignments more closely to the strategic operational requirements.

Key international assignments are often handled as unique events. It is true, of course, that each case is different, but not so different that the organisation cannot learn from the accumulation of cases, nor so different that it cannot develop generic guides based upon past experience. Very often the "one-off" approach arises because, except in the very largest organisations, there is no coherent framework on which to base decisions. Each situation becomes a problem and the line manager has to use his or her personal knowledge of individuals to try to fill the gap. This is partly why the research into expatriate selection often fails to identify any systematic approach. The reality is that such decisions are often taken (or at least initiated) in the corridor or at a social gathering as the result of one manager "knowing" one person who could fill their company's one vacancy.[41]

While some managers are happy to exploit the sense of patronage that this gives them, many others are uncomfortably aware that this is far from ideal: the organisation is sending expensive expatriates out when it would be better served employing local staff; there may well be excellent candidates completely overlooked by such an approach (it is probable that this is not entirely unrelated to the very low proportion of female expatriates); and accusations of favouritism and unfairness spread through the organisation. Such an approach is becoming increasingly untenable as financial demands increase, as potential expatriates become ever more demanding, and as other countries cease to be quite so welcoming to a continuous stream of foreigners in crucial positions.

Not all assignments are undertaken for the same reason; some are to enhance the control of the centre; some to underline the importance of the country to the local government; some to provide skills not existing in that geographical location; others to provide opportunities for management development or to internationalise the managerial cadre.

Assessing postings on the basis of their size and growth potential allows organisations to make rational policy choices about the staffing of those posts. Using size and growth potential as the axes (Figure 8.1) gives four kinds of postings. These categories were developed from work with international organisations on both Information Systems work (see, for example, Edwards *et al.*)[42] and the staffing of international assignments. The similarities with the Boston Consulting Group matrix (see Buzell & Gale; Hambrick *et al.*; Hedley)[43-45] are unsurprising, given that the issues which we identified as differentiating policies in these areas relate to strategic impact and growth, factors which have much in common with the BCG's market share and growth axes. We will take a brief look at Figure 8.1.

- **High potential: assignments that are currently small but may be critical to achieving future business strategy**. Assignments categorised in this quadrant exhibit the essential feature of a high degree of uncertainty, which may manifest itself in the nature of the venture or the host country. For example, the parent organisation may be a knowledgeable oil explorer but experience in extreme deep-sea operations may be low; or the venture could be a perfectly ordinary technical task but be required in a difficult political climate, for example an organisation's attempt to break into a new and difficult country. The essential feature of

Figure 8.1 The assignment portfolio

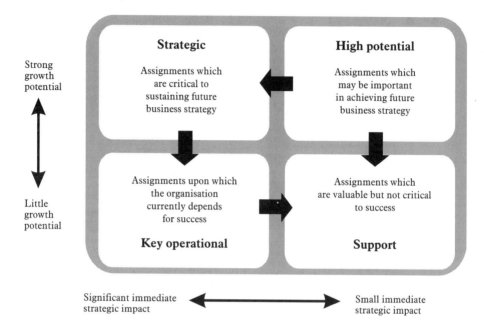

Strong
growth
potential

Little
growth
potential

Strategic

Assignments which
are critical to
sustaining future
business strategy

High potential

Assignments which
may be important
in achieving future
business strategy

Assignments upon which
the organisation
currently depends
for success

Key operational

Assignments which
are valuable but not critical
to success

Support

Significant immediate
strategic impact

Small immediate
strategic impact

SOURCE: Brewster, C. & Edwards, C. Do you need expatriates? Managing the international assignment. EIASM 2nd European Workshop on International Staffing and Expatriate Management, Braga, Portugal, June 1995. Used with permission.

this type of assignment is the underlying uncertainty inherent in the task, which could, if well managed, lead to substantial gains – but could also lead to no profit whatsoever. This would suggest a small operation, in the context of the parent business, which has a high degree of delegated authority. The secondary purpose is then to communicate the outcome directly to the parent organisation, so that exploitation plans can be formed quickly if the assignment is successful and a pull-out can be organised if it is not.

- **Strategic: assignments that are critical to sustaining future business strategy.** Assignments categorised in this quadrant are known to be vitally important to the parent organisation's future plans and aspirations. Much of the uncertainty exhibited in the previous quadrant has been reduced or eliminated by experimentation while the assignment was in that quadrant. By definition, even the largest organisations will have few of these assignments, although organisations always welcome more! The primary purpose of such assignments is to exploit to the maximum the proven potential of such opportunities.

- **Key operational: assignments upon which the organisation currently depends for success, but which are unlikely to grow very much bigger**. Assignments categorised in this quadrant are core day-to-day operations and provide the present income. They are important to the organisation but substantial growth of the business in such assignments is not likely. The primary purpose of such assignments is to avoid losing existing market share or profit, and to sustain existing income into the future.
- **Support: assignments that are valuable but not critical to success.** Assignments categorised in this quadrant are of some importance to the parent but could not reasonably be described as strategic or key operational. It is necessary to manage these assignments effectively, but a constant eye must be maintained upon the efficiency of the local operation; managing the total cost of the assignments is therefore vital. Speculation about selling such ventures is often ongoing.

Assignments do not remain in a single quadrant forever; they migrate around the portfolio through time. High-potential assignments either succeed and become strategic, or fail and are closed. Maybe a failed high potential shows a little promise, but will never become strategic – and hence the original high-potential assignment becomes a support assignment. Strategic assignments eventually mature and become key operational; in time, with the advent of a larger parent, even these may become support assignments.

8.4.1 Managing assignments in each quadrant

International organisations use expatriates in a number of roles (see Figure 8.2): as CEO, managerial, technical specialist, developmental, and "other" (this last category is an example of academic caution). Typically, assignments in each role (or even all roles) have been assumed to be much the same and have been managed in the same way. But they are not the same. As an example of the way organisations can use the matrix outlined in Figure 8.1, we take the role of CEO of a country subsidiary.

- **High potential**. Clearly, the description of the role identifies the need here for a bright, sparky, company-committed and highly motivated individual. It is not particularly important that they see the organisation's big picture or that they are very senior in the parent organisation. However, it is vital that such individuals are fully committed to the

Figure 8.2 The collection of portfolios

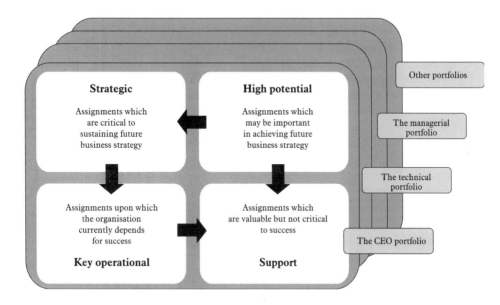

SOURCE: Brewster, C. & Edwards, C. Do you need expatriates? Managing the international assignment. EIASM 2nd European Workshop on International Staffing and Expatriate Management, Braga, Portugal, June 1995. Used with permission.

organisation and see a future for themselves within the organisation, otherwise they may be tempted to use any success by marketing themselves to third parties or by setting up in business on their own account, thus invalidating the whole purpose of the assignment. The organisation can afford to be generous in the way that it manages such assignments. Though a comparatively small operation, the possibly considerable pay-off means that it would be foolish of the organisation to stint on its use of resources. This would apply, for example, to expense accounts. The organisation may not wish to have too much detail about how these have been used – in the exploratory assignments the CEO may have to use money in ways that a rigorous expenses control system might not allow – but the total figures are likely to be a small percentage of the organisation's spending. It could afford to provide this post-holder with considerable facilities and back-up, and with expansive terms and conditions of employment. Not only would this give post-holders the necessary focus, by taking away as many non-task-related causes of complaint as possible; it would also motivate them and commit them to the idea that, should things work out well, this is the organisation's success and not just their own, and therefore also encourage them to remain committed to ensuring that the organisation reaps the fruits of its risk and investment.

- **Strategic**. The nature of the strategic country assignment means that the CEO probably needs some skills that are rather different from those of the CEO in a high-potential assignment. The incumbent here should be a steady long-term operator, able to see the big picture and to motivate others. They will need to manage growth and be orientated towards long-term results. They may well have a major representational role, dealing perhaps with other senior members of the country's hierarchy; they should be comfortable with and respected in governmental circles, for example. Such an individual may well be a board member of the parent organisation. Since the strategic assignment will form a substantial part of the parent organisation's main direction for the future, it is to be expected that, here again, the organisation will be generous, both in its provision of back-up facilities and in its employment package. It is important that this provision is manifest as a sign of the importance attached to such a manager.

- **Key operational**. The key operational assignments are important to the income stream of the organisation but, since any significant growth or development is unlikely, they need a different kind of CEO. Such a person may not necessarily be close to the board, but they will have to be a significant player in the host community. They will probably have to stay with the role for a number of years, establishing by their presence a "localisation" of the operation. In the best cases, the population is often unaware that this is a foreign company. This is a role generally best taken by a senior, well-respected *local* manager. Direct control from the parent will usually be established through financial measures; this should be relatively easy since the business should be well established and any significant change in the pattern of spending will be obvious in the accounts. Unlike the spending in the high-potential assignments, for example, for the key operational assignment financial issues become very important. The corollary is that control via an expatriate becomes of less value. In these key operational cases, there is an important role for cost control. This will apply, within the constraints of maintaining an impressive profile within the country, to the role and package applied to the CEO.

- **Support**. Countries falling within the support box are also likely to have a local CEO. The limited but nonetheless useful income from the territory does not have any organisationally strategic impact. Furthermore, the small profits that are made may not support the high cost of an expatriate. These positions are good management development opportunities, allowing younger managers the chance to "run their own show" and show how they handle a full range of responsibilities (albeit as a big fish in a small pond). Where these assignments are used for the development of people from the home base, however, there is a strong case for making HQ, rather than the subsidiary business unit, responsible for the costs. At the very least, the parent should pay any excess over local rates if it chooses to use the assignment as a development opportunity for an expatriate.

8.4.2 Managing assignments through time

A central issue for organisations, as subsidiaries grow, concerns the transition from one stage to the next. With CEOs in particular, this can be a crucial issue. The world, and the literature, is littered with cases of brilliant designers, inventors or entrepreneurs who have built up their organisations from nothing, but who then find it almost impossible to adjust to a different style of management and so become a brake on the development of the company. Clearly, one implication of our portfolio approach is that different styles of CEO are required in each quadrant. One advantage of expatriate appointments is that they come with a built-in assumption of a time limit.

Thus, the CEO operating in a high-potential environment will have identified the result of entry into that market, probably within the span of one assignment. If there is no scope for the organisation to develop activities in the original territory, because the assignment has reached its expected termination point, the expatriate manager can be returned to HQ or another assignment with little loss (of face or finance!). The corporation's exposure has been limited, as required for high-potential assignments. On the other hand, it might be determined that this territory could be a small, but useful, addition to the MNE's operation, producing tidy if limited profits, but which is never going to be crucial to the overall success of the organisation. In such a case, the MNE would not want one of its brighter and sparkier high-flyers, on an expensive package, running the company. The end of the expatriate assignment provides the perfect opportunity, if it is well managed, for the operation to be handed over to a trusted local manager as described above for the support assignment that this will have become. If the high-potential assignment actually delivers its potential, the organisation has a different requirement: a steady and senior "safe pair of hands" rather than a risk-taking, narrowly focused individual with a high commitment to a particular task. Almost certainly, we are looking at a board executive: someone who understands the importance of the market to the organisation's global strategy and has sufficient authority to ensure that the organisation puts its resources behind the growing enterprise. It is not easy to make this transition from a sharp, focused entrepreneur to a world-level player in a domestic setting: even within one country it can be fraught with problems. Almost by definition, the entrepreneurial characters who create such successes are unconvinced by arguments that now they have built up the business it is time for a change and they should relinquish their position to someone more senior. The same problems would apply to international operations where the market has been built up by a locally appointed manager. With an expatriate assignment, however, the expectation on the part of the manager, their family and their colleagues is that, after an appropriate period, there will be a replacement CEO. The transition problem becomes much less serious.

Similar issues surround the other critical transition point: from strategic to key operational. As the territory changes from a strategic, developmental position within the organisation to one which, while it may be significant and important, has become safe, steady, unremarkable and with little scope for expansion, so the nature of the CEO required to run such a country changes too. The need is for someone who will retain the image of importance commensurate with the contribution that the country makes to the MNE, and who will be prepared to spend a lengthy period holding the business together, even if nothing particularly exciting is going to happen. Such a major contributing territory will require a "significant player" at its head – but, rather than one of the key international corporate players, this can now be a position for a favoured organisational leader just prior to retirement – many of the more attractive locations in Europe and such countries as Australia seem to be used this way. Equally, it can be a position for a well-regarded expatriate from outside the headquarters country, or for a favoured local. The CEO in these cases is likely to have to spend a lot of time maintaining relationships: networks in the government, suppliers, customers and even competitors need to be massaged and supported. Frequently, these people will be looking to the MNE to emphasise its commitment to the country at this stage in its development by downplaying the international aspects, by upgrading its "national" profile within the country through its location of research and development and its marketing – and often by its appointment of a local CEO. This may well be someone who has worked abroad in the company, even perhaps at headquarters, but the appointment of a local in such an obviously powerful and important position sends very clear and positive messages to the country.

In terms of staffing and managing the appointments, therefore, this analysis would lead to the pattern outlined in Figure 8.3. By examining the range of situations that MNEs face, we have been able to outline four discrete forms of international assignments. A different type of CEO is needed to make a success of the different types of assignments.

Figure 8.3   The CEO portfolio

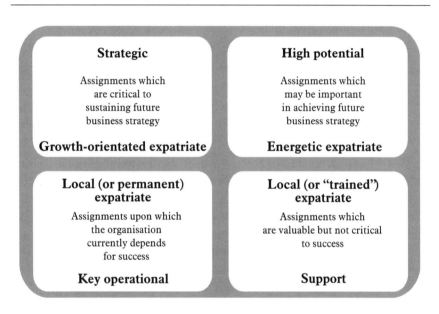

SOURCE: Brewster, C. & Edwards, C. Do you need expatriates? Managing the international assignment. EIASM 2nd European Workshop on International Staffing and Expatriate Management, Braga, Portugal, June 1995. Used with permission.

This conclusion stands in stark contrast to the many, perhaps somewhat naive, attempts to establish universal criteria for "the effective international manager". Not surprisingly, such attempts invariably come up with long lists of remarkable qualities – someone who is tough, dedicated, culturally aware, committed to the organisation, global thinking, and so on.[46-49] It is hard not to think that, should we be able to find such a close approximation to Superman, or Superwoman, we would put them in charge of the whole global corporation – at least ... This analysis provides a means for international organisations to identify the different qualities required for different assignments. In short, the framework enables organisations to take more cost-effective decisions about international assignments.

8.5   International HRM: cheaper and/or better

8.5.1   Doing it cheaper: alternatives to expatriation

Expatriation is always expensive. Expatriates tend to be paid more than other staff, even at the same level, get substantially more benefits, and involve a disproportionate amount of specialist HR support and senior management time. Many established MNEs are looking carefully at their budgets and trying to reduce the costs involved.

One approach is to *negotiate more toughly*. There are many organisations using "salary clubs" (groups of international organisations sharing pay and cost-of-living information) which in effect allow them to set the terms and conditions of staff – for particular locations and levels of staff. This is increasingly being challenged: while MNEs see the benefits of ensuring that their staff are able to "hold their own" with other equivalent-level expatriates, they are also seeing the benefits of negotiating hard about terms and conditions – "if you are the right person, and really want this job, you will take it on these terms: if not we will look elsewhere". At the same time, expatriates themselves are getting more "streetwise" about their employability. They know that good expatriates are in short supply and intend to negotiate a good deal. The result is that the standard deal of a set package for a set job in a set location is breaking down, and being replaced by the kind of negotiation that goes on elsewhere.

There has been increasing interest in the use of *third-country nationals* (TCNs): individuals who are neither from headquarters nor from the host country. They have a number of advantages: they take the organisation away from criticism as ethnocentric; they emphasise the organisation's commitment to develop and use talent wherever it may be; they are usually considerably cheaper; and they often have a cultural awareness which can be beneficial. Thus, Muslims working in Arab countries can have an advantage over Europeans. On the other hand, assumptions here can be dangerous: there are innumerable stories of overseas Chinese being sent in to the Peoples' Republic of China, for example, and, because they have fewer excuses, receiving a much rougher ride than Westerners would have done.

Increasingly, international organisations are employing expatriates *on local terms and conditions*. This is of particular relevance in the European Union and is happening both among university graduates (biochemists recruited from Italy to work in eastern England, for example, on the same terms as if they had come from Scotland) and managerial employees. Restricted job markets, the rough equivalence of living standards and facilities, and the absence of legal formalities and constraints in the EU mean that this approach is becoming increasingly widespread. A particular group of employees of MNEs, which has been little studied, is the many who end up working for one of their national organisations after having made their own way to the host country. This group of self-initiated foreign employees (SFEs) is probably much bigger than had previously been understood and is only now beginning to be researched.[50]

Another group of expatriates that seems to be becoming more common is that of *temporary employees* (see Chapter 10). With the shortages of appropriate candidates for expatriation that are being reported,[51] and the pressure to use this expensive resource only when strictly necessary, some companies are resorting to the use of short-term appointments to overcome temporary gaps in their requirements. Typically, these are "old hands" who have previously worked in those countries or in the industry.

More significantly, particularly in terms of the numbers involved, are frequent travellers. There are a number of different forms: commuters, loyalty card travellers and project teams. In each case, we are considering people who may spend up to 200 days a year outside their own country without ever relocating. These are the people who are constantly in airport lounges and in the business-class section of the aeroplane. In many ways they share the same stresses as expatriates, particularly in terms of their social lives and family pressures, and yet never move home or receive the benefits of expatriation. In Europe, especially, with so many countries so close to each other, the Eurocommuter phenomenon has taken hold: managers live at home in, for example, Austria during the weekend and travel to, say, Hungary every Monday, returning home every Thursday night or Friday morning. There are many more people throughout the world travelling frequently, visiting company operations or customers in other countries for a few hours or days on a regular basis. The cost to the organisation and the benefits that such travel brings are debatable and a subject for further empirical research. And some organisations have teams of people flying around the world on regular assessment projects, enabling them to balance central knowledge with local control.[52]

The cheapest option, of course, is usually the employment of locals. There is a strong case to be made that the reason that this is so rare in management circles has less to do with internationalising the management cadre than with the remnants of colonialism or racial assumptions of superiority.[53] The argument that international assignments are part of developing international awareness and understanding in the management team would be stronger if there were better evidence that organisations utilise and exploit the knowledge they can gain from these arrangements: in fact it seems that international assignments are usually seen as little more than an interlude away from headquarters. It is assumed that it is at headquarters that the real action takes place. International experience is discounted.[54] In practice there is little doubt that most organisations fail to realise the capabilities and expertise of their local employees.

A key related issue concerns the use of the senior local managers, who are responsible for making sure that each successive expatriate manager is able to understand the local environment, is introduced to the important people and steered to the key decisions. These are crucial people for the organisation, people whose career path is blocked by the same expatriates. The issues involved in managing these staff members need further research – and further attention by the MNEs.

The argument has also been made that the development of *information and communication technology* (ICT) will render both international transfers and international travelling redundant. Why go to a country when it is much easier and cheaper to video-conference with the people there? As with the growth of ICT in individual economies, the argument has some strength – undoubtedly there will in the future be more video-conferencing and more use of e-mail, etc. However, the same arguments apply: in many cases, face-to-face meetings are more effective. That ICT technology has made a comparatively limited difference to working practices within individual countries – like the fact that business travel has grown significantly just as the international ICT has developed – may be less a function of ignorance (or the desire for foreign travel) than of a recognition that the social side of management is critical to success. Our understanding of negotiating skills, for example, tells us that it is more difficult to say "No" face-to-face than it is by fax or e-mail. In these circumstances, international travel by the sellers makes a lot of sense. And we all know that teamwork is better fostered by meetings than by even the best video-conferencing.

8.5.2 Doing it better: the expatriate cycle

If the decision is made that expatriation is appropriate in any particular case, the research still has some interesting things to tell us. Research into expatriation has, in general, followed the traditional expatriate "cycle", with, interestingly, early attention on the earlier stages of the assignment and a successively developing focus on the later and more complex issues of adjustment, monitoring performance and repatriation. This section summarises, briefly, the contribution of research in each area of the cycle.

Research into the *selection* of expatriates has generally been focused on the more "visible" aspects of this issue, such as the criteria used in such decisions.[55-56] Researchers[57] have found that in practice technical expertise and domestic track record are by far the two dominant selection criteria.

Factors such as language skills and international adaptability come further down the list in all studies, though there is some evidence that these have more importance for European than for US organisations.[58-59] Recent research into recruitment systems indicates that these criteria are constructs of the international HR department: in practice decisions on expatriation are taken by line managers – who often simply ignore the criteria.[60] Bonache & Fernandez[61] and Bonache & Brewster[62] utilise the theoretical framework of the resource-based theory of the firm to identify the types of knowledge transfer needed in each instance and hence the type of selection strategy required.

Training and development programmes for expatriates are, surprisingly, more apparent by their absence than their presence. They do appear to be more common in European than in US MNEs;[63-65] in Europe they include some interesting and cost-effective alternatives to formal training pro-grammes such as pre-appointment visits and briefings by returned expatriates.[66-67]

Pay and rewards are critical components in ensuring maximum return from human resources throughout the whole international organisation; but, as "technical" issues related to tax and pension regimes, they have tended to be the domain of consultants rather than researchers. Recent writing in Europe has been concerned with pay policies and their link to business goals, while allowing for sensitivity to business, cultural and other influences at subsidiary unit level. Differences in international rewards are seen as not just a consequence of cultural differences, but also as reflecting differences in institutional influences, national business systems and the role and competence of managers in the sphere of HRM.[68-69]

The whole question of *performance measurement* and management in multinational companies involves a complex range of issues,[70] and research to date suggests that rigorous performance appraisal systems for expatriates are far from universal.[71] This is perhaps surprising given the high costs of expatriate underperformance and the growing tendency to see expatriates as key human assets.[72] European firms, in particular, seem to be paying more attention to this aspect of expatriation.[73] In part this reflects the growing use of international assignments for development purposes in European multi-nationals[74] and the greater integration of expatriation into the overall career development process in European firms.[75]

The *repatriation* of expatriates has been identified as a major problem for multinational companies,[76-79] but is still comparatively under-researched.[80] Interestingly, concern over re-entry was cited as a significant reason affecting expatriate performance in UK MNEs.[81] For many MNEs this problem has become more acute in recent years because expansion of foreign operations had taken place at the same time as the rationalisation of HQ operations: there are few unfilled positions suitable for expatriates in the majority of companies. From the repatriate perspective, other problems associated with reintegrating into the home country are loss of status, loss of autonomy, loss of career direction and a feeling that international experience is undervalued by the company.[82] There is growing recognition that where companies are seen to deal unsympathetically with the problems faced by expatriates on re-entry, managers will be more reluctant to accept the offer of international assignments.[83] Many expatriates leave their company on return, with a consequent loss of investment and expertise.[84] Yet, while it is widely accepted that the costs of expatriate turnover are considerable, very few firms have effective repatriation programmes. Recent research in Europe has situated repatriation in the context of career development and loss of corporate knowledge. [85-86]

8.6   Strategy and attention to detail

Evans & Doz[87] discuss the concept of the *dualities* that are at the core of complex organisations and apply this to building international competencies. They argue that HRM is a critically important tool for building dualistic properties into the firm. In terms of HRM, the key mechanism through which this can happen is layering. Layering involves building new capabilities and qualities into the organisation's culture while reinforcing its past cultural strengths. Organisations which are deeply layered often operate more informally than can be seen from an examination of rules, hierarchies or management processes. Layering often occurs through the long-term development of key managers and professionals who are recruited for careers rather than short-term jobs, and therefore the HRM functions of recruitment and selection, development, retention and reward management are vital regulators of this process.

These dualities are a reflection of the complications involved in managing HRM generally, and the extra level of complexity added by internationalism. There are unlikely to be exact or final answers to the questions raised by IHRM, therefore. However, there is much that can be done by senior executives in multinational enterprises to ensure that their organisations are learning from the available research understandings. (And, incidentally, there is much that the researchers can learn by paying closer attention to the experience and expertise within the MNEs). Many international organisations struggle with the issue of which elements of their HR policies and practices can be centralised and which decentralised. There is an ongoing debate in the literature about the extent to which MNEs bring new HRM practices into a country, in comparison to the extent to which they adapt their own practices to those of the local environment. In practice, of course, there is always an interplay between the two, and both factors apply to some degree. The focus has tended to be on expatriation and even more narrowly on the pay and conditions of the expatriates. HR managers in MNEs have to start examining their use of human resources internationally on the same criteria that they would apply to national HRM: what kind of people do we need working for us in these locations? How do we ensure that we get the best people in the most cost-effective manner? How do we ensure that we are monitoring their performance and unlocking their potentialities as fully as possible? And, in this particular context, would this involve the international transfer of people; and, if so, what is the best mechanism for making this effective? Where MNEs ask themselves these basic questions they will be able to improve the way in which they manage their human resources internationally.

8.7 Summary

This chapter has examined the additional complexities created for HR managers when business is conducted internationally. It has addressed the critical issues of what can be managed from the centre and what has to be held locally. In some cases the international transfer of employees will be appropriate, and the second half of the chapter has considered what is necessary to make such processes cost-effective.

References

1 Pucik, V. 1984. White collar human resource management in large Japanese manufacturing firms. *Human Resource Management*, vol. 23, no. 3, pp. 257–276.

2 Dowling, P.J. 1986. Human resource issues in international business. *Syracuse Journal of International Law and Commerce*, vol. 13, no. 2, pp. 255–271.

3 Laurent, A. 1986. The cross-cultural puzzle of international human resource management. *Human Resource Management*, vol. 25, no. 1, pp. 91–102.

4 Evans, P.A.L. & Lorange, P. 1989. The two logics behind human resource management. In Evans, P.A.L., Doz, Y. &

Lorange, P. (eds.), *Human Resource Management in International Firms, Change, Globalization, Innovation.* London, Macmillan.

5 Hossain, S. & Davis, H.A. 1989. Some thoughts on international personnel management as an emerging field. In Nedd, A., Ferris, G.R. & Rowland, K.M. (eds.), *Research in Personnel and Human Resources Management – International Human Resources Management.* Greenwich, Connecticut, JAI Press.

6 Nedd, A., Ferris, G.R. & Rowland, K.M. 1989. *Research in Personnel and Human Resources Management – International*

Human Resources Management. Greenwich, Connecticut, JAI Press.

7   Shaw, B.B., Deck, J.E., Ferris, G.R. & Rowland, K.M. 1990. *Research in Personnel and Human Resource Management – International Human Resources Management*. Greenwich, Connecticut, JAI Press.

8   Mendenhall, M. & Oddou, G. (eds.) 1991. *International human resource management*. Boston, PWS-Kent.

9   Weber, W. & Festing, M. 1991. Entwicklungstendenzen Im Internationalen Personalmanagement: Personalfuhrung Im Wandel. *Gablers Magazin*, 2 S. pp. 10–16.

10 Dowling, P., Schuler, R. & Welsch, D. 1994. *International dimensions of human resource management* (second edition). Belmont CA, Wadsworth.

11 Scherm, E. 1995. *Internationales Personalmanagement.*, Munchen, Wien, Oldenbourg.

12 Boxall, P. 1995. *The challenge of human resource management*. London, Longman Publishing Group.

13 Kochan, T., Batt, R. & Dyer, L. 1992. International human resource studies: A framework for future research. In Lewin, D. *et al.* (eds.), *Research frontiers in industrial relations and human resources*. Madison, Industrial Relations Research Association.

14 Brewster, C. 1991. *The management of expatriates*. London, Kogan Page.

15 Black, J.S., Gregerson, H. & Mendenhall, M. 1993. *Global assignments*. San Francisco, Jossey-Bass.

16 Dowling *et al.* 1994.

17 Adler, N. & Ghadar, F. 1990. International strategy from the perspective of people and culture: The North American context. In Rugman, A. (ed.), *Research in global strategic management* (vol. 1). Greenwood, Connecticut, JAI Press.

18 Heenan, D. & Perlmutter, H. 1979. *Multinational organisation development*. Reading MA, Addison-Wesley.

19 Evans, P.A.L. & Lorange, P. 1989. The two logics behind human resource management. In Evans, P.A.L., Doz, Y. &

Lorange, P., *Human resource management in international firms: Change, globalisation, innovation*. London, Macmillan.

20 Mayrhofer, W. & Brewster, C. 1996. In praise of ethnocentricity: Expatriate policies in European multinationals. *International Executive*, vol. 38, no. 6 (November/December), pp. 749–778.

21 Schuler, R., Dowling, P.J. & De Cieri, H. 1993. An integrative framework of strategic international human resource management. *International Journal of Human Resource Management*, vol. 4, no. 4, pp. 717–764.

22 Sundaram, A.K. & Black, J.S. 1992. The environment and internal organization of multinational enterprises. *Academy of Management Review*, vol. 17, no. 4, pp. 729–757.

23 Adler, N.J. & Bartholomew, S. 1992. Managing globally competent people, *Academy of Management Executive*, vol. 6, no. 1, pp. 52–64.

24 Schuler *et al.* 1993.

25 Punnett, B.J. & Ricks, D.A. 1992. *International business*. Boston, Mass, PWS-Kent.

26 Ghoshal, S. 1987. Global strategy: An organizing framework. *Strategic Management Journal*, vol. 8, pp. 425–440.

27 Galbraith, J.R. 1987. Organization design. In Lorsch, J. (ed), *Handbook of organization behavior*. Englewood Cliffs, NJ, Prentice-Hall, pp. 343–357.

28 Kobrin, S.J. 1994. Is there a relationship between a geocentric mind-set and multinational strategy. *Journal of International Business Studies*, vol. 3, pp. 493–512.

29 Perlmutter, H. 1969. The tortuous evolution of the multinational corporation. *Columbia Journal of World Business*, vol. 1, pp. 9–18.

30 Taylor, S., Beechler, S. & Napier, N. 1996. Toward an integrative model of strategic international human resource management. *Academy of Management Review*, vol. 21, no. 4, pp. 959–965.

31 Pucik, V. 1992. Globalization and human resource management. In V. Pucik *et al.*,

Globalizing management. London, John Wiley & Sons.

32   Taylor *et al.* 1996.

33   Lado, A.A. & Wilson, M.C. 1994. Human resource systems and sustained competitive advantage. *Academy of Management Review*, vol. 19, no. 4, pp. 699–727.

34   Torbiorn, I. 1982. *Living abroad: Personal adjustment and personnel policy in an international setting*. Chichester, John Wiley & Sons.

35   Brewster, C.J. 1999. Different paradigms in strategic HRM: Questions raised by comparative research. In Wright, P., Dyer, L., Boudreau, J. & Milkovich, G. (eds.), *Research in personnel and HRM*. Greenwich, Connecticut, JAI Press Inc.

36   Brewster, C. & Scullion, H. 1997. Expatriate HRM: An agenda and a review. *Human Resource Management Journal*, vol. 7, no. 3 (July), pp. 32–41.

37   Brewster, C. & Harris, H. (eds.) 1999. *International HRM: Contemporary issues in Europe*. London, Routledge.

38   Rosenzweig, P.M. & Nohria, N. 1994. Influences on human resource management practices in multinational corporations. *Journal of International Business Studies*, vol. 25, no. 2, pp. 229–251.

39   Porter, M. 1986. *Competition in global industries*. Boston, Harvard Business School Press.

40   Prahalad, C.K. & Doz, Y. 1987. *The multinational mission: Balancing global demands and global vision*. New York, Free Press.

41   Harris, H. & Brewster, C.J. 1999. The coffee machine system: How international selection really works, *International Journal of Human Resource Management* (forthcoming).

42   Edwards, C., Bytheway, A. & Ward, J. 1995. *The essence of information systems* (second edition). Englewood Cliffs, Prentice Hall.

43   Buzzell, R.B. & Gale, B.T. 1987. *The PIMS principles: Linking strategy to performance*. New York, Free Press/Macmillan.

44   Hambrick, D.C., Macmillan, I.A. & Day, D.L. 1982. Strategic attributes and performance in the BCG matrix: A PIMS based analysis of industrial product business. *Academy of Management Journal*, vol. 7, no. 3 (September), pp. 510–531.

45   Hedley, B. 1997. Strategy and the business portfolio. *Long Range Planning*, vol. 22, no. 1 (February), pp. 7–16.

46   Business International Corporation 1991. *Developing effective global managers for the 1990s*. New York.

47   Barham, K. & Devine, M. 1991. *The quest for the international manager: A survey of global human resource strategies*. London, The Economist Intelligence Unit.

48   Coulson-Thomas, C. 1990. *Professional development of and for the Board*. London, Institute of Directors.

49   Birchall, D., Hee, T. & Gay, K. 1996. *Competencies for international managers*. Singapore Institute of Management (January), pp. 1–13.

50   Suutari, V. & Brewster, C. 1999. Expatriate management practices and their perceived relevance: Evidence from Finnish expatriates. *Personnel Review* (forthcoming).

51   Scullion, H. 1995. International human resource management. In Storey, J. (ed.), *Human resource management: A critical text*. London, Routledge.

52   Bonache, J. & Cervino, J. 1997. Global integration without expatriates. *Human Resource Management Journal*, vol. 7, no. 3, pp. 89–100.

53   Hailey, J. 1999. Localization as an ethical response to internationalization. In Brewster, C. & Harris, H. (eds.), *International HRM: Contemporary issues in Europe*. London, Routledge.

54   Bonache, J. & Brewster, C. 1999. Knowledge transfer and the management of expatriation. *Journal of Management Studies* (forthcoming).

55   Dowling, P., Schuler, R. & Welch, D. 1994. *International dimensions of human resource management* (second edition). Belmont CA, Wadsworth.

56 Mendenhall, M. & Oddou, G. 1985. The dimensions of expatriate acculturation: A review. *Academy of Management Review*, vol. 10, no. 1, pp. 39–487.

57 *Ibid.*

58 Tung, R.L. 1982. Selection and training procedures of US, European, and Japanese multinationals. *California Management Review*, vol. 25, no. 1 (Fall), pp. 57–71.

59 Suutari, V. & Brewster, C. 1998. The adaptation of expatriates in Europe: Evidence from Finnish companies. *Personnel Review*, vol. 27, no. 2, pp. 89–103.

60 Brewster, C. & Harris, H. 1999. An integrative framework for pre-departure preparation. In Brewster, C. & Harris, H., *International HRM: Contemporary issues in Europe.* London, Routledge.

61 Bonache, J. & Fernandez, Z. 1997. Expatriate compensation and its link to the subsidiary strategic role: A theoretical analysis. *International Journal of Human Resource Management*, vol. 8, no. 4, pp. 457–475.

62 Bonache *et al.* 1999.

63 Tung, R.L. 1982, pp. 57–71.

64 Torbiorn, I. 1982.

65 Brewster, C. 1991.

66 Pickard, J. & Brewster, C. 1994. Evaluating expatriate training. *International Studies of Management and Organisation*, vol. 24, no. 3, pp. 18–35.

67 Suutari, V. & Brewster, C. 1998. The adaptation of expatriates in Europe: Evidence from Finnish companies. *Personnel Review*, vol. 27, no. 2, pp. 89–103.

68 Bradley, P., Hendry, C. & Perkins, S. 1999. Global or multi-local? The significance of international values in reward strategy. In Brewster, C. & Harris, H. (eds.), *International HRM: Contemporary issues in Europe.* London, Routledge.

69 Sparrow, P.R. 1986. The erosion of employment in the UK: The need for a new response. *New Technology, Work and Employment*, vol. 1, no. 2, pp. 101–112.

70 Schuler, R.S., Fulkerson, J.R. & Dowling, P.J. 1991. Strategic performance measurement and management in multinational corporations. *Human Resource Management*, vol. 30, no. 3, pp. 365–392.

71 Schuler *et al.* 1991.

72 Adler, N.J. & Bartholomew, S. 1992. Managing globally competent people. *Academy of Management Executive*, vol. 6, no. 1, pp. 52–64.

73 Lindholm, N., Tahvanainen, M. & Bjorkman, I. 1998. Performance appraisal of host country employees: Western MNEs in China. In Brewster, C. & Harris, H., *International human resource management, contemporary issues in Europe.* London, Routledge.

74 Scullion, H. 1995. International human resource management. In Storey, J. (ed.), *Human resource management: A critical text.* London: Routledge.

75 Hamil, I.J. 1989. Expatriate policies in British multinationals. *Journal of General Management*, vol. 14, no. 4, pp. 18–33.

76 Harvey, M.C. 1989. Repatriation of corporate executives: An empirical study, *Columbia Journal of World Business*, vol. 20, no. 1, pp. 131–144.

77 Johnston, J. 1991. An empirical study of repatriation of managers in UK multinationals. *Human Resource Management Journal*, vol. 1, no. 4, pp. 102–108.

78 Scullion, H. 1993. Creating international managers: Recruitment and development issues. In Kirkbride, P. (ed.), *Human Resource Management in Europe.* London, Routledge.

79 Peltonen, T. 1999. Repatriation and career systems: Finnish public and private sector repatriates in their career lines. In Brewster, C. and Harris, H. (eds.), *International HRM: Contemporary issues in Europe.* London, Routledge.

80 Pickard, J. & Brewster, C. 1995. Repatriation: Closing the circle. *International HR Journal*, vol. 4, no. 2, pp. 45–49.

81 Scullion, H. 1993. Creating international managers: Recruitment and development issues. In Kirkbride, P. (ed.), *Human resource management in Europe.* London, Routledge.

82 Johnston, J. 1991. An empirical study of repatriation of managers in UK

multinationals. *Human Resource Management Journal*, vol. 1, no. 4, pp. 102–108.

83 Scullion, H. 1993. Creating international managers: Recruitment and development issues. In Kirkbride, P. (ed.), *Human Resource Management in Europe*. London, Routledge.

84 Adler, N. 1987. Pacific Basin managers: A *gaijin*, not a woman. *Human Resource Management*, vol. 26, no. 2, pp. 169–192.

85 Peltonen, T. 1999. Repatriation and career systems: Finnish public and private sector repatriates in their career lines. In Brewster, C. and Harris, H. (eds.), *International HRM: Contemporary issues in Europe*. London, Routledge.

86 Bonache, J. & Brewster, C. 1999. Knowledge transfer and the management of expatriation. *Journal of Management Studies* (forthcoming).

87 Evans, P.A.L.& Doz, Y. 1993. The dualistic organization. In Evans, P.A.L., Doz, Y. & Lorange, P., *Human Resource Management in International Firms, Change, Globalization, Innovation*. London, Macmillan.

9

Labour relations in multinational firms

9.1 Introduction

Before we examine the key issues in labour relations as they relate to multinational firms, we need to consider some general points about the field of international labour relations.[1] First, it is important to realise that it is difficult to compare industrial relations systems and behaviour across national boundaries; a labour relations concept may change considerably when translated from one industrial relations context to another.[2] The concept of collective bargaining, for example, is understood in the United States to mean negotiations between a labour union local and management; in Sweden and Germany the term refers to negotiations between an employers' organisation and a trade union at the industry level. Cross-national differences also emerge as to the objectives of the collective bargaining process and the enforceability of collective agreements. Many European unions view the collective bargaining process as an ongoing class struggle between labour and capital, whereas in the United States union leaders tend towards a pragmatic rather than ideological economic view of collective bargaining. Second, it is generally recognised in the international labour relations field that no industrial relations system can be understood without an appreciation of its historical origin.[3-4] As Schregle[5] has observed:

> A comparative study of industrial relations shows that industrial relations phenomena are a very faithful expression of the society in which they operate, of its characteristic features and of the power relationships between different interest groups. Industrial relations cannot be understood without an understanding of the way in which rules are established and implemented and decisions are made in the society concerned.

An interesting example of the effect of historical differences may be seen in the structure of trade unions in various countries. Poole[6] has identified several factors that may underlie these historical differences:

- the mode of technology and industrial organisation at critical stages of union development;
- methods of union regulation by government;
- ideological divisions within the trade union movement;
- the influence of religious organisations on trade union development; and
- managerial strategies for labour relations in large corporations.

As Table 9.1 shows, union structures differ considerably among Western countries. They include industrial unions, which represent all grades of employees in an industry; craft unions, which are based on skilled occupational groupings across industries; conglomerate unions, which represent

Table 9.1 Trade union structure in leading Western industrial societies

Australia	general, craft, industrial, white-collar
Belgium	industrial, professional, religious, public sector
Canada	industrial, craft, conglomerate
Denmark	general, craft, white-collar
Finland	industrial, white-collar, professional and technical
Great Britain	general, craft, industrial, white-collar, public sector
Japan	enterprise
The Netherlands	religious, conglomerate, white-collar
Norway	industrial, craft
Sweden	industrial, craft, white-collar and professional
Switzerland	industrial, craft, religious, white-collar
United States	industrial, craft, conglomerate, white-collar
West Germany	industrial, white-collar

SOURCE: Poole, M. 1986. *Industrial Relations: Origins and patterns of national diversity.* London, Routledge & Kegan Paul, p. 79. Used with permission.

members in more than one industry; and general unions, which are open to almost all employees in a given country. These differences in union structures have had a major influence on the collective bargaining process in Western countries. Some changes in union structure are evident over time; for example, enterprise unions are increasingly evident in industrialised nations. Enterprise unions are common in Asian-Pacific nations, although there are national variations in their functions and in the proportion of enterprise unions to total unions.[7-8]

The less one knows about how a structure came to develop in a distinctive way, the less likely one is to understand it. As Prahalad & Doz[9] note, the lack of familiarity of multinational managers with local industrial and political conditions has sometimes needlessly worsened a conflict that a local firm would have been likely to resolve.[10] Increasingly, multinationals are recognising this shortcoming and admitting that industrial relations policies must be flexible enough to adapt to local requirements. This is evidently an enduring approach, even in firms that follow a non-union labour relations strategy where possible, as the following case study shows.

IHR in the news:
Advice for companies going global

The key to successfully expanding overseas is to become one with the culture of the location, even if it means unionisation of employees, Michael R. Quinlan, chairman and chief executive officer of McDonald's Corp., tells conferees at a meeting of the Human Resources Management Association in Chicago.

After opening fast-food restaurants in 53 nations, McDonald's has learned that it must follow the established practices of a foreign country to succeed there, Quinlan says. For example, a number of European countries and Australia have very strict unionisation standards, and operations there are unionised as a condition of doing business. Acknowledging that McDonald's has had some "horrible union fights around the world," Quinlan advises employers considering expansion into other nations to "do it their way, not your way".

The main implication of dealing with unions is the increased cost of wages and benefits, according to Quinlan. Still, he adds that he does not feel unionisation has interfered with employees' loyalty to McDonald's, or to the company's philosophy of service and employee motivation. Declaring that unions do not "bring much to the equation" of the employee/employer relationship, Quinlan says McDonald's is "basically a nonunion company" and intends to stay that way.

Another source of difficulty for McDonald's in its expansion overseas lies in the fact that fast-food restaurants are unfamiliar in most nations. Opening the first

McDonald's inside the Communist bloc, in Yugoslavia, took 12 years, Quinlan notes. He also points out that the company's policy is to staff its restaurants, from crew through management, only with nationals – for the 3 300 foreign outlets, the corporation employs only 35 expatriate US citizens, and its goal is to have 100 per cent local employees within five years.

SOURCE: The Bureau of National Affairs, *Bulletin to Management*, 7 March 1991, pp. 66-67 (P.O. Box 40949, Washington D.C., 20016-0949). Used with permission.

9.2   Key issues in international labour relations

The focus of this chapter is on the labour relations strategies adopted by multinationals rather than the more general topic of comparative labour relations.[11-15] A central question for labour relations in an international context is that of the orientation of multinational firms to organised labour.

Because national differences in economic, political and legal systems produce markedly different labour relations systems across countries, multinationals generally delegate the management of labour relations to their foreign subsidiaries. However, a policy of decentralisation does not keep corporate headquarters from exercising some co-ordination over labour relations strategy. Generally, corporate headquarters will become involved in or oversee labour agreements made by foreign subsidiaries, because these agreements may affect the international plans of the firm and/or create precedents for negotiations in other countries. Furthermore, Marginson, Armstrong, Edwards & Purcell[16-17] found that the majority of the firms in their study monitored labour performance across units in different countries. Comparison of performance data across national units of the firm creates the potential for decisions on issues such as unit location, capital investment, and rationalisation of production capacity. The use of comparisons would be expected to be greatest where units in different countries undertake similar operations.

Much of the literature on the labour relations practices of multinationals tends to be at a more cross-national or comparative level. There is, however, some research on labour relations practices at the firm level. Empirical research has identified a number of differences in multinational approaches to labour relations. For example, a series of studies by Hamill[18-20] found that US firms were less likely than their British counterparts to recognise trade unions, preferred not to join employer associations, had more highly developed and specialised personnel departments at plant level, and tended to pay higher wages and offer more generous employee fringe benefits than local firms. Marginson, Armstrong, Edwards & Purcell investigated the potential consequences of firm strategies for the management of labour, using a 1992 survey of multinationals operating in Britain.[21] They found a tendency for strategic decisions that affect the interests of employees to be made beyond national jurisdictions. Indeed, a number of studies have examined differences in the propensity of multinational headquarters to intervene in, or to centralise control over, matters such as industrial relations in host locations. Multinational headquarters' involvement in labour relations is influenced by several factors, as detailed below.

9.2.1   The degree of inter-subsidiary production integration

According to Hamill,[22] a high degree of integration was found to be the most important factor leading to the centralisation of the labour relations function within the firms studied. Labour relations throughout a system become of direct importance to corporate headquarters when transnational sourcing patterns have been developed – that is, when a subsidiary in one country relies on another foreign subsidiary as a source of components or as a user of its output.[23-24] In this context, a co-ordinated labour relations policy is one of the key factors in a successful global production strategy.[25] One example of the development of an international policy for labour relations can be seen in the introduction of employee involvement across Ford's operations.[26]

9.2.2   Nationality of ownership of the subsidiary

There is evidence of differences between European and US firms in terms of headquarters' involvement in labour relations.[27-31] A number of studies have revealed that US firms tend to exercise greater centralised control over labour relations than do British or other European firms.[32-34] US firms tend to place greater emphasis on formal management controls and a close reporting system (particularly within the area of financial control) to ensure that planning targets are met. In his review of empirical research of this area, Bean[35] showed that foreign-owned multinationals in Britain prefer single-employer bargaining (rather than involving an employer association), and are more likely than British firms to assert managerial prerogative on matters of labour utilisation. Further, Hamill[36] found US-owned subsidiaries to be much more centralised in labour relations decision making than British-owned firms. Hamill attributed this difference in management procedures to the more integrated nature of US firms, the greater divergence between British and US labour relations systems than between British and other European systems, and the more ethnocentric managerial style of US firms.

9.2.3 International human resource management approach

As indicated in Chapter 8, the IHRM literature uses four terms to describe MNE approaches to managing and staffing their subsidiaries. These terms are taken from the seminal work of Perlmutter,[37] who claimed that it was possible to identify among international executives three primary attitudes – ethnocentric, polycentric, and geocentric – towards building a multinational enterprise, based on top management assumptions upon which key product, functional and geographical decisions were made. To demonstrate these three attitudes, Perlmutter used aspects of organisational design; such as decision making, evaluation and control, information flows and complexity of the organisation. He also included "perpetuation", which he defined as "recruiting, staffing, development". A fourth attitude – regiocentric – was added later.[38] The four approaches are:

- **Ethnocentric.** Few foreign subsidiaries have any autonomy; strategic decisions are made at headquarters. Key positions at the domestic and foreign operations are held by headquarters' management personnel. In other words, subsidiaries are managed by expatriates from the home country (parent-country nationals, abbreviated as PCNs).
- **Polycentric.** The MNE treats each subsidiary as a distinct national entity with some decision-making autonomy. Subsidiaries are usually managed by local nationals (host-country nationals, abbreviated as HCNs) who are seldom promoted to positions at headquarters. Likewise, PCNs are rarely transferred to foreign subsidiary operations.
- **Geocentric.** Here, the MNE is taking a worldwide approach to its operations, recognising that each part (subsidiaries and headquarters) makes a unique contribution with its unique competence. It is accompanied by a worldwide integrated business, and nationality is ignored in favour of ability. For example, the CEO of the Swedish multinational Electrolux claims that, within this global company, there is not a tradition of hiring managing directors from Sweden, or locally, but to find the person best suited for the job.[39] That is, the colour of one's passport does not matter when it comes to rewards, promotion and development. PCNs, HCNs and third-country nationals (TCNs) can be found in key positions anywhere, including those at senior management level at headquarters and on the board of directors.
- **Regiocentric.** This reflects the geographic strategy and structure of the multinational. Like the geocentric approach, it utilises a wider pool of

managers, but in a limited way. Personnel may move outside their countries, but only within the particular geographic region. Regional managers may not be promoted to headquarters positions but enjoy a degree of regional autonomy in decision making. It may be seen as a precursory step towards geocentrism.

While these attitudes have been a useful way of demonstrating the various approaches to staffing foreign operations, it should be stressed that the above categories refer to managerial attitudes that reflect the socio-cultural environment in which the internationalising firm is embedded, and are based on Perlmutter's study of US firms.

These approaches have implications for international labour relations. Interestingly, an ethnocentric predisposition is more likely to be associated with various forms of labour relations conflict.[40] Conversely, it has been shown that more geocentric firms will bear more influence on host-country industrial relations systems, due to their greater propensity to participate in local events.[41]

9.2.4 MNE prior experience in labour relations

European firms have tended to deal with labour unions at industry level (frequently via employer associations) rather than at firm level. The opposite is more typical for US firms. In the US, employer associations have not played a key role in the industrial relations system, and firm-based labour relations policies are the norm.[42-44]

9.2.5 Subsidiary characteristics

Research has identified a number of subsidiary characteristics to be relevant to centralisation of labour relations. First, subsidiaries that are formed through acquisition of well-established indigenous firms tend to be given much more autonomy over labour relations than are greenfield sites set up by a multinational firm.[45] Second, according to Enderwick, greater intervention would be expected when the subsidiary is of key strategic importance to the firm and the subsidiary is young.[46] Third, where the parent firm is a significant source of operating or investment funds for the subsidiary (that is, where the subsidiary is more dependent on headquarters for resources), there will tend to be increased corporate involvement in labour relations and human resource management.[47] Finally, poor subsidiary performance tends to be accompanied by increased corporate involvement in labour relations.

Where poor performance is due to labour relations problems, multinationals tend to attempt to introduce parent-country labour relations practices aimed at reducing industrial unrest or increasing productivity.[48]

9.2.6 Characteristics of the home product market

An important factor is the extent of the home product market.[49] If domestic sales are large relative to overseas operations (as is the case with many US firms), it is more likely that overseas operations will be regarded by the parent firm as an extension of domestic operations. This is not the case for many European firms, whose international operations represent the major part of their business. The lack of a large home market is a strong incentive to adapt to host-country institutions and norms. There is evidence of recent change in the European context: since the implementation of the Single European Market in 1993, there has been growth in large European-scale companies (formed via acquisition or joint ventures) that centralise management and strategic decision making. However, processes of operational decentralisation with regard to labour relations are also evident. [50-51]

9.2.7 Management attitudes towards unions

An additional important factor is that of management attitudes or ideology concerning unions.[52] Knowledge of management attitudes concerning unions may provide a more complete explanation of multinational labour relations behaviour than could be obtained by relying solely on a rational economic model. Thus, management attitudes should also be considered in any explanation of managerial behaviour along with such factors as market forces and strategic choices. This is of particular relevance to US firms, since union avoidance appears to be deeply rooted in the value systems of American managers.[53]

As Table 9.2 shows, the US has one of the lowest union-density rates (the percentage of wage and salary employees who are union members) in the Western world. Hence, US managers are less likely to have extensive experience with unions than managers in many other countries. Worldwide trade union membership has fallen over the past decade, although the decline is not universal. This decline in union density in many countries may be explained by economic factors such as reduced public sector employment, reduced employment in manufacturing industries as a share of total employment, and increased competition; it is also suggested to be associated with decentralisation of labour relations to business unit level, changes in governance and legislative changes. For example, the sharpest drop in union

Table 9.2 Union membership for selected countries

	Union density		Proportionate changes in union density (%)	Rank order of union density[c]	
	1985	1995	1985-95	1985	1995
Australia[d]	46	33	-28	2	4
Canada[e]	35	35	0	6	3
France[d]	15	11	-27	9	10
Germany[e]	36[a]	30	-16	5	5
Italy[d,e]	42	38	-10	4	2
Japan[d,e]	29	24	-18	7	7
Korea[f]	12	13	+8.3	10	9
Sweden[d]	85	83	-2.2	1	1
UK[d]	45	29	-35	3	6
USA[g]	18	15[b]	-12	8	8

NOTES:
a   1991.
b   1993.
c   Rank order of union density of the 10 countries listed.
d   Replies by governments.
e   Replies by workers' organisations.
f   Replies from Korea Labour Statistics Department.
g   Adjusted density rate.
ILO unpublished data (1996); Australia ABS Cat. No.6325.0.

SOURCE: Bamber, G.J., Ross, P. & Whitehouse, G. 1998. Employment relations and labour market indicators in ten industrialised market economies: Comparative statistics. *International Journal of Human Resource Management*, vol. 9, no. 2, Table 14. Used with permission.

density (almost 36 per cent over the past decade) has been in Central and Eastern Europe, and may be explained by political and economic changes associated with the dissolution of the Soviet bloc and the end of compulsory union membership. Union membership decline is also linked to the introduction of new forms of work organisation, globalisation of production, and changes in workforce structure.[54-56]

Although there are several problems inherent in data collection for a cross-national comparison of union-density rates, several theories have been suggested to explain the variations among countries. Such theories consider economic factors such as wages, prices and unemployment levels, social factors such as public support for unions, and political factors. In addition, studies indicate that the strategies utilised by labour, management and governments are particularly important. [57-59]

9.2.8 Industrial disputes

Another key issue in international labour relations is that of industrial disputes. Hamill[60] examined strike-proneness of multinational subsidiaries and indigenous firms in Britain across three industries. Strike-proneness was measured via three variables: strike frequency, strike size and strike duration. There was no difference across the two groups of firms with regard to strike frequency, but multinational subsidiaries did experience larger and longer strikes than local firms. Hamill suggests that this difference indicates that foreign-owned firms may be under less financial pressure to settle a strike quickly than local firms – possibly because they can switch production out of the country.

Overall, it is evident that international labour relations are influenced by a broad range of factors. Commenting on the overall results of his research, Hamill[61] concluded that:

> general statements cannot be applied to the organisation of the labour relations function within MNCs. Rather, different MNCs adopt different labour relations strategies in relation to the environmental factors peculiar to each firm. In other words, it is the type of multinational under consideration which is important rather than multinationality itself.

9.3   Labour unions and international labour relations

Labour unions may limit the strategic choices of multinationals in three ways: (1) by influencing wage levels to the extent that cost structures may become uncompetitive; (2) by constraining the ability of multinationals to vary employment levels at will; and (3) by hindering or preventing global integration of the operations of multinationals.[62] We shall briefly examine each of these potential constraints.

- **Influencing wage levels.** Although the importance of labour costs relative to other costs is decreasing, labour costs still play an important part in determining cost competitiveness in most industries. The influence of unions on wage levels is therefore important. Multinationals that fail to successfully manage their wage levels will suffer labour cost disadvantages that may narrow their strategic options.

- **Constraining the ability of multinationals to vary employment levels at will.** For many multinationals operating in Western Europe, Japan and Australia, the inability to vary employment levels at will may be a more serious problem than wage levels. Many countries now have legislation that limits considerably the ability of firms to carry out plant closure, redundancy or lay-off programmes unless it can be shown that structural conditions make these employment losses unavoidable. Frequently, the process of showing the need for these programmes is long and drawn out. Plant closure or redundancy legislation in many countries also frequently specifies that firms must compensate redundant employees through specified formulae such as two week's pay for each year of service. In many countries, payments for involuntary terminations are rather substantial, especially in comparison to those in the United States.

  Labour unions may influence this process in two ways: by lobbying their own national governments to introduce redundancy legislation, and by encouraging regulation of multinationals by international organisations such as the Organisation for Economic Co-operation and Development (OECD). (Later in this chapter we describe the *Badger* case, which forced Raytheon to finally accept responsibility for severance payments to employees made redundant by the closing down of its Belgian subsidiary.) Multinational managers who do not take these restrictions into account in their strategic planning may well find their options severely limited. In fact, recent evidence shows that multinationals are beginning to consider the ability to dismiss employees to be one of the priorities when making investment location decisions.[63]

- **Hindering or preventing global integration of the operations of multinationals.** In recognition of these constraints, many multinationals make a conscious decision not to integrate and rationalise their operations to the most efficient degree, because to do so could cause industrial and political problems. Prahalad and Doz[64] cite General Motors as an example of this "suboptimisation of integration". GM was alleged in the early 1980s to have undertaken substantial investments in Germany (matching its new investments in Austria and Spain) at the demand of the German metalworkers' union (one of the largest industrial unions in the Western world) in order to foster good labour relations in Germany. One observer of the world auto industry suggested that car manufacturers were suboptimising their manufacturing networks partly to placate trade unions and partly to provide redundancy in sources to prevent localised social strife from paralysing their network. This suboptimisation led to unit manufacturing costs in Europe that were 15 per cent higher, on average, than an economically optimal network would have achieved. Prahalad and Doz drew the following conclusion from this example:[65]

> Union influence thus not only delays the rationalisation and integration of MNCs' manufacturing networks and increases the cost of such adjustments (not so much in the visible severance payments and "golden handshake" provisions as through the economic losses incurred in the meantime), but also, at least in such industries as automobiles, permanently reduces the efficiency of the integrated MNC network. Therefore, treating labour relations as incidental and relegating them to the specialists in the various countries is inappropriate. In the same way as government policies need to be integrated into strategic choices, so do labour relations.

9.4   The impact of multinationals upon trade union and employee interests, and the response of labour unions

Labour union leaders have long seen the growth of multinationals as a threat to the bargaining power of labour because of the considerable power and influence of large multinational firms. While it is recognised that multi-nationals are "neither uniformly anti-union nor omnipotent and monolithic bureaucracies",[66] their potential for lobbying power and flexibility across national borders creates difficulties for employees and trade unions endeavouring to develop countervailing power. There are several ways in which multinationals have an impact upon trade union and employee interests. Kennedy[67] has identified the following seven characteristics of MNEs as the source of labour unions' concern about multinationals:

- **Formidable financial resources**. This includes the ability to absorb losses in a particular foreign subsidiary that is in dispute with a national union and still show an overall profit on worldwide operations. Union bargaining power may be threatened or weakened by the broader financial resources of a multinational. This is particularly evident where a multinational has adopted a practice of transnational sourcing and cross-subsidisation of products or components across different countries. "The economic pressure which a nationally based union can exert upon a multinational is certainly less than would be the case if the company's operations were confined to one country".[68]

- **Alternative sources of supply**. This may take the form of an explicit "dual sourcing" policy to reduce the vulnerability of the multinational to a strike by any national union. Also, temporary switching of production in order to defeat industrial action has been utilised to some extent, for example in the automotive industry.[69]
- **The ability to move production facilities to other countries**. A reported concern of employees and trade unions is that job security may be threatened if a multinational seeks to produce abroad what could have or previously has been manufactured domestically. National relative advantages provide MNEs with a choice in the location of units. Within the EU, for example, evidence suggests that multinational managements are locating skill-intensive activities in countries with national policies promoting training and with relatively high labour costs. Conversely, semi-skilled, routinised activities are being located in countries with lower labour costs.[70] Threats by multinationals, whether real or perceived, to reorganise production factors internationally, with the accompanying risk of plant closure or rationalisation, will have an impact on management–labour negotiations at a national level. However, technical and economic investments would reduce a multinational's propensity to relocate facilities.
- **A remote locus of authority (i.e. the corporate head office management of a multinational firm)**. While many multinationals report decentralisation and local responsiveness of HRM and industrial relations, trade unions and works councils have reported that the multinational decision-making structure is opaque and the division of authority obscured. Furthermore, employee representatives may not be adequately aware of the overall MNE organisational strategy and activities.[71]
- **Production facilities in many industries**. As Vernon[72] has noted, most multinationals operate in many product lines.
- **Superior knowledge and expertise in labour relations**.
- **The capacity to stage an "investment strike"** whereby the multinational refuses to invest any additional funds in a plant, thus ensuring that the plant will become obsolete and economically non-competitive.

Another issue reported by labour unions is their claim that they have difficulty accessing decision makers located outside the host country and obtaining financial information. For example, according to Martinez Lucio & Weston:

> Misinformation has been central to the management strategy of using potential investment or disinvestment in seeking changes in certain organisations. For example, in companies such as Heinz, Ford,

Gillette and General Motors, workers have established that they had on occasions been misinformed by management as to the nature of working practices in other plants. [73]

The response of labour unions to multinationals has been threefold: to form international trade secretariats (ITSs); to lobby for restrictive national legislation; and, finally, to try to achieve regulation of multinationals by international organisations.

9.4.1 International Trade Secretariats (ITSs)

There are 15 ITSs, which function as loose confederations to provide world-wide links for the national unions in a particular trade or industry (e.g. metals, transport and chemicals). The secretariats have mainly operated to facilitate the exchange of information.[74-75] One of the fastest growing of the ITSs is the International Federation of Commercial, Clerical, Professional and Technical Employees (generally known by its French initials, FIET) which is focused on the service sector.[76] The long-term goal of each ITS is to achieve transnational bargaining with each of the multinationals in its industry. Each ITS has followed a similar programme to achieve the goal of transnational bargaining.[77] The elements of this programme are (1) research and information, (2) calling company conferences, (3) establishing company councils, (4) company-wide union–management discussions, and (5) co-ordinated bargaining. Overall, the ITSs have met with limited success, which Northrup[78-79] attributes to (1) the generally good wages and working conditions offered by multinationals, (2) strong resistance from multinational firm management, (3) conflicts within the labour movement, and (4) differing laws and customs in the labour relations area.

9.4.2 Lobbying for restrictive national legislation

On a political level, labour unions have for many years lobbied for restrictive national legislation in the US and Europe. The motivation for labour unions to pursue restrictive national legislation is based on a desire to prevent the export of jobs via multinational investment policies. For example, in the US, the AFL-CIO has lobbied strongly in this area.[80-81] A major difficulty for unions when pursuing this strategy is the reality of conflicting national economic interests. In times of economic downturn, this factor may become an insurmountable barrier for trade union officials. To date, these attempts have been largely unsuccessful, and, with the increasing internationalisation of business, it is difficult to see how governments will be persuaded to legislate in this area.

9.4.3 Regulation of multinationals by international organisations

Attempts by labour unions to exert influence over multinationals via international organisations have met with some success. Through trade union federations such as the European Trade Union Confederation (ETUC) and the International Confederation of Free Trade Unions (ICFTU), the labour movement has been able to lobby the International Labour Organisation (ILO), the United Nations Conference on Trade and Development (UNCTAD),[82-83] the Organisation for Economic Co-operation and Development (OECD), and the European Union (EU). The ILO has identified a number of workplace-related principles that should be respected by all nations: freedom of association, the right to organise and collectively bargain, abolition of forced labour, and non-discrimination in employment. In 1977 the ILO adopted a code of conduct for multinationals (Tripartite Declaration of Principles Concerning MNEs and Social Policy).[84-85] The ILO code of conduct, which was originally proposed in 1975, was influential in the drafting of the OECD guidelines for multinationals, which were approved in 1976. These voluntary guidelines cover disclosure of information, competition, financing, taxation, employment and industrial relations, and science and technology.[86-87]

A key section of these guidelines is the *umbrella* or *chapeau clause* (the latter is the more common term in the literature) that precedes the guidelines themselves. This clause states that multinationals should adhere to the guidelines "within the framework of law, regulations and prevailing labour relations and employment practices, in each of the countries in which they operate". Campbell & Rowan[88] state that employers have understood the chapeau clause to mean that compliance with local law supersedes the guidelines, while labour unions have interpreted this clause to mean that the guidelines are a "supplement" to national law. The implication of this latter interpretation is significant: a firm could still be in violation of the OECD guidelines even though its activities have complied with national law and practice. Given the ambiguity of the chapeau clause and the fact that the OECD guidelines are voluntary, it is likely that this issue will remain controversial.

There is also some controversy in the literature as to the effectiveness of the OECD guidelines in regulating multinational behaviour.[89] This lack of agreement centres on assessments of the various challenges to the guidelines.

The best-known of these challenges is the *Badger* case. The Badger Company is a subsidiary of Raytheon, a US-based multinational. In 1976 the Badger Company decided to close its Belgian subsidiary, and a dispute arose concerning termination payments.[90] Since Badger (Belgium) NV had filed for bankruptcy, the Belgian labour unions argued that Raytheon should assume the subsidiary's financial obligations. Raytheon refused, and the case was brought before the OECD by the Belgian government and the International Federation of Commercial, Clerical, Professional and Technical Employees (FIET), an international trade secretariat. The Committee on International Investments and MNEs (CIIME) of the OECD indicated that paragraph six of the guidelines (concerned with plant closures) implied a "shared responsibility" by the subsidiary and the parent in the event of a plant closing. Following this clarification by the CIIME and a scaling-down of initial demands, Badger executives and Belgian government officials negotiated a settlement of this case.

Blanpain[91] concludes that the *Badger* case made clear the responsibility of the parent company for the financial liability of its subsidiary, but that this responsibility is not unqualified. As to whether the *Badger* case proved the "effectiveness" of the OECD guidelines, Jain[92] and Campbell & Rowan[93] point out that the Belgian unions devoted considerable resources to make this a test case and had assistance from both American unions (which, through the AFL-CIO, lobbied the US State Department) and the Belgian government in their negotiations with the OECD and Badger executives. Liebhaberg[94] is more specific in his assessment:

> Despite an outcome which those in favor of supervision consider to be positive, the Badger Case is a clear demonstration of one of the weaknesses in the OECD's instrument, namely that it does not represent any sort of formal undertaking on the part of the twenty-four member states which are signatories to it. The social forces of each separate country must apply pressure on their respective governments if they want the guidelines applied.

Recognising the limitations of voluntary codes of conduct, European labour unions have also lobbied the Commission of the European Union to regulate the activities of multinationals.[95-96] Unlike the OECD, The Commission of the EU can translate guidelines into law, and has developed a number of proposals concerning disclosure of information to make multinationals more "transparent".[97-99] These are discussed in more detail in the next section.

9.5   Regional integration: the European Union (EU)

Regional integration such as the development of the European Union (EU) has brought significant implications for international labour relations.[100-101] In the Treaty of Rome (1957) some consideration was given to social policy issues related to the creation of the European Community. In the EU, the terms "social policy" or "social dimension" are used to cover a number of issues – including, in particular, labour law and working conditions, aspects of employment and vocational training, and social security. There have been a number of significant developments in EU social policy over the past four decades. The Social Charter of the Council of Europe came into effect in 1965. In 1987, the major objective of the implementation of the Single European Act was to establish the Single European Market (SEM) on 31 December 1992, in order to enhance the free movement of goods, money and people within the SEM.[102] Hence, the social dimension aims to achieve a large labour market by eliminating the barriers that restrict freedom of movement and the right of domicile within the SEM. The European Community Charter of the Fundamental Social Rights of Workers (often referred to simply as the Social Charter) was introduced in 1989, and has guided the development of social policy in the 1990s.[103] Naturally, the social dimension has been the subject of much debate: proponents defend the social dimension as a means of achieving social justice and equal treatment for EU citizens, while critics see it as a kind of social engineering.[104-106]

At the signing of the Treaty on European Union in Maastricht in February 1992, Britain was allowed to opt out of the social policy agreements. The other 11 member states were party to a protocol (The Social Policy Protocol), which allows them to agree on their own directives without Britain's partici-pation.[107-109] With the election of the Blair Labour government in Britain in 1997, this anomaly was resolved when all members of the EU signed the Treaty of Amsterdam on 17 June 1997. This means that there now exists a single coherent legal basis for action by the EU member states with regard to social policy.

The Social Chapter in the Treaty of Amsterdam opens with a general statement of objectives.[110] Its first Article (Article 117 of the EC Treaty), drawn largely from Article 1 of the Maastricht Social Agreement, begins with a reference to fundamental social rights such as those in the European Social Charter of 1961 and the Social Charter of 1989. It then sets out the objectives for the EU: to support and complement the activities of the member states in a number of listed areas. These include improvement of working conditions and of the working environment in the interest of workers' health and safety, information and consultation of workers, integration of persons excluded from the labour market, and equality of opportunity, and at work, between men and women. However, the treaty excludes matters of pay, the right of association and the right to strike or to lock out.

The European Commission department responsible for social policy is known as Directorate-General V (often abbreviated to "DG V"). The following text summarises the six directorates of DG V and the different areas of social policy covered by each directorate.

Implementation of social policy in the European Union

Introduction
Based in Brussels and Luxembourg, DG V is the European Commission department responsible for social policy. It is made up of six directorates responsible for different areas of social policy.

Directorate-General
Directorate A: is responsible for employment policies, labour market policies, employment services (EURES), and local development and readaptation.

Directorate B: is responsible for policy development of the European Social Fund, information on the Fund, assessment of the political impact of the Fund, the Community Initiatives, technical assistance and innovation studies, and adaptation to industrial change.

Directorate C: is responsible for the operation of the European Social Fund in the Member States.

Directorate D: is responsible for relations with the social partners and organisation of the social dialogue, industrial relations and labour law, co-ordination of social security for migrant workers, migration policy and promotion of free movement for workers, equal opportunities for women and men, and family policy.

Directorate E: is responsible for analysis of and research on the social situation, social security and actions in the social field, and integration of disabled people. It also deals with external relations, international organisations, information and publications on behalf of the whole Directorate-General.

Directorate F: (based in Luxembourg) is responsible for analysis, co-ordination and development of policies and programmes in the field of public health, implementation of action programmes targeted on diseases, health promotion and disease surveillance, and health and safety at work. It also provides the permanent secretariat for the Advisory Committee on Safety, Hygiene and Health Protection at the Workplace.

Directorate G: is responsible for the management of human and financial resources for the Directorate-General, for audit and inspection, and evaluation.

SOURCE: http://europa.eu.int/comm/dg05/index en.htm. Used with permission.

9.5.1 Disclosure of information and European Works Councils

The EU has introduced a range of directives related to the social dimension. Of the directives concerned with multinationals, the most contentious has been the Vredeling Directive (associated with Henk Vredeling, a former Dutch member of the EU Commission).[111] The Seventh (Vredeling) Directive's requirement of disclosure of company information to unions faced strong opposition led by the British government and employer representatives. They argued that employee involvement in consultation and decision making should be voluntary.

More recently, the European Works Councils (EWC) Directive was approved on 22 September 1994 and implemented two years later. Under the terms of the Treaty of Amsterdam, this directive applies to all EU member states. This is the first pan-European legislation that regulates collective relationships between multinationals and employees. The directive requires EWCs to be established in multinationals with at least 1 000 employees and with 100 or more employees in each of two member states. According to Chesters, more than 1 000 multinationals, including around 200 US-based firms, are affected by the EWC Directive.[112-115] The directive is designed to provide coverage to all employees, whether unionised or not. The EWC Directive aims to enhance employees' rights to information and consultation in general, and provide rights to information regarding international corporate decisions that would significantly affect workers' interests.[116-117] Partly in response to the EWC Directive, firms such as General Motors and Heinz have subsidised visits of worker representatives to other plants and provided information and forums for discussion at the European level.[118]

Obviously all firms will need to become familiar with EU directives and keep abreast of changes. While harmonisation of labour laws can be seen as the ultimate objective, Michon[119-120] argues that the notion of a European social community does not mean a unification of all social conditions and benefits – or, for that matter, of all social systems. However, the EU does aim to establish minimal standards for social conditions that will safeguard the fundamental rights of workers.

9.5.2 Social "dumping"

One of the concerns related to the formation of the SEM was its impact on jobs. There was alarm that those member states that have relatively low social security costs would have a competitive edge and that firms would locate in those member states that have lower labour costs. The counter-alarm was that states with low-cost labour would have to increase their labour costs, to the detriment of their competitiveness.[121] There are two industrial relations issues here: the movement of work from one region to another, and its effect on employment levels; and the need for trade union solidarity to prevent workers in one region from accepting pay cuts to attract investment, at the expense of workers in another region. There is some (although not as much as was expected) evidence of "social dumping" in the EU.[122] It is likely that this issue will be a contentious one in Europe for some time, and multinationals need to be aware of this debate when doing business in Europe.

9.6   Regional integration: the North American Free Trade Agreement (NAFTA)

Another important regional economic integration involves the formation of a free trade zone between the United States, Canada and Mexico. The Canada-United States Free Trade Agreement (FTA) went into effect in January 1989, and a draft accord to create NAFTA, which brought Mexico into the trading bloc, was announced in August 1992. The NAFTA agreement was signed by the governments of the United States, Mexico and Canada in December 1992, ratified by the US Congress in November 1993, and came into force on January 1994.[123-125] It is important to stress here that NAFTA differs from the Single European Market in that it is a free trade zone and not a common market. NAFTA deals only with the flow of goods, services and investments among the three trading partners. It does not address labour mobility or other common policies of the SEM.[126] However, in an effort to manage the social dimension of NAFTA, the North American Agreement on Labour Co-operation (NAALC) came into effect in 1993. Although it has been criticised as weak and ineffective, this accord has introduced new institutions to process complaints of violations of labour laws, and has committed each of the three nations to introduce a set of 11 labour rights principles.[127]

There are significant HR implications in NAFTA that must be considered by HR managers in North American firms. While NAFTA does not include workplace laws and their enforcement, as was discussed in the context of the

SEM, the country with the least restrictive workplace laws will have a competitive advantage.

Organised labour in the US and Canada responded to the passage of NAFTA with substantial opposition, based on fear of job losses due to the transfer of production to Mexico to take advantage of lower wage rates and lax enforcement of social and labour legislation.[128-129] In other words, the concern about social dumping is similar to the concern at the formation of the SEM, but there is a difference. In the case of NAFTA, jobs are able to cross borders, but workers are not.[130] Although there has been a general lack of co-ordination between labour organisations of the NAFTA countries, examples in telecommunications, trucking and electrical industries show that NAFTA has stimulated some strategic cross-border collaboration among individual labour unions and their allies.[131-133]

The EU and NAFTA provide examples of regional integration which present many issues for international labour relations. As regional integration and inter-regional integration develop in other parts of the world, issues will continue to emerge for international labour relations.[134-135]

9.7   Summary

The literature reviewed in this chapter and the discussion surrounding the formation of regional economic zones such as the European Union and the North American Free Trade Agreement support the conclusion that transnational collective bargaining has yet to be attained by labour unions.[136-137] As Enderwick[138] has stated:

> The international operations of MNCs do create considerable impediments in effectively segmenting labour groups by national boundaries and stratifying groups within and between nations. Combining recognition of the overt segmentation effects of international business with an understanding of the dynamics of direct investment yields the conclusion that general multinational collective bargaining is likely to remain a remote possibility.

Enderwick argues that labour unions should opt for less ambitious strategies in dealing with multinationals, such as (1) strengthening national union involvement in plant-based and company-based bargaining; (2) supporting research on the vulnerability of selective multinationals; and (3) consolidating the activities of company-based ITSs. Despite setbacks, especially with the regional economic integration issues discussed in this chapter, it is likely that labour unions and the ILO will pursue these strategies and continue to lobby for the regulation of multinationals via the European Commission and the United Nations.

Recent research on multinationals and labour relations has provided useful information on the issues and challenges related to this aspect of international HRM.[139-141] Further research is needed on how multinationals view developments in international labour relations and whether these developments will influence the overall business strategy of the firm. Research is also needed on how global firms implement labour relations policy in various countries.

References

1   These introductory comments are drawn from Schregle, J. 1981. Comparative industrial relations: Pitfalls and potential. *International Labour Review*, vol. 120, no. 1, pp. 15–30.

2   This point is also referred to as the emic-etic problem. For a detailed discussion see Chapter 1 of Dowling, P.J., Welch, D.E. & Schuler, R. 1999. *International human resource management: Managing people in a multinational context* (third edition), Cincinnati, Ohio, USA, South-Western.

3   Kahn-Freund, O. 1979. *Labour relations: Heritage and adjustment*. Oxford, Oxford University Press.

4   Peterson, R.B & Sargent, J. 1997. Union and employer confederation views on current labour relations in 21 industrialized nations. *Relations Industrielles*, vol. 52, no.1, pp. 39–59.

5   Schregle, J. 1981, p. 28.

6   Poole, M. 1986. *Industrial relations: Origins and patterns of national diversity*. London, Routledge.

7   Jeong, J. 1995. Enterprise unionism from a Korean perspective. *Economic and Industrial Democracy*, vol. 16, no. 2, pp. 253–273.

8   Kuruvilla, S. & Venkataratnam, C.S. 1996. Economic development and industrial relations: The case of South and Southeast Asia. *Industrial Relations Journal*, vol. 27, no. 1, pp. 9–23.

9   Prahalad, C.K. & Doz, Y.L. 1987. *The multinational mission: Balancing local demands and global vision*. New York, The Free Press.

10   Many US multinational firms are reducing the number of expatriates on overseas assignment (see Kobrin, S.J. 1988. Expatriate reduction and strategic control in American multinational corporations. *Human Resource Management*, vol. 27, no. 1, pp. 63–75). With regard to labour relations, this reduction has the effect of reducing the opportunities of US managers to gain first-hand experience of labour relations in various countries.

11   Kennedy, T. 1980. *European labour relations*. Lexington, Mass., Lexington Books.

12   Bean, R. 1985. *Comparative industrial relations: An introduction to cross-national perspectives*. New York, St. Martin's Press.

13   Bamber, G. & Lansbury, R. 1998. International and comparative employment relations. London, Sage.

14   Rothman, M., Briscoe, D. & Nacamulli, R. 1993. *Industrial relations around the world: Labour relations for multinational companies*. Berlin, De Gruyter.

15   Locke, R., Kochan, T. & Piore, M. 1995. Reconceptualizing comparative industrial relations: Lessons from international research. *International Labour Review*, vol. 134, no. 2, pp. 139–161.

16 Marginson, P., Armstrong, P., Edwards, P.K. & Purcell, J. 1995. Extending beyond borders: Multinational companies and the international management of labour. *International Journal of Human Resource Management*, vol. 6, no. 3, pp. 702–719.

17 Martinez Lucio, M. & Weston, S. 1994. New management practices in a multinational corporation: The restructuring of worker representation and rights. *Industrial Relations Journal*, vol. 25, pp. 110–121.

18 Hamill, J. 1983. The labour relations practices of foreign-owned and indigenous firms. *Employee Relations*, vol. 5, no. 1, pp. 14–16.

19 Hamill, J. 1984 (a). Multinational corporations and industrial relations in the UK. *Employee Relations*, vol. 6, no. 5, pp. 26–36.

20 Hamill, J. 1984 (b). Labour relations decision-making within multinational corporations. *Industrial Relations Journal*, vol. 15, no. 2, pp. 30–34.

21 Marginson *et al.* 1995.

22 Hamill, J. 1984 (b).

23 Robock, S.H. & Simmonds, K. 1989. *International business and multinational enterprises* (fourth edition). Homewood, Illinois, Irwin.

24 Marginson *et al.* 1995.

25 Hefler, D.F. 1981. Global sourcing: Offshore investment strategy for the 1980s. *Journal of Business Strategy*, vol. 2, no. 1, pp. 7–12.

26 Starkey, K. & McKinlay, A. 1993. *Strategy and the Human Resource. Ford and the Search for Competitive Advantage*. Oxford, Blackwell.

27 Roberts, B.C. & May, J. 1974. The response of multinational enterprises to international trade union pressures. *British Journal of Industrial Relations*, vol. 12, pp. 403–416.

28 Hamill, J. 1983.

29 Hamill, J. 1984 (a).

30 Hamill, J. 1984 (b).

31 Hyman, R. & A. Ferner, A. 1992, cited in Bean, R. 1985.

32 La Palombara, J. & Blank, S. 1976. *Multinational corporations and national elites: A study of tensions*. New York, The Conference Board.

33 Sim, A.B. 1977. Decentralized management of subsidiaries and their performance: A comparative study of American, British and Japanese subsidiaries in Malaysia. *Management International Review*, vol. 17, no. 2, pp. 45–51.

34 Shetty, Y.K. 1979. Managing the multinational corporation: European and American styles. *Management International Review*, vol. 19, no. 3, pp. 39–48.

35 Bean, R. 1985..

36 Hamill, J. 1984 (b).

37 Perlmutter, H.V. 1969. The tortuous evolution of the multinational corporation. *Columbia Journal of World Business*, vol. 4, no. 1, pp. 9–18.

38 Heenan, D.A. & Perlmutter, H.V. 1979. *Multinational organization development*, Reading, Mass., Addison-Wesley.

39 Electrolux in-house magazine, *Appliance*, E-26, (1995).

40 Marginson, P. 1992. European integration and transnational management-union relations in the enterprise. *British Journal of Industrial Relations*, vol. 30, no. 4, pp. 529–545.

41 Martinez Lucio & Weston, 1994.

42 See Bean, R. 1985.

43 Bok, D. 1971. Reflections on the distinctive character of American labour law. *Harvard Law Review*, vol. 84, pp. 1394–1463.

44 Windmuller, J.P. & Gladstone, A. (eds) 1984. *Employers associations and industrial relations: A comparative study*. Oxford, Clarendon Press.

45 Hamill, J. 1984 (b).

46 Enderwick, P. 1984. The labour utilization practices of multinationals and obstacles to multinational collective bargaining. *Journal of Industrial Relations*, vol. 26, no. 3, pp. 354–364.

47 Rosenzweig, P.M. & Nohria, N. 1994. Influences on human resource management practices in multinational corporations. *Journal of International*

Business Studies, vol. 25, no. 2, pp. 229–251.

48   Hamill, J. 1984 (b).

49   Bean, R. 1985.

50   Marginson, P., Buitendam, A., Deutschmann, C. & Perulli, P. 1993. The emergence of the Euro-company: Towards a European industrial relations? *Industrial Relations Journal*, vol. 24, no. 3, pp. 182–190.

51   Marginson, P. & Sisson, K. 1994. The structure of transnational capital in Europe: The emerging Euro-company and its implications for industrial relations. In Hyman, R. & Ferner, A. (eds.), *New frontiers in European industrial relations*. Oxford, Blackwell.

52   For a lucid discussion of the importance of understanding ideology, see Lodge, G.C. 1985. Ideological implications of changes in human resource management. In Walton, R.E. & Lawrence, P.R., *HRM trends and challenges*. Boston, Harvard Business School Press.

53   Kochan, T.A., McKersie, R.B. & Cappelli, P. 1984. Strategic choice and industrial relations theory. *Industrial Relations*, vol. 23, no. 1, pp. 16–39.

54   Frazee, V. 1998. Trade union membership is declining globally. *Workforce*, vol. 3, no. 2, p. 8.

55   World Labour Report 1997–98. *Industrial relations, democracy and social stability*. Geneva, ILO.

56   Groot, W. & Van den Berg, A. 1994. Why union density has declined. *European Journal of Political Economy*, vol.10, no. 4, pp. 749–763.

57   Bean, R. 1985.

58   Poole, M. 1986.

59   Visser, J. 1988. Trade unionism in Western Europe: Present situation and prospects. *Labour and Society*, vol. 13, no. 2, pp. 125–182.

60   Hamill, J. 1984 (a).

61   Hamill, J. 1984 (b), p. 34.

62   This section is based in part on Chapter 5, The impact of organized labour, in Prahalad and Doz, 1987.

63   For example, the decision by Hoover to shift some of its production from France to Scotland in the early 1990s appeared to be influenced by the ease with which the employer could implement lay-offs. See Goodhart, D. 1993. Ground rules for the firing squad. *Financial Times* (15 February), p. 8.

64   Prahalad and Doz, 1987.

65   *Ibid.*, p. 102.

66   Allen, M. 1993. Worldly wisdom. *New Statesman and Society*, vol. 6, pp. xii.

67   Kennedy, T. 1980.

68   Bean, R. 1985, p. 191.

69   Bean, R. 1985.

70   Marginson *et al.*, 1995.

71   Mahnkopf, B. & Altvater, E. 1995. Transmission belts of transnational competition? Trade unions and collective bargaining in the context of European integration. *European Journal of Industrial Relations*, vol. 1, no. 1, pp. 101–117.

72   Vernon, R. 1977. *Storm over the multinationals: The real issues*. Cambridge, Mass., Harvard University Press.

73   Martinez Lucio, M. & Weston, S. 1995. Trade unions and networking in the context of change: Evaluating the outcomes of decentralization in industrial relations. *Economic and Industrial Democracy*, vol. 16, p. 244.

74   For a detailed analysis of ITSs, see Neuhaus, R. 1982. *International trade secretariats: Objectives, organization, activities* (second edition). Bonn, Friedrich-EbertStiftung.

75   For an overview of international labour politics and organizations, see Boswell, T. & Stevis, D. 1997. Globalization and international labour organizing: A world-system perspective. *Work and Occupations*, vol 24, no. 3, pp. 288–308.

76   For further information on the FIET, see their web page at www.fiet.org/fiet-doc1.html.

77   Willatt, N. 1974. *Multinational unions*. London, Financial Times.

78   Northrup, H.R. 1978. Why multinational bargaining neither exists nor is desirable.

Labour Law Journal, vol. 29, no. 6, pp. 330–342.

79   Gallagher, J. 1997. Solidarity forever. *New Statesman & Society*, p. 10.

80   Kennedy, T. 1980.

81   Helfgott, R.B. 1983. American Unions and Multinational Enterprises: A case of misplaced emphasis. *Columbia Journal of World Business*, vol. 18, no. 2, pp. 8–16.

82   Up to 1993 there was a specialised UN agency known as the United Nations Centre on Transnational Corporations (UNCTC), which had published a number of reports on MNEs (see for example, Transborder data flows: Transnational corporations and remote-sensing data, New York, 1984, and Transnational corporations and international trade: Selected issues, New York, 1985). Since 1993, the responsibilities of the UNCTC have been assigned to UNCTAD. For further information, see the UNCTAD website at www.unicc.org/unctad/en/aboutorg/inbrief.htm.

83   See Boswell & Stevis, 1997, for more information on these international organisations.

84   Leonard, B. 1997. An interview with Anthony Freeman of the ILO. *HR Magazine*, vol. 42, no. 8 (August), pp. 104–109.

85   For coverage of the ongoing debate on international labour standards and globalisation, see Lee, E. 1997. Globalization and labour standards: A review of issues. *Management International Review*, vol. 136, no. 2, pp. 173–189.

86   For a detailed description and analysis of the OECD guidelines for multinational enterprises, see Campbell, D.C. & Rowan, R.L. 1983. *Multinational Enterprises and the OECD Industrial Relations Guidelines*. Philadelphia, The Wharton School Industrial Relations Research Unit, University of Pennsylvania.

87   Blanpain, R. 1985. *The OECD guidelines for multinational enterprises and labour relations, 1982–1984: Experiences and review*. Deventer, The Netherlands, Kluwer.

88   Campbell and Rowan, 1983.

89   Rojot, J. 1985. The 1984 revision of the OECD guidelines for multinational enterprises. *British Journal of Industrial Relations*, vol. 23, no. 3, pp. 379–397.

90   For a detailed account of this case see Blanpain, R. 1977. *The Badger Case and the OECD Guidelines for Multinational Enterprises*. Deventer, The Netherlands, Kluwer.

91   R. Blanpain, R. 1979. *The OECD guidelines for multinational enterprises and labour relations, 1976–1979: Experience and review*. Deventer, The Netherlands: Kluwer.

92   Jain, H.C. 1980. Disinvestment and the multinational employer – A case history from Belgium. *Personnel Journal*, vol. 59, no. 3, pp. 201–205.

93   Campbell and Rowan, 1983.

94   Liebhaberg, B. 1980. *Industrial relations and multinational corporations in Europe*. London, Gower, p. 85.

95   Jensen, C.S., Madsen, J.S. & Due, J. 1995. A role for a pan-European trade union movement? Possibilities in European IR-regulation. *Industrial Relations Journal*, vol. 26, no. 1, pp. 4–18.

96   Mahnkopf & Altvater, 1995.

97   Latta, G.W. & Bellace, J.R. 1983. Making the corporation transparent: Prelude to multinational bargaining. *Columbia Journal of World Business*, vol. 18, no. 2, pp. 73–80.

98   Addison, J.T. & Siebert, W.S. 1994. Recent developments in social policy in the new European Union. *Industrial and Labour Relations Review*, vol. 48, no. 1, pp. 5–27.

99   Donnelly, N. & Rees, C. 1995. *Industrial relations and multinational companies in the European Community: The work of the international companies network*. Warwick Papers in Industrial Relations no. 54, Warwick Business School, United Kingdom.

100 Teague, P. 1994. EC social policy and European human resource management. In Brewster, C. & Hegewisch, A. (eds.),

Policy and practice in European human resource management. London, Routledge.

101 Ulman, L., Eichengreen, B. & Dickens, W.T. (eds.) 1993. *Labour and an Integrated Europe.* Washington, D.C., The Brookings Institution.

102 De Cieri, H. & Dowling, P.J. 1991. An examination of the implications of the social dimension for entry of Australian firms to the single European market. Paper presented at the 17th annual meeting of the European International Business Association, Copenhagen (15-17 December), p. 2.

103 Commission of the European Communities, Community Charter of the Fundamental Social Rights of Workers. Luxembourg, Office for Official Publications of the European Communities, 1990.

104 Lodge, J. 1989. Social Europe: Fostering a people's Europe? In Lodge, J. (ed.), *European Community and the Challenge of the Future.* London, Pinter.

105 Addison, J. & Siebert, S. 1991. The social charter of the European Community: Evolution and controversies. *Industrial and Labour Relations Review,* vol. 44, no. 4, pp. 597–625.

106 Hall, M. 1994. Industrial relations and the social dimension of European integration: Before and after Maastricht. In Hyman, R. & Ferner, A. (eds.). *New frontiers in European industrial relations.* Oxford, Blackwell.

107 Pickard, J. 1992. Maastricht Deal Worries the Multinationals, *PM Plus* (January), p. 4.

108 Fitzpatrick, B. 1992. Community social law after Maastricht. *Industrial Law Journal,* vol. 21, no. 3, pp. 199–213.

109 Bercusson, B. & Van Dijk, J.J. 1995. The implementation of the protocol and agreement on social policy of the treaty on European Union. *The International Journal of Comparative Labour Law and Industrial Relations,* vol. 11, no.1, pp. 3–30.

110 The Treaty of Amsterdam revised the treaties on which the European Union was founded. For further information see

http://europa.eu.int/abc/obj/amst/en/index.htm and http://www.europarl.eu.int/basicdoc/en/default.htm.

111 For a detailed analysis of the Vredeling Directive, see Van Den Bulcke, D. 1984. Decision making in multinational enterprises and the information and consultation of employees: The proposed Vredeling Directive of the EC Commission. *International Studies of Management and Organization,* vol. 14, no. 1, pp. 36–60.

112 See Chesters, A. 1997. What you need to know about works councils. *Workforce* (July), pp. 22–23.

113 Anonymous. 1996. New legislation on EWCs and collective bargaining. *European Industrial Relations Review* (December), pp. 15–16.

114 Gold, M. & Hall, M. 1994. Statutory European works councils: The final countdown? *Industrial Relations Journal,* vol. 25, no. 3, pp. 177–186.

115 Marginson, P. 1992.

116 Addison & Siebert, 1994.

117 Knutsen, P. 1997. Corporatist tendencies in the Euro-policy: The EU Directive of 22 September 1994, on European Works Councils. *Economic and Industrial Democracy,* vol. 18, no. 2, pp. 289–323.

118 Martinez Lucio & Weston, 1995.

119 Michon, F. 1990. The 'European Social Community': A common model and its national variations? Segmentation effects, societal effects. *Labour and Society,* vol. 15, no. 2, pp. 215–236.

120 Szyszczak, E. 1995. Future directions in European Union social policy law. *Industrial Law Journal,* vol. 24, no. 1, pp. 19–32.

121 Nicoll, W. & Salmon, T.C. 1990. *Understanding the European Community.* Hertfordshire, UK, Philip Allan, p. 191.

122 Erickson, C.L. & Kuruvilla, S. 1994. Labour costs and the social dumping debate in the European Union. *Industrial and Labour Relations Review,* vol. 48, no. 1, pp. 28–47.

123 For more detail on the FTA and NAFTA, see Adams, R. 1997. The impact of the movement towards hemispheric free trade

on industrial relations. *Work and Occupations*, vol. 24, no. 3, pp. 364–380.

124 Cook, M. & Katz, H. (eds.) 1994. Regional integration and industrial relations in North America. Ithaca, NY, ILR Press.

125 For more detail on NAFTA see http:// iepnt1.itaiep.doc.gov/nafta/nafta2.htm; http://www.nafta.net/.

126 Society for Human Resource Management 1993. *Briefing paper on the North American Free Trade Agreement*. Washington, D.C., International Division, Institute of International Human Resources (January), p. 1.

127 Adams, R. 1997.

128 *Ibid.*

129 Daniels, D. & Radebaugh, L.H. 1992. *International business: Environments and operations* (sixth edition). Reading, Mass., Addison-Wesley.

130 Society for Human Resource Management, Briefing Paper.

131 See Boswell and Stevis, 1997.

132 Cook, M.L. 1997. Cross-border labour solidarity. *Dissent*, vol. 44, no. 1, p. 49.

133 Adams, R. 1997.

134 Verma, A., Kochan, T.A. & Lansbury, R.D. 1995. *Employment relations in the growing Asian economies*. London, Routledge.

135 Turner, D. 1996. Investment is key to EU-Asia future. *Europe Business Review*, vol. 1, no. 4, pp. 6–7.

136 Ramsey, H. 1997. Solidarity at last? International trade unionism approaching the millennium. *Economic and Industrial Democracy*, vol. 18, no. 4, pp. 503–537.

137 Jensen *et al.* 1995.

138 Enderwick, P. 1984, p. 357.

139 Hamill, J. 1983.

140 Hamill, J. 1984 (a).

141 Marginson *et al.* 1995.

10

The future role of human resource management

10.1 Introduction

From the discussion in the chapters thus far, it has become clear that the world of work has changed dramatically, and continues to do so. This has an impact not only on employees' working lives, but also on their future survival. In this book, issues and activities through which to address these changes have been discussed, but the question now is, how will the future work environment look, and specifically, what impact will it have on the HR professional and the HR department? In this chapter we will address the following important issues:

- The new millennium workplace.
- The redesign of the HRM role.
- The skills required of the future HR professional.
- The structure of the future HR department.

10.2 The new millennium workplace

In this section we will look at the important work done by Robert Barner and published in his article "The new millennium workplace: Seven changes that will challenge managers and workers",[1] as well as the work done by Christopher Barnatt and published in his article "Office space, cyberspace and virtual organisation".[2] Barner's research identifies seven changes due to take place over the next number of years that will reshape the work environment. These include:[3]

- the virtual organisation;
- a just-in-time workplace;
- the ascendancy of knowledge workers;
- computerised coaching and electronic monitoring;

- growth of worker diversity;
- an ageing workforce; and
- the birth of a dynamic workforce.

Many of these issues have already been mentioned in chapters 2 to 9, but to understand their HR implications better, a closer investigation is necessary.

10.2.1 The virtual organisation

As indicated earlier in this book, organisational members are already being linked at different work sites by means of electronic technology, and are communicating with each other via these systems. This type of operation is known as a virtual organisation. Virtual organisations exhibit a number of characteristics. For example, it can be noted that virtual organisations:[4]

- will be reliant on the medium of cyberspace (cyberspace refers to the medium in which electronic communications flow and computer software operates);
- will be enabled via new computing and communications developments; and
- will initially exist only across conventional organisational structures.

The growth in this area can be attributed to a number of developments:[5]

- the rapid evolution of electronic technology in the area of video, audio and text information;
- the spread of computer networks over the world as a result of globalisation; and
- the growth of home offices (telecommuting).

For management as well as HR professionals, these developments hold a number of important challenges for the future.

From a management perspective, issues such as effective communication and planning will need attention as the face-to-face approaches which have worked well over the years disappear. In addition, to capitalise on the flexibility and speed that is possible through these networks, managers and team members will have to form clear agreements from the outset regarding issues such as (1) performance expectations, (2) team priorities, (3) communication links and (4) resource allocation.[6] Other problems that may arise include possible misunderstandings and interpretations as a result of electronic mail (e-mail) correspondence. By means of this system messages and computer files can be sent electronically from computer to computer over a network. The advantage of e-mail is that it cuts down on paper use and increases the speed of messages.[7] According to Barnatt, the computer giant Microsoft sees its e-mail system as the carrier of its culture. The company is expanding so rapidly that it is reliant on e-mail as the glue to hold its employees together.[8-10]

The redistribution of power within the organisation can also be problematic. For example, with electronic networks, individuals can skip levels in the chain of command and give senior managers direct feedback on problems or successes, which is not the case in many conventional organisations.[11]

As a result of the computer networks, faster decision making and easier access to company information are also possible. However, the speed of decision making may place great pressure on individuals who do not possess the necessary skills to function within such environments. At the same time, those who thrive in such an environment will find themselves in a strong competitive position in the networked marketplace.[12]

From an HRM point of view the virtual organisation also holds a number of challenges. For example, the way recruitment and career development have been approached in the past will change rapidly. More companies and employees are using the Internet to match jobs and candidates.[13] If the information on individuals is up to date and correct, no skill within a company will be able to go unnoticed. It also helps management to put people together with specific skills via cross-functional teams to solve problems. This was impossible in the past with outdated information systems and rigid organisational structures. Flexibility is thus the new goal.

Easy access to relevant information will mean that individuals will also be able to plan their own career moves within the company, thus utilising the available talent to the benefit both of the company and of the individual.[14]

With multiple teams, the rigid traditional job description will also have to disappear. Job descriptions are not flexible enough for the constantly changing world of new strategies, customer requirements and membership of multiple teams. To fill this gap, companies will follow the competency-based approaches more enthusiastically. Competencies can and should be organised into menus that individuals and teams can use to describe their work and conduct people practices.[15]

With workers at distant work sites, problems can also arise regarding the appraisal system to be used and the manner in which these individuals are compensated. Innovative methods will have to be devised by HR managers to address these unique situations.

10.2.2 The just-in-time workforce

The growth in temporary workers, just-in-time workers, and the outsourcing of a large number of organisational functions have resulted in companies using more temporary workers.

HR professionals utilising these types of workers will have to find new ways to motivate them, as serious problems in performance and morale will occur. Research in the US has indicated that conflict between permanent and temporary staff can easily occur where, for example, permanent staff are paid for production outputs while temporary employees are given a flat hourly rate, as mentioned earlier in the book.[16] Due to their employment contract, temporary workers cannot be motivated by the traditional methods of promotion, merit increases or even profit-sharing programmes. To overcome these problems, management and HR professionals will have to spend more time and money on providing training, giving such workers greater access to company information and a bigger role in decision making. Thus, in tomorrow's workplace, HR professionals will have to look at issues such as orientation and training of just-in-time workers.[17]

10.2.3 The ascendancy of knowledge workers

As the world is moving rapidly away from manufacturing into the services sector, HR managers will have to rethink their traditional approaches to directing, coaching and motivating employees. Thus the emerging knowledge worker in this new environment will be an unique individual who must be nurtured to enable the organisation to gain the competitive edge it desires.[18]

As companies continue to become flatter, individuals who do not add value will be retrenched. Gone are the days when individuals will be paid only for performing managerial tasks. Managers and employees will have to make a strong commitment to lifelong learning and skill advancement to achieve job security in the new work environment. As these new knowledge workers become more mobile, HR managers will have to continually educate and train new employees in company culture and values.[19]

10.2.4 Computerised coaching and electronic monitoring

The growth in electronic systems over the next number of years will allow employees to become fully independent. Easier control by managers over work performed may result in employees feeling manipulated and exploited, placing the relationship between the manager and employee under great pressure.[20] Employees will also be able to learn more rapidly, for example by placing solutions to problems in a central database which can be accessed globally. Employees will also become less dependent on managers for coaching, training and performance feedback, resulting in the redesign of managers' jobs. The operation of the electronic networks 24 hours a day will make it difficult for employees to draw a line between work and home, which may result in domestic problems. Employees' right to privacy may also be invaded as a result of the permanent presence of the network system in the home environment.[21]

10.2.5 The growth of worker diversity

The mobility of workers between countries has increased enormously over the years. Individuals with specific skills (e.g. computer specialists, chartered accountants) are sought throughout the world.[22] Increasingly, companies are setting up manufacturing and assembly plants worldwide and smaller companies are expanding into international markets. For the first time, managerial staff will come into contact with multicultural groups and will need to adapt to different work expectations and communication styles. Workers who are able to operate successfully in these diverse environments will be highly valued by companies.[23] For HR professionals it will be necessary to provide sensitivity training to help managers understand the needs and perspectives of different members in these work groups.

10.2.6 The ageing workforce

In the past, companies were to a large extent reluctant to employ older workers, as they saw them as less productive, less flexible and more expensive.[24] Older workers were also denied challenging jobs. However, with the lack of skills in numerous areas, older workers are again being employed because of their experience and maturity. These workers are also more flexible about taking part-time and odd-hour shifts than younger workers. However, the implications would be that younger managers may find themselves threatened when managing older staff. In this situation, HR managers must arrange for these managers to undergo training in managing teams and in communication skills, to enable them to extract the best efforts from older teams.[25]

10.2.7 The birth of the dynamic workforce

One fact is true: the processes and methods of performing work are no longer fixed but fluid. This situation requires workers to adapt continuously. Thus, over the next few years, managerial performance will be based less on the ability to direct and co-ordinate work functions and more on improving key work processes through innovative thinking on a continuous basis.[26] This new dynamic environment will require workers to jump quickly into new ventures and manage temporary projects.

10.3 The redesign of the HRM role

From the previous discussion it is obvious that if HRM is to address these changes successfully, the traditional role it has played until now will not work in the future. Therefore, the redesign of the HRM role is necessary. Galbraith,[27] as quoted by Gregory Kesler,[28] argues that the function must be repositioned much in the same way as a company would reposition itself to become more competitive.

One method to achieve this has been through the re-engineering of HR processes. However, although re-engineering will reduce waste and result in more satisfied internal clients, it will not change the fundamental role that HR professionals play in the business or the value they add to shareholders.[29]

Research suggests that, to be successful, HR professionals must first work with top management to contract for a new or realigned role, before pursuing the re-engineering route. Thus this must take place after the contract process. Kesler identifies three tactics that can be followed to achieve success.[30]

- **contracting** with line management for a new role for HR;
- identifying and developing new HR **competencies;** and
- **redesigning** HR work, systems and organisation.

All these components cannot achieve change alone, but need to be done in conjunction with one another. As Kesler remarks:[31]

> Contracting for new roles without competencies to deliver is pointless; redesigning or eliminating work without a consensus from the client organisation leads to confusion and dissatisfied clients; building competencies based on historic assumptions about the role risks obsolescence and disappointment.

What do these individual elements entail? A brief look at each will be taken.

10.3.1 Contracting new roles

When contracting new roles to be performed, it is important to involve the internal clients who will be served. Thus, several stakeholders need to be approached. These can include employees, middle management, functional top executives, HR and top line management. The process must also be a two-way dialogue in which the client managers influence and are influenced by their HRM providers. A process needs to be developed by which HR priorities for the business are identified through intense involvement of both HR and line management.[32]

Establishing the priority HR practice areas and outputs desired by line managers is not enough. HR and line managers must also agree on how the HR role will actually change in the new environment, beyond the re-engineering effort of the HR processes. The question that must be asked is: what value will HR truly add?[33] For example, in the case of training and development, will the HR role be to enable employees to be better business people or will it merely deliver a number of individual training programmes?[34] Thus, establishing this fundamental orientation of HR work is critical if it is truly going to redesign itself for the new challenges.

A "performance capabilities (PC)" model[35] that will help in this regard has been proposed by Kesler (see Table 10.1).

As can be seen, the model consists of a continuum of six value-adding roles, each of which is a distinct competency. The roles from left to right in the model are:[36]

- catalytic influence;
- diagnostic and fact-based analysis;
- innovating business structures and processes;
- assuring standards;
- administration and services; and
- problem solving.

Roles 1 to 3 generally exert more leverage, as indicated in the model. Here a partnership between HR and line people creates benefits for the line organisation that are greater than the immediate efforts of the HR staff member.[37] Roles 4 to 6, however, have less leverage because they are more transactional in nature and are less likely to add value to the money invested. Most HR departments are of the opinion that their current activities and resources fall in the "controlling, administering and problem-solving" roles. However, the value of the various roles can be determined only in the context of a given company and its needs.[38] But to be successful the business strategy must be supported more directly by the partnership-orientated performance capabilities (roles 1 to 3) than by the service transactions portion of the continuum (roles 4 to 6). The most effective use of resources is served when the continuum is utilised effectively.[39]

Activating the left side of the model first will normally reduce the resources consumed on the right side of the continuum later, according to Kesler.[40] For

Table 10.1 The performance capabilities model: defining the fundamental role of HR

Greater leveraged roles ← - → Less leveraged roles					
1 **Catalytic** **influence**	**2** **Diagnostic** **assessment**	**3** **Innovating** **processes,** **structure**	**4** **Assurance** **of standards**	**5** **Administra-** **tion and** **services**	**6** **Problem** **solving**
"Partnering role"			**"Transactional role"**		
• Enable others • Knowledge-based • Performance-based quality • Distributed resources • Enhance business performance • Knowledge transfer to line • Highly integrated with business process • Non-linear work – focus design on outcomes and competencies • Early life cycle			• Service others (or remove administrative barriers) • System-based • Conformance-based quality • Consolidated resources • Economy of scale/cost (commodity) • Few specialists/admin transferred to line • Parallel, stand-alone • Linear work – process map and redesign (for consolidation, elimination, automation) • Late in the life cycle		

SOURCE: Kesler, G.C. 1995. A model and process for redesigning the HRM role, competencies, and work in a major multinational corporation. *Human Resource Management.* vol. 34, no. 2 (Summer), p. 237. Reprinted by permission of Wiley-Liss, Inc., a subsidiary of John Wiley & Sons, Inc.

example, labour relations planning and joint labour management process facilitation will usually result in less labour relations problem solving. Thus, to be effective, the HR role which normally starts on the right side of the model (roles 4 to 6) must move to the left-hand roles (1 to 3) where conditions are best accomplished. Thus both halves of the model must be delivered to the appropriate extent and in a highly competent manner to be successful.[41]

To practically implement the discussion between line and HR managers, Kesler provides a further extension of his model in Table 10.1 by placing HRM practice areas and the performance capabilities on an HR processes grid in which a dialogue can take place in order to:[42]

- contract for priority, value-added roles, while influencing the expectations of internal clients;
- identify a set of required competencies that reflect those priorities; and
- redesign the work and processes.

See Table 10.2 for Kesler's HR grid, which was completed by the US company Whirpool's North American Appliance Group (NAAG). This grid will provide a tool for repositioning the HRM function by answering the following questions:[43]

- What is the HR work that needs to be performed?
- Who are the best people to perform it?
- Where does the HR organisation clearly add the most value?
- What are the specific outputs required, and in what time frames?
- What is the relationship between line and HR staff in these major practice areas?
- How are we allocating resources among the cells of the grid?
- What can we stop doing?

Getting answers to these questions for the future state will form the basic contract with the line organisation. The process by which to obtain these answers can consist of scanning for competitive success factors to implement the business strategy, benchmark visits to other companies, interviews with focus groups within the company (e.g. managers across diverse units and group functions) and surveys among the staff using questionnaires on the HR process grid.[44] For example, respondents can be asked to identify which cells in the grid should be further emphasised and which should be de-emphasised over the next number of years, given specific business strategies. Other questions can also be asked to determine what activities could be eliminated, consolidated or automated, either at the business unit or other levels. After gathering the data, feedback meetings must be held and final decisions made. It is interesting to note that, in the Whirpool case, middle management emphasised the maintenance or service-orientated portions of the grid. The team involved in this process must try to use the information from other more successful companies to increase the support for the partnering (the left side of the model) elements of the grid. After the discussions a two-to-five year plan can be drawn up, HR processes re-engineered and staff competencies developed.[45]

10.3.2 Competencies

Besides determining what new roles must be developed, additional skills to support this new role – for example leadership, strategic planning and

Table 10.2 HR grid at Whirlpool's North American Appliance Group (NAAG)

	Catalytic influence	Diagnostic and analysis	Innovate process, structure and plans	Assurance of standards	Admin and service	Problem solving
Organisation design	Increase	Increase	Increase	No change	Increase	Decrease
Talent pool management	Increase	No change	Increase	No change	Increase	Decrease
Training and education	Increase	Increase	Increase	No change	Decrease	Decrease
Employee involvement	No change	No change	Increase	No change	Increase	Decrease
Rewards and recognition	No change	Increase	Increase	Decrease	Decrease	No change
Well-being and morale	No change	Increase	Increase	Decrease	No change	Decrease
Communication	No change	No change	No change	Decrease	No change	No change

Key:

Increase   No change   Decrease

Future emphasis

SOURCE: Kesler, G.C. 1995. A model and process for redesigning the HRM role, competencies, and work in a major multinational corporation. *Human Resource Management*, vol. 34, no. 2 (Summer), p. 244. Reprinted by permission of Wiley-Liss, Inc., a subsidiary of John Wiley & Sons, Inc.

business know-how – must also be developed, as indicated earlier. In many HR organisations these skills will be unknown to the HR staff.[46] See section 10.4 for more details in this area.

10.3.3 Redesign of HR process and structure

The final step is the redesign of the HR function. Here re-engineering plays a vital role, as it does in the other functional areas within the organisation. In most organisations the re-engineering action redirects the staff responsibilities away from functional work to client-centred consulting, while the HR structure is realigned to focus on administrative service centres and internal HR consulting organisations.[47] See section 10.5 for more details.

10.4 The skills required of the future HR professional

As indicated earlier, one of the tactics by which to reposition the HRM function includes the development of competencies for the HR employees. Competency refers to an individual's demonstrated knowledge, skills or abilities.[48] The literature indicates that little work has been done to conceptually or empirically identify competencies required of HR professionals.[49] Many companies follow the approach where competencies for HR professionals may be defined either by the insights of senior managers or by other internal customers.

Ulrich, Brockbank, Yeung & Lake propose that HR professionals demonstrate competence when they add value to their business. This can be done by delivering ideas, programmes and initiatives to their business which can assist it to compete. Thus, the value of HR professionals resides in their ability to create a competitive advantage. If HR professionals develop the competencies to design and deliver practices which build organisational capability, they create and sustain unique sources of competitive advantage.[50]

Based on an overview of the literature and their view that HR professionals must add value, Ulrich *et al.* have developed a three-domain framework for conceptualising HR competencies (see Figure 10.1). The framework consists of (1) knowledge of business, (2) delivery of HR practices, and (3) management of change processes.[51-55] A brief look will be taken at these elements.

10.4.1 Knowledge of business

Value can be added to an organisation when HR understands the business and adapts its HR activities to the changing business conditions. To be able to perform this task successfully, the HR professional must know the financial, strategic, technological and organisational capabilities of the business. Thus it

Figure 10.1 Framework for HR competencies

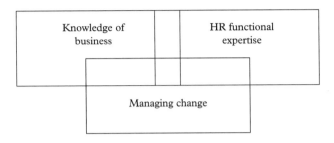

SOURCE: Ulrich, D., Brockbank, W., Yeung, A.K. & Lake, D.G. 1995. Human resource competencies: An empirical assessment. *Human Resource Management*, vol. 34, no. 4, p. 475. Reprinted by permission of Wiley-Liss, Inc., a subsidiary of John Wiley & Sons, Inc.

will not be sufficient only to have excellent knowledge of the HR discipline; a broader perspective is required. (This broader knowledge does not have to be direct operational experience, but the HR professional must have the ability to understand the issues.[56])

10.4.2 Delivery of HR practices

As mentioned earlier, the HR professional must be an expert in HRM. Knowing and being able to deliver state-of-the-art innovative HR practices to organisational members builds the credibility of HR professionals. Credibility and professional respect evolve from HR professionals being seen as competent in their unique area of expertise.[57]

10.4.3 Management of change processes

Success can be achieved only if the changes taking place outside the organisation are matched by changes taking place internally. Thus companies with a greater capacity for change will naturally be more competitive over time. By possessing competencies to manage these change processes, HR professionals can help other organisational members manage change, thus creating an overall organisational capacity for change as a key source of competitive advantage.[58-59] HR professionals who are successful in this area will demonstrate the attributes of a change agent, which will include the ability to diagnose problems, build relationships with clients, articulate a vision, set a leadership agenda, solve problems and implement goals. Thus the competencies exhibited in the management of change are: knowledge (of change processes), skills (as change agents), and abilities (to deliver change).[60] If HR professionals can demonstrate competence in each of the areas indicated in Figure 10.1 they will be perceived by their colleagues as effective.

In their research, Tom Lawson and Vaughan Limbrick have identified a list of required skills, personal attributes and capabilities that senior HR managers should possess to be successful. These include:[61]

- interpersonal skills;
- progressive/proactive decision making;
- teaming skills;
- communication and persuasion skills;
- creative/innovative thinking;
- HR technical knowledge;
- business knowledge;
- strategic focus;
- leadership and planning skills;
- sense of urgency/initiative;
- visioning/initiative sense;
- aggressiveness;
- flexibility/adaptiveness;
- change-orientated;
- opportunism;
- intellectual independence;
- approachability; and
- general business skills.

Having identified the different roles to be played by the new HR department and the different competencies required by the HR professional, all that now remains is to determine how the structure looks within which the HR professional will operate.

10.5 The structure of the future HR department

For the HR department to function successfully and survive the tremendous changes taking place within organisations, it needs to undergo major restructuring. Thus, reorganisation should better position the function to enable it to provide support for the changing business needs. This view is shared by Hilborn, an associate of William M. Mercer in Philadelphia, USA, who remarks:[62]

HR departments have been evolving away from a traditional functional design to a team based model. The traditional design typically includes a vice president of HR, then a manager of compensation and benefits, a manager of HRIS and payroll, a manager of employment and so on. However, the emerging model is more like a three-legged stool.

Hilborn's emerging HR organisational model appears in Figure 10.2. In the model the three legs described in the above paragraph can be clearly distinguished, namely (1) an administrative service centre, (2) a centre of excellence and (3) business partners.[63] The administrative service centre is responsible for processing the payroll, benefits and other administrative aspects, and also focuses on the efficiency of transaction functions. The second leg – that is, the centre of excellence – concentrates on design rather than transactions and will have line managers as its customers. The emphasis here is on effectiveness.[64] The third leg comprises the HR business partners. These employees do not get involved in transactions but instead act as consultants and planners, linking the business with appropriate programmes.[65-67]

Figure 10.2 Emerging HR organisational model

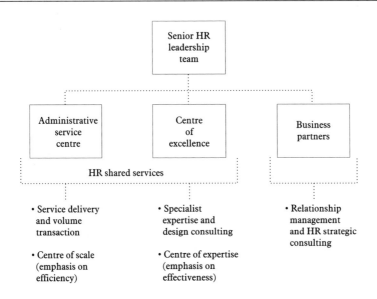

SOURCE: Republished with permission of *HR Magazine*, from Changing Shapes. Joinson, C. Vol. 44, No. 3. March 1999, p. 44. Permission conveyed through Copyright Clearance Center, Inc.

10.6 Summary

This chapter has looked at the important changes that will take place over the next few years within the workplace. It has also indicated the role to be played by the HR function. To be successful, the HR function will have to be repositioned. A number of tactics have been identified which can assist with this process. Issues pertaining to the skills needed by the HR professional to manage the new HR function were highlighted, as well as the new HR structure which will accommodate these changes.

References

1 Barner, R. 1996. The new millennium workplace: Seven changes that will challenge managers and workers. *Futurist*, vol. 30, no. 2 (March/April), pp. 14–18. Article obtained from http://gateway.ovid.com/server5/ovidweb.

2 Barnatt, C. 1995. Office space, cyberspace and virtual organisation. *Journal of General Management*, vol. 20, no. 4 (Summer), pp. 78–91.

3 Barner, R. 1996, p. 1.

4 Barnatt, C. 1995, p. 83.

5 Barner, R. 1996, p. 2.

6 *Ibid.*

7 Barnatt, C. 1995, p. 83.

8 *Ibid.*

9 Pruitt, S. & Barrett, T. Corporate virtual workspace. In Benedikt, M. (ed.), *Cyberspace: first steps*. Cambridge, MA, MIT Press, 1993.

10 Lloyd, B. 1990. Office productivity – time for a revolution. *Long Range Planning*, vol. 23, no. 1, pp. 66–79.

11 Barner, R. 1996, p. 2.

12 *Ibid.*

13 *Ibid.*, p. 3.

14 *Ibid.*

15 Mc Lagan, P.A. 1997. Competencies: the next generation. *Training & Development*, vol. 51, no. 5, p. 2. Article obtained from http://gateway.ovid.com/ server3/ ovidweb.

16 Barner, R. 1996, p. 3.

17 *Ibid.*, p. 4.

18 *Ibid.*

19 *Ibid.*

20 *Ibid.*, p. 5.

21 *Ibid.*

22 *Ibid.*

23 *Ibid.*

24 *Ibid.*

25 *Ibid.*, p. 6.

26 *Ibid.*

27 Galbraith, J. 1992. Positioning human resources as a value-adding function: The case of Rockwell International. *Human Resource Management*, vol. 31, no. 4, pp. 287–300.

28 Kesler, G. C. 1995. A model and process for redesigning the HRM role, competencies, and work in a major multinational corporation. *Human Resource Management*, vol. 34, no. 2 (Summer), pp. 229–252.

29 *Ibid.*, p. 230.

30 *Ibid.*

31 *Ibid.*

32 *Ibid.*, p. 231.

33 *Ibid.*, p. 236.

34 *Ibid.*

35 *Ibid.*

36 *Ibid.*

37 *Ibid.*

38 *Ibid.*

39 *Ibid.*

40 *Ibid.*

41 *Ibid.*

42 *Ibid.*, p. 238.

43 *Ibid.*

44 *Ibid.*, pp. 239–246.

45 *Ibid.*

46 *Ibid.*, pp. 231–232.

47 *Ibid.*, p. 232.

48 Ulrich, D., Brockbank, W., Yeung, A.K. & Lake, D.G. 1995. Human resource competencies: An empirical assessment. *Human Resource Management*, vol. 34, no. 4, pp. 473–495.

49 *Ibid.*, p. 474.

50 *Ibid.*

51 Ulrich *et al.* 1995, p. 475.

52 Mansfield, R.S. 1996. Building competency models: Approaches for HR professionals. *Human Resource Management*, vol. 35, no. 1 (Spring), pp. 7–18.

53 Kockanski, J.T. & Ruse, D.H. 1996. Designing a competency-based human resources organisation. *Human Resource Management*, vol. 35, no. 1, pp. 19–34.

54 Gorsline, K. 1996. A competency profile for human resources: No more shoemaker's children. *Human Resource Management*, vol. 35, no. 1, pp. 53–66.

55 McLagan, P.A. 1997. Competencies: The next generation. *Training & Development*, vol. 51, no. 5, pp. 40–47.

56 Ulrich *et al.* 1995, pp. 475–476.

57 *Ibid.*, p. 476.

58 *Ibid.*

59 Blancero, D., Boroski, J. & Dyer, L. 1996. Key competencies for a transformed human resource organisation: Results of a field study. *Human Resource Management*, vol. 35, no. 3, pp. 383–403.

60 Ulrich *et al.* 1995, p. 476.

61 Lawson, T.E. & Limbrick, V. 1996. Critical competencies and developmental experiences for top HR executives. *Human Resource Management*, vol. 35, no. 1, p. 74.

62 Quoted in Joinson, C. 1999. Changing shapes. *HR Magazine*, vol. 44, no. 3, pp. 41–48.

63 *Ibid.*, p. 44.

64 *Ibid.*

65 *Ibid.*

66 Bobrow, W. 1998. Is your HR Department in shape to support your business strategies? *Bobbin*, vol. 39, no. 8, pp. 64–68.

67 Peters, J. 1997. A future vision of human resources. In Ulrich, D., Losey, M.R. & Lake, G. (eds.), *Tomorrow's HR Management*. New York, John Wiley, pp. 250–258.

Subject index

Author index